LOCKDOWN WALES

How Covid-19 Tested Wales

LOCKDOWN WALES

How Covid-19 Tested Wales

WILL HAYWARD

Seren is the book imprint of
Poetry Wales Press Ltd,
Suite 6, 4 Derwen Road, Bridgend, Wales, CF31 1LH

www.serenbooks.com
facebook.com/SerenBooks
Twitter: @SerenBooks

ISBN: 9781781726013
Ebook: 9781781726006

A CIP record for this title is available from the British Library.

The publisher acknowledges the financial assistance
of the Welsh Books Council.

Printed by Severn, Gloucester

CONTENTS

Introduction

Do you ever just take a moment among all the noise, announcements, changes to restrictions and just ask yourself: What has happened?

As I write this, Wales is in a two-week 'firebreak' and England is heading into a one month lockdown to try and get on top of spiraling cases. In the space of just six months, all our worlds have changed. We now think twice about hugging friends and family we don't live with. People we used to see every day now only appear in our lives as pixels on a screen. Diaries that were full of trips, visits and occasions are empty, after all, what is the point in making plans too far ahead?

In the middle of something so seismic, so enormous, and frankly, so horrible, it is hard to fully grasp what has happened. There is just so much depressing news. The temptation can naturally be to just try and let it wash over you. To just push your headphones deeper into your ears to drown out the relentlessness of it all.

That is why I wrote this book. It is not written for epidemiologists. It is not written for policy boffins. It is certainly not written for politicians or self styled 'politicos' in Cardiff Bay and Westminster. This book is written as an aid for people in Wales to understand what has happened to themselves, their families and their lives.

And it is important that we do understand. In the age of fake news, when people would have us believe that facts are open to interpretation, an understanding of an issue prevents misinformation from flooding in to fill the gaps. But understanding is most important because the issue isn't just *what* happened to us, but why.

Hearing politicians speak you would be under the impression that the loss of lives, jobs and futures was inevitable – an act of nature. The virus of course was inevitable. Even if it had not been Covid-19, it was only a matter of time before a new and emerging infectious disease emerged to threaten us. The virus was inevitable, but an appalling lack of preparation as well as an initially sluggish and anaemic response was not.

A pandemic had long been identified as one the biggest threats facing society. In 2016, the UK government conducted 'Exercise Cygnus', a simulation to test readiness for a pandemic, and found us lacking. But as this book and our own lived experience shows us, four years later, we were not ready. As other countries have demonstrated, the number of deaths and the economic catastrophe that followed were not because of the virus, they were the result of decisions.

If we fail to understand fully what happened to us and why, we fail to hold to account those responsible. In not holding the decision makers to account we also doom ourselves to repeat this suffering in the future.

But this is not ultimately a story about politicians or Covid-19. This is a story about the people of Wales – and how both the virus and decisions made by politicians affected them. It is about how people in Wales both suffered and died, but also rose magnificently to the challenge.

The theme that will come up time and again throughout this book is not that Covid-19 wreaked havoc on a thriving United Kingdom. The UK in 2020 was a road with hundreds of small potholes. They could have been filled in while the sun was shining but they were not. Covid was the water that filled those potholes and then froze overnight, cracking open the shortcomings in our society into fissures. These potholes will not come as a surprise. An under-funded health service, a political culture that scorns collaboration and long term planning, a hodge-podge approach to social care as well huge economic, gender and racial inequality to name but a few.

This book is divided into two parts. The first is a chronology, tracking how the virus developed in Wales from December 2019 to July 2020. The second looks at the key themes and issues that arose in the first wave of the virus.

The book records and explores events up until July 6 – the first day that no deaths were announced in Wales since the lockdown began. In many ways this is a shame. There were dozens of other circumstances subsequently that fall outside the scope of the book that I would love to have covered: the A-level and GCSE result saga, the failures in the UK Government's Lighthouse Labs and the October firebreak lockdown with the Welsh Government's ban on the sale of non-essential goods.

At time of writing Wales and the wider UK sadly seem to be entering a second wave. Though this is not covered in the book, the events of March through July are the foundations of everything that has come since. If the outbreak in March had been handled better, perhaps the UK wouldn't be preparing for a socially dis-tanced Christmas.

At the beginning of February 2020 I was offered the job of acting Political Editor at WalesOnline and the *Western Mail* – the national newspaper of Wales. The current political editor was going on maternity leave for around twelve months from the end of March and I was asked to step into the role from my post as Social Affairs Correspondent.

When the Editor-in-Chief and I spoke about the subjects I

would look to cover over this period all the discussion was about issues like poverty, the end of the Brexit transition period and ways to make politics accessible and relevant to readers. We had no idea that from the start of March almost every story I would cover for the next six months would be about just one thing.

Through my new position I was able to interview on a near daily basis the people making the decisions that changed all our lives. I hope I am able to provide insight into what has happened to us all.

This book is not intended to make a political point. It is about how Covid-19 affected the people of Wales. However, political decision-making is intrinsically linked to this, and criticism and analysis of our politicians' performance is inevitable.

No one is doubting how hard the task before them was. However it is my strongly held belief that to put oneself forward as a Member of Parliament or a Member of the Senedd (or any elected representative for that matter), is an act of supreme confidence. You are standing before people and telling them that you, and only you, are best placed to make their lives better. You are asking to be trusted with power over their lives, to decide how their children are educated and how they will be treated when they are old. You and your political party are asking for permission to tax their wages on the understanding that you will use the proceeds to make their society better. You are saying that you can guide them through any crises. It shows total self assuredness. Because of this, you must be held to a higher standard. On morality, integrity and simple competence it is not enough to be 'not too bad'. That is the standard I am applying within this book.

There are two final points to make. The first is to note that this is an incredibly fast moving situation. The science of this virus is progressing every single day. It is perfectly possible that some of the analysis I do within these pages will eventually be out of date as our understanding grows. Frankly, I really hope that is the case because it means we are better placed to stop Covid having such a hold on our lives.

The second point is that no single book can cover all of the issues that the coronavirus pandemic raised. With a fast moving situation, it was often necessary to only touch on very worthy subjects for the sake of a coherent narrative. For that I can only apologise.

The crisis has changed Wales, the UK and in all likelihood the entire course of human history. Understanding what has happened to us and why is the first step in ensuring that, in the longer term, it is change for the better.

Introducing Covid-19

Allow me to introduce severe acute respiratory syndrome coronavirus 2, or SARS-CoV-2 for short. On February 11, 2020, this was the name given to the virus which has turned our lives upside down.

Viruses and the subsequent diseases they cause, are often named differently. The virus HIV causing AIDS is one example of this. SARS-CoV-2 is the virus which causes the disease called Covid-19.

Though it is a virus which up until December 2019 we had never seen before, we are very familiar with its family. Coronaviruses are a large family of viruses that often cause mild or moderate illnesses in the upper-respiratory tract: the nasal cavities, sinuses, pharynx, tonsils, and larynx. There are four coronaviruses that cause mild or moderate disease in humans and the chances are you will contract one of them over the course of your life.

There are also three that can cause more serious or deadly disease. One of them, SARS coronavirus (SARS-CoV,) emerged in November 2002 and caused severe acute respiratory syndrome (SARS). That virus disappeared by 2004. Middle East respiratory syndrome (MERS) is caused by the MERS coronavirus (MERS-CoV) that came from camels in 2012, and is still seen in localised outbreaks.

If you become infected with Covid-19 it has most likely entered your body after inhaling an infected person's virus-laden droplets, though you may have touched an infected surface and then touched your face. In the early stage the virus then multiples at the back of the throat.

There is a reasonable chance that you may not get any symptoms at all. The exact probability is hard to calculate because people with no symptoms are far less likely to be tested. If symptoms do develop they can be wide-ranging: fever, body ache, dry cough, fatigue, chills, headache, sore throat, loss of appetite, and loss of smell. Some people also experience neurological symptoms, muscle weakness, tingling or numbness in the hands and feet, dizziness, confusion, delirium, seizures, and stroke. There are also those who have gastrointestinal symptoms, such as nausea, vomiting, diarrhea, and abdominal pain or discomfort.

The virus can badly affect your lung cells, binding on to an enzyme called ACE2 which is the surface of some of the cells in the air sacs of the lungs. The virus uses the ACE2 to gain entry and attack the cells causing inflammation leading to pneumonia.

It is estimated around 6% of cases become critically ill (these estimates do vary). Some patients have suffered strokes and seizures with some developing severe pneumonia and dying from respiratory failure. Covid-19 patients have ultimately died from several causes including from low blood oxygen levels, organ failure, heart failure, respiratory failure and severe blood clotting and embolisms.

The long term effects of the virus on those who survive is unknown but many have experienced long term issues affecting the respiratory system, the brain, cardiovascular system and heart, the kidneys, the gut, the liver, and the skin.

It is a horrible, nasty disease. One thing to be thankful for is that it did not seem to affect children as severely. Emerging in late 2019 in Wuhan China, it was circulating in every part of Wales in a matter of months.

PART I

1. Around the World in 60 Days

At the start of December 2019, when we were all concentrating on getting Brexit done, a general election and who had won the *Apprentice* final, doctors in the Chinese city of Wuhan were concerned about a spike in pneumonia cases there.

On December 30 a doctor named Li Wenliang messaged[1] his old medical school classmates on WeChat, a private messaging app, after reading case reports showing seven people with what seemed to be a new type of coronavirus. He told his friends, "There are seven confirmed cases of SARS at Huanan Seafood Market" before sending pictures of the diagnosis reports. One of the others in the group warmed him to 'be careful' writing about something like that in a private message group. But Li replied: "The latest news is, it has been confirmed that they are coronavirus infections, but the exact virus is being subtyped. Don't circulate the information outside of this group; tell your family and loved ones to take precautions."

In an example of what was to become the global dismissal and underplaying of evidence, where perceived political expedience and maintaining power took precedence over the health of humanity, Li was given a formal written warning by the Wuhan Public Security Bureau for publishing untrue statements and made to sign a letter promising not to do it again. On February 7, as the total deaths in China went through the 600 mark, Dr Li Wenliang died from the virus he tried to warn people about[2].

The situation had developed. On January 1 the seafood market, the likely centre of the outbreak, was closed – two days later China officially notified the World Health Organisation about a 'viral pneumonia of unknown cause'[3]. By January 14, travellers leaving Wuhan's airports and railway stations were being screened for the virus but it was becoming clear how far its tendrils had already travelled from the city, a major transport hub.

On January 23 the Chinese government imposed a lockdown on Wuhan and other cities in Hubei province. Unfortunately, despite how hard they were now slamming the door, the virus and its spike proteans, had already bolted. The very next day Malaysia, France, Vietnam and Nepal all confirmed their first cases, the USA confirmed its second and the following day Australia and Canada also confirmed their first. January 25 would see the beginning of a trend that would in a matter of months become a familiar news report in Wales – Liang Wudong, a doctor who had been on the front line of the fight against the virus became the first doctor to die from it.

In the UK the risk level was raised from 'very low' to 'low' meaning that Heathrow Airport increased surveillance on the three direct flights a week from Wuhan while the authorities began trying to trace the 2,000 people who had already flown into the UK over the preceding fourteen days.

It is easy in retrospect, months and even years later, to think that in those early days we didn't really know what we were dealing with yet. If we do this, or allow policy makers to suggest this was the case after the fact, we will be complicit in the rewriting of history. Health Minister Vaughan Gething was challenged at length about the threat posed by coronavirus in the Senedd as early as January 29. The questions being asked by a member of the Senedd at the time reflected a real and genuine concern from MSs. Caroline Jones said: "The threat we face from this new strain of coronavirus is of grave concern" and Conservative MS Angela Burns enquired: "does Wales have any emergency treatment centre planning in place, in case we get to a situation where this does develop further?" It was also common knowledge at the time that someone could carry the virus for a considerable time before noticing symptoms, with Janet Finch-Saunders stating: "My concerns, Minister, are that the virus seems to be spreading like a normal flu during its incubation period and before any symptoms appear."[4]

Mr Gething stressed that the Welsh Government was not being complacent but he was certain he didn't "want to add to the impression that a more significant health risk is on its way than is likely." He added that "it's worth reflecting that the 'flu makes people severely unwell and kills people every year, and yet, we still can't persuade people who are in a category where they can receive a free NHS vaccine, to take that up in the numbers we'd want them to. So, let's have some perspective on it." In the same debate Vaughan Gething described 'quarantine' as "a dreadful, old-fashioned word" – we couldn't know that it would soon become part of our vernacular along with 'furlough', 'social distancing', 'ramp up' and 'flattening the curve'.

What this debate demonstrated was that as early as January it was known that Covid-19 was a threat, that it could incubate for a considerable amount of time, that it was killing people and that both the UK and Welsh Government had time to prepare. As we moved into February life went on, Coronavirus was a news item, but not *the* news item. Wales hosted Italy in the Six Nations at the Principality Stadium in February. No one knew that the virus had already started to take root in the Lombardy area, with Italy soon to see the first mass outbreak and then lockdown in Europe. On the 21st the first lockdowns covering ten municipalities in the province of Lodi in Lombardy and one in the province of Padua in Veneto began, covering around 50,000 people. But even then, as an advanced healthcare system began to be overwhelmed – still life went on. The very next day Italy hosted Scotland in the Six Nations at the Stadio Olimpico in Rome – Scotland fans travelled to watch the game. Just two weeks later on March 8 the lockdown would cover the entire north of the country before being extended to the whole of Italy the following day.

On March 1, 62 days after Dr Li Wenliang's warning, Wales had its first known case of the virus – a person from the Swansea area who had recently returned from northern Italy. This took the UK total to 35[5] with some identified as originating in Italy and Iran. A cause for concern was that it was unclear how some of the infected people had contracted it, suggesting community transmission.

On the same day the *Daily Telegraph* broke the news that Number 10 had vetoed the UK staying inside the EU's Early Warning and Response System (EWRS) established in 1988 to respond to viruses which had been vital in tackling the bird flu outbreak[6]. The Department for Health had wanted to remain in the system but Downing Street, under the control of the Prime Minister and Dominic Cummings, had insisted. It was an early, but sadly not solitary, example of how political expediency took precedence over keeping people safe. health secretary Matt Hancock was also not allowed to travel to a meeting of EU health ministers following the UK's exit from the EU a month before.

The Prime Minister told the country on March 2 that the UK Government were 'well prepared' for a pandemic. That statement was completely debunked by Exercise Cygnus in 2016[7] (the study that found the UK was not ready for a large pandemic) and by the events of the next six weeks. This is not to suggest that the PM was being deliberately misleading, given the reports that Mr Johnson likes to have his notes limited to two sides of A4 it is entirely possible he hadn't actually read Exercise Cygnus[8]. Either way, were these the safest pair of hands in which to be nestled?

Regardless, Mr Johnson himself did not seem to care about the safety of his hands. The following day he proudly told a press conference[9] that he "was at a hospital the other night where there were actually a few coronavirus patients and I shook hands with everybody, you will be pleased to know".

It is worth reflecting that when the Prime Minister (the Prime Minister!) spoke these words of pure idiocy, across the world more than 90,000 people in over forty countries had been infected with coronavirus. Of these, 3,119 had died. China had built huge field hospitals, the virus was transmitting in the community in the very country Johnson governed and Italy had been in a partial lockdown for over a week. But this throwaway remark demonstrates far greater shortcomings in our political system than the fact that our leader behaves like a buffoon.

There are three things worthy of attention. First is the idea of British exceptionalism which seems to have blinded the Government to the reality of the situation. Italy and China had both already seen parts of their country overwhelmed and their citizens die. These are not developing countries, they had all the tools the UK had to combat the virus and were often better equipped, yet still there was a sense of 'this couldn't happen to us'. In the same way that not being successfully invaded for a millennium makes some people disdainful of the values of organisations like the EU, so too does the fact that previous outbreaks like Sars and Ebola never took hold in the UK made us lax in our response to Covid-19. We believed we were one of the exceptions, and in a way we were, but in all the worst ways.

The Government was not alone in holding this view. In Cardiff people of Asian heritage reported suffering abuse as a result of the coronavirus. The Premier League footballer Dele Ali issued an apology after mocking an Asian man. It was seen to be (using Trump's horrible expression) a 'Chinese virus'. It wasn't for us, because apparently we are different – exceptional.

Secondly, the apparent revelling in ignorance and disdain for the rules and science. The entire tone of the Prime Minister appeared to be one of nonchalant disdain for the science being presented around a virus which was killing people. There is a growing trend amongst some of our elected officials to actually embrace the perception of ignorance. Like the kids in school who didn't want to try because then they could be seen as having failed. This troubling trend is more ingrained in parts of US politics but it is also clearly present in the UK. Similarly the reaction to the overwhelming evidence of climate change – utter disinterest with the occasional quip of 'what happened to global warming?' when it snows.

Finally was the reaction of the scientist alongside the Prime Minister at the March 3 press conference. Upon hearing a statement that was clearly not conducive to public health, Chief Scientific Officer Sir Patrick Vallance did not attempt to publicly rebuke what was clearly terrible advice. He was instead very diplomatic, looking exasperated and simply saying 'wash your hands'. From now on scientific experts would regularly flank UK Government Ministers to add their expertise to statements but they too would come in for criticism for becoming a 'PR wing' of the government. Perhaps scientists shouldn't be criticised for not calling out the Prime Minister on national television – they are scientists not politicians. However, there would be legitimate concerns that the lines between the two would blur at times during the upcoming crisis.

As the amount of cases began to increase daily other countries were heading into some form of lockdown, with schools closing and in many places heavy fines for those found to be breaking the restrictions. But in the UK (and it is important to remember at this stage there was a uniform UK-wide approach) things were different. This is when the phrase 'herd immunity' became mainstream and would shortly become one of the most fought-over parts of the narrative around the early days of the virus.

The concept of herd immunity is that if enough people are immune to the virus it will break the lines of future transmission, meaning the end of the epidemic. Ideally this is done with a vaccine (which at this point was considered to be at least a year away). Without a vaccine the other option is to allow people to catch the virus while sheltering those most at risk. Speaking on Friday March 13 Patrick Vallance said: "Communities will become immune to it and that's going to be an important part of controlling this longer term. About 60% is the sort of figure you need to get herd immunity."[10]

You don't need to be an epidemiologist or a doctor to realise the risks of doing this with a new virus. First, this policy will still lead to the deaths of hundreds of thousands of people. There are 66 million people in the UK meaning that if you allow 60% infection you are allowing roughly 40 million people to get the virus. At a 1% mortality rate you are allowing 400,000 people to die. This is a greater number than Britain had military dead in World War Two. To put that in a Welsh context it is 18,600 – more than the population of Aberystwyth.

Secondly, there was no concrete evidence that long term immunity was even possible from the virus – this was a new disease and not fully understood. Government advisor and disease modeller Graham Medley advocated the policy on *Newsnight* on March 12 suggesting that in an ideal world you would put all the vulnerable people in the north of Scotland and everyone else down in Kent to have a 'nice big epidemic'[11]. The backlash was immediate and strong. Anthony Costello, professor of health and sustainable development at University College London and a former director of maternal and child health at the WHO, branded the whole idea unethical. Professor Costello tweeted: "Is it ethical to adopt a policy that threatens immediate casualties on the basis of an uncertain future benefit?" This dalliance with herd immunity (which the Government would later deny) was pointed to by many as the reason the UK was slow going into lockdown. While other countries were battening down the hatches and closing schools we were just being told to wash your hands while singing 'happy birthday' twice. ('The Gambler' by Kenny Rogers was also a popular choice.)

At this stage the UK Government had a four phase plan to respond to Covid: contain, delay, research, mitigate. The contain phase was defined as: detect early cases, follow up close contacts, and prevent the disease taking hold in this country for as long as is reasonably possible. Delay entailed slowing the spread in this country, and if it did take hold, lowering the peak impact and pushing it away from the winter season.

On the 12th the Government announced it was moving out of the 'contain' phase into the 'delay' phase. The risk level was raised to high, and anyone with symptoms was asked to self-isolate for a week. They abandoned attempts to contact and trace people (they didn't have the capacity to deal with the number of cases) who may have the virus and instead focussed on 'flattening the curve'. The idea was that if you could spread the peak of the virus over a longer period, the number of cases at any one time would remain lower and within the NHS's capacity.

Despite this, still no lockdown was ordered and there was confusion in the messaging coming from Government. Incredibly, with all of this going on, the Wales against Scotland rugby match was still planned to go ahead in Cardiff on March 14. Dr Jenny Harries, the Deputy Chief Medical Officer for England, said: "In general, those sorts of events and big gatherings are not seen to be something which is going to have a big effect, so we don't want to disrupt people's lives."[12] But people were scared and, frankly, desperate to have their lives disrupted and see some leadership on this issue. Two days before the match the other two Six Nations games were cancelled, Wales' football match against the USA on March 30 was also cancelled, with the Premier League put on hold until at least April. But Health Minister Vaughan Gething said: "There is little medical reason at the moment to ban such events." People were incredulous. Ireland, a country of 4.83 million, had 43 cases and had just ordered all schools to close. Wales, a county of 3.139 million had 25 cases, had decided to allow 70,000 people to gather in one place. This is not to mention all the social gatherings that would occur in towns and villages across Wales to watch the match. With just 24 hours to go and up to 20,000 Scots travelling to Cardiff for the match, the game was called off by the Welsh Rugby Union. The Scotland fans were already packed into bars and restaurants in the Welsh capital – the late notice was widely condemned but many were also relieved the decision had been made.

The same day a joint press conference was held by First Minister Mark Drakeford, Health Minister Vaughan Gething and NHS Wales chief executive Andrew Goodall. They announced the suspension of non-urgent outpatient and surgical care in Wales due to the coronavirus outbreak. This would allow staff, beds and other resources to be reallocated in priority areas as emergency service staff prioritised coronavirus. Speaking at the press conference Mr Gething said the estimate by scientists was for 20,000 possible coronavirus deaths in Wales with a maximum figure of 25,000.

Crucially this move would also fast-track placement to care-homes by suspending the protocol which allows a choice of homes. The decision gave the Welsh NHS a head start preparing for the storm that was already stirring but begged the question for many why their cancer consultation had been cancelled when thousands of Scottish rugby fans had been allowed to travel into Wales on the very same day.

If people were incredulous about the rugby match going ahead, they were downright furious when a planned concert by the Stereophonics went ahead over the weekend of Friday, March 14 and Saturday 15. On Saturday evening the band tweeted a picture of a packed Motorpoint Arena in Cardiff city centre with the phrase 'Cardiff is rockin'!'. People stood shoulder to shoulder like the contents of a vacuum-packed travel case in ways that just weeks later would be unthinkable. Doctors were publicly calling on the band to cancel the gig, with a huge social media backlash labelling them and the people who attended 'irresponsible' and 'selfish'. Many mass gatherings had already been cancelled and legitimate criticism could be levelled at the band. However, it should also be pointed out that other countries had taken the decisions out of the hands of organisers, with governments stepping in to do the right thing. It seems outrageous that important operations (and what operation on the NHS isn't ultimately important to the person receiving it?) were cancelled to protect the NHS but large gatherings that would directly increase the pressure on the health service were allowed to continue.

On March 16 Wales saw its first death from coronavirus after a 68-year-old with underlying health conditions died at Wrexham Maelor Hospital. This phrase 'underlying health condition' became something of a mantra for those still looking to underplay the danger of the virus. Every death that was announced alongside the phrase 'they had an underlying health condition' was perceived as being a crumb of comfort by many, as if to say 'don't worry, this virus isn't really dangerous to most of us, these people would have died anyway' – it was perverse. There were thousands of examples of the kindness and selflessness of humanity during this crisis but the idea that we should take comfort in the fact that this virus would only kill the old and vulnerable showed how quickly we cling to any form of hope in hard times, and was unpleasant to see. It was also monumentally short-sighted. Underlying health condition did not just mean someone was on a ventilator already and the virus finished them off – it applies to people overweight (35.6% of the UK), with diabetes (6%), or asthmatic (12%). What adult over the age of forty does not have some kind of underlying health condition?

March 16 also saw first use of another phrase that would repeatedly come back to haunt many unprepared and slow-to-act governments around the world. In a broadcast, World Health Organisation head Dr Tedros Adhanom Ghebreyesus lamented the fact that there had not been an urgent enough escalation in testing, isolation and contact tracing, which should be the 'backbone' of the global response – 'Test, test, test' he demanded.

The next day 'vulnerable people' were told to isolate for twelve weeks – this list included pregnant women (as a precaution because the evidence was unclear how they would be affected), those aged over 70 and those under 70 with underlying health conditions (which at this point included everyone eligible for the flu jab on medical grounds). At the same time Patrick Vallance was telling the Health Select Committee that under 20,000 deaths would be 'a good outcome'.[13]

It was on March 17 that I took my computer and screens home from work. Along with millions of others I was to begin a long battle with wifi, noisy neighbours and back pain as I struggled to work remotely. As I left my desk, neighbour and then Chief Reporter at the *Western Mail* shouted after me: "See you at the Christmas party!"

On the 20th the Deputy Chief Medical Officer for England Jenny Harries told the UK that "the country has a perfectly adequate supply of PPE" and that supply pressures had now been 'completely resolved'.[14] The falsehood of this statement was clear at the time from anecdotes, borne out by subsequent evidence and mortality rates. It was an example of a growing trend of scientists making statements that appeared more like a Government press release than the scientific assessment of available information.

In what was becoming the norm, the public would gather round the television every day at 5pm to watch the Prime Minister give the latest bulletin on the virus, with a Union Jack backdrop and flanked by scientists (the government would tell you they were following the science at every available opportunity). Each time, the situation and the messaging was more dire and it was becoming increasingly clear from news reports and anecdotes on the frontline that the country was not remotely prepared for what was now happening.

Also on the 20th it was announced that cafés, pubs, bars, clubs, restaurants, gyms, leisure centres, nightclubs, theatres and cinemas must close that night. It gave people the chance for one last night out before the closure. Though it was quieter than usual on the Friday night, Newport in particular saw substantial crowds in some bars, well into the night. Sadly for all those people who had just had their last big piss-up for months, panic buying had left supermarkets with no toilet roll or hand sanitiser. Videos began to surface of NHS staff arriving at supermarkets after shifts to find empty shelves and supermarkets began introducing limits on how much of each product people could buy. The same day the Welsh Government announced it would provide funding to get all homeless people a bed in hotel rooms, student blocks and B&Bs to keep them safe during the crisis. On the one hand this was great, but it also begged the question why this had not been the case all along?

Schools followed next. Established science had long said that the closure of schools was one of the big steps a government could take that would have a meaningful impact on the spread of the virus – but it was not that simple. If children were not in school, they needed looking after. Parents would normally turn to grandparents for childcare but they were likely the people most at risk if they caught the disease. Still, on March 20 all schools in Wales were closed.

As the virus marched on it swiftly became clear that south east Wales around Newport was by far the worst area. On March 21 Wales had 280 cases of the virus, 145 of them were in the Gwent area whilst, in comparison, Powys had only 9.

Most of Western Europe was now in some form of lockdown and yet one had still to be ordered in the UK. There was a resistance from Boris Johnson to dictate to people that they must stay home, with some lingering hope that just strongly suggesting it would be enough. There was a huge amount of goodwill at the time and most people understood the social distancing rules but simple guidance was clearly not going to be enough. People were writing furious Facebook posts accompanied by pictures of rammed parks and busy play areas. One Cardiff doctor called me in despair after driving past a busy Pontcanna fields in the city. He had heard from colleagues what the situation was like in London and knew the storm that was coming. Finally, on March 23 Boris Johnson accepted the inevitable and ordered us to 'stay home, protect the NHS, save lives'.

2. Stay Home, Protect the NHS, Save Lives

March 23 to March 29
Wales' confirmed Covid-19 cases – 418
Wales deaths – 16
UK confirmed cases – 5,683
UK deaths – 281

"It is still true that many lives will sadly be lost," said Prime Minister Boris Johnson as he announced the UK going into lockdown. The PM was absolutely correct. From Downing Street, back-dropped by an enormous Union Jack flag, a stately fireplace and polished wooden floors, the PM gravely said that "though huge numbers are complying with the advice to stay home, more is needed. From this evening I must give the British people a very simple instruction – you must stay home."

The phrase 'fast moving situation' is perhaps overused in political journalism (alongside 'a perfect storm') but the last week in March was incredibly fast moving.

The key message in the government's lockdown was that the public should stay at home. It was permissible to go out only to shop for basic necessities, exercise once a day, any medical need, to provide care or to help a vulnerable person (which in two months will become known as the 'Cummings get out of jail free card') and travelling to and from work when this cannot be done from home. The PM encouraged people to try to do their grocery shopping online which led to several supermarket websites crashing[1].

Life as we knew it was stopped immediately. All those things that simply are life: the school run, young people being educated, meeting friends, weddings, taking your kids to a play area, all halted.

On the same day as the lockdown was announced those still holding on to that common but reprehensible thought, 'it doesn't matter it will only affect the elderly', were brought down to earth when an 18-year-old died of the virus. They were the youngest person to have died so far in the UK[2]. Sadly this would not be a record that would stand for long.

In the face of the dramatic lockdown announcement it didn't register that Johnson's messages to the 'British people' would become a flash point and source of frustration to politicians in Cardiff Bay and Hollyrood as the crisis progressed. Though in this speech he was correct in addressing the British people as a whole, the rules of lockdown were decided by the devolved nations[3]. Though at this time, when nations of the UK were 'walking in lockstep' (another phrase to become overused in the following weeks and months), differentiating between English rules and UK rules was not an issue. However in about six weeks, when we have English holiday-makers turning up on rural Welsh beaches this is going to become a problem.

Operation 'flatten the curve' was now fully underway across the UK. In a statement the same day Public Health Wales officials said that the virus was now circulating in 'every part of Wales'[4]. Cardiff and Vale Health board put out temporary job adverts for what seemed like, every job imaginable. Housekeeping, catering, hospital portering, health care support workers, administration and clerical staff, drivers, allied health professionals and clinical scientists, doctors, nurses and IT experts were all called upon to sign up[5]. A tough task given that there was hardly a surplus of nurses and doctors before the crisis.

Suddenly sport stadia were no longer cauldrons of competitive atmosphere. Whereas just days before we had been debating whether it was the best move to bring 70,000 rugby fans into the Principality with a closed roof (screw you Eddie Jones, we will shut it if we want), on March 27, less than a week later, plans were announced to turn the iconic pitch into a huge 2,000-bed hospital.

It wasn't just the Millennium, sorry Principality, that was seeing changes. Llanelli Scarlets handed over the Parc y Scarlets to the Welsh NHS to become a 250 bed field hospital, named Ysbyty Enfys Scarlets with Enfys (rainbow), a reflection of the symbol of hope chosen for the pandemic which was now showing up in windows across the country.

From a Welsh perspective, one of the biggest stories of the first lockdown period was not just how many cases there were, but where they were located. New case figures released on the 23rd confirmed that Gwent was the epicentre of Covid-19 in Wales and had the highest UK rates of the disease outside London. Of the 418 confirmed cases in Wales that day 220 of them were within the Aneurin Bevan Health Board.

Eighty year old Marita Edwards was among them. A retired cleaner and keen golfer, she had gone into Newport's Royal Gwent hospital for a routine gallbladder operation at the end of February. She caught the disease and according to reports at the time was told she had pneumonia. Three weeks later she died of the virus and was believed to be the first person to die from a hospital-acquired infection of Covid-19.

Marita's case was significant for several reasons and, in micro-cosm, illustrated the predictability of the unfolding disaster. She was an early example of the failure to test. For a considerable period she was not tested for the disease. The issue of testing capacity, who to test and when to test is one of the recurring themes of the crisis. What can be measured can be managed. Without testing, how could public health officials possibly be expected to manage the disease?

For almost three weeks, Marita was inside a hospital and could have had coronavirus for most of that time. She was cared for by hospital staff and visited by family. All of whom could have been exposed to the disease. Those staff will have probably also have come into contact with dozens of people over the following days.

It was hugely significant that she caught the disease in hospital. It very quickly became apparent how dangerous hospitals were becoming for sick people. To suggest that we didn't know that hospitals would be the places most at risk from the virus is laughable. It is the exact location where people who have a severe form of the virus would go and exactly where many people at risk with an underlying health condition would be also.

Marita Edwards' case was also significant as an early example of how hospitals tried to cope with new situations arising from the virus. According to her son, she was isolated in the last week of her life once there was a suspicion that she had the virus. She was moved to an isolation ward. Her family could only visit wearing masks, gloves and aprons. This was the case all over the country. In the Gwent ICU they actually started using iPads so that people could speak to their family digitally without catching the virus.

It wasn't recognised at the time, but Marita's death marked something else, outside her personal experience. Her individual case was reported in the media. In the early part of the pandemic in Wales, because numbers were low, news organisations were able to treat each death as the individual tragedy it was, if the family desired such coverage.

In Marita's case her son Stuart Loud posted the story on Facebook and spoke in moving radio interviews saying: "If she had not been in hospital she would be still be alive. Clearly there was a coronavirus infection in the hospital which claimed my mum's life. I sit here, heartbroken by the loss of my beautiful mum. I sat for hours holding her hand and an oxygen mask to her face, as this extremely aggressive killer took control of her. Her death was horrific and a mental picture I can't forget. Please, please take this virus seriously. I don't want anyone else to endure what our family is going through. The legacy is an uncertainty about the funeral and tribute she so deserved and my wedding in four weeks, which she was so looking forward to. All because of this virus."

Marita had a son, daughter and granddaughter. She was going to attend her son's wedding in a month's time.

Throughout the crisis, at 2pm every day, Public Health Wales would release the latest figures for confirmed cases and deaths. We would report those figures as soon as they were released. Very quickly we moved from one or two deaths a day to dozens.

It is a tragic quirk of news reporting that as death tolls increase often our feeling of empathy for those who have lost their lives can diminish because we are talking about numbers instead of people. A report that "John Smith, 48, healthy father of three, died after a sudden, heart attack in Caerphilly" is one to which readers will empathise. They may think "I know (or I am!) a person in their late forties" or "I have children, imagine if they were without a dad". Not to mention that they know where it happened: "Caerphilly? I have been there! My mate Dai is from Caerphilly."

As the extent of the epidemic grew the victims stopped being Marita Edwards of Gwent and became one of tens or hundreds or thousands reported. The dead became anonymous to the general public, and the public began to feel desensitised. People respond to people, not numbers.

Take the example of illegal migration. Over 27,000 migrants have died at sea trying to get into Europe since 1993. I know, just as any decent person does, that those figures are appalling. I know that every single one of those numbers is a human being. I know they are doing exactly as I would do in their circumstances (though I don't think I would have half the courage they have).

Yet that figure does not stir a fraction of the emotion in me as one image of two-year-old Alan Kurdi (initially reported as Aylan), facedown in the sand on the Turkish beach at Bodrum. I can still tell you what he was wearing off the top of my head. Blue shorts, red t-shirt and tiny little shoes. That is a human being. He has a name. He looks like my little cousins and the children I see as I jog round a park. For parents that reaction is going to be a hundred fold more intense.

There is a reason that image conjured up more emotion and calls for change than the figure of 27,000. It is the same reason that George Floyd dying under the knee of an officer sparked global protests more than any dry figures about stop and search ever could – people respond to people.

To return to Marita Edwards, it is really important to remember that, no matter how high the death toll, we are always talking about people. When Chief Scientific Officer Sir Patrick Vallance[6] told the Health Select Committee just before lockdown that 20,000 deaths or below being 'a good outcome', he was talking about 20,000 human beings. When the death toll goes over 40,000 and the Prime Minister says in PMQs that he is proud of the government's record, remember that is 40,000 human beings, just like Marita Edwards or Alan Kurdi.

In the first few weeks of the lockdown the big story in terms of the Welsh outbreak really was all about the Aneurin Bevan Health

Board. So why was Gwent so bad? The definitive answer will have to wait until the inevitable public enquiry and swarms of epidemiologists are able to dig into the data. However there are a few theories.

The theory was put forward by Wales' Chief Medical Officer Frank Atherton in a press conference on March 26 was that it was close to England[7]. He suggested that the area's proximity to the border was an issue although this didn't explain why it was worse than areas such as Bristol which, on April 9 had 46 cases per 100,000 compared to Newport's 286.

There was also speculation that it was because of a rugby match. On March 6 there was a game between Newport Gwent Dragons and Italian side Benetton leading some to suggest that it was seeded here from Italy which had far more cases of the virus than elsewhere. However Dr Andrew Freedman, expert in infectious diseases and an honorary consultant physician at Cardiff University School of Medicine, said that given that only 2,000 people attended that game and it was five days after Wales' first case, it is likely the virus was already spreading in communities.

More light was shed as we neared the end of the month and Gwent had 514 cases (Cardiff and Vale had the next highest number on 282). Mark Drakeford said the reason for the spike was a combination of an infected health worker and increased testing. The health worker was diagnosed quite early and was found to have passed the disease on to several colleagues. This in turn led to an increase in testing in the Gwent area, and to more confirmed cases.

However, other indicators of high virus levels, such as ICU admittance and GP contacts, were also higher in Gwent than many other parts of Wales, suggesting that there were other factors in addition to more testing. Good luck to the swarming epidemiologists with that one.

As the virus established itself, it quickly became clear how lacking in PPE the Welsh NHS was. I conducted several interviews with healthcare professionals in the first two weeks of lockdown. Though from different hospitals and professions they all told the same story. They were exhausted, didn't have enough PPE and were terrified for their families. They all echoed the same perception that the health service was simply not prepared for this kind of epidemic. The PPE chapter discusses this in more detail.

One woman, who I interviewed on the 27th, worked in the University Hospital of Wales. She was on the edge of tears when I spoke to her. Describing the NHS as 'self-harming' she painted a bleak picture of what was happening in Wales' biggest hospital. She told me: "People are walking around with no masks at all. People working around people who have coronavirus just have surgical masks and no protective equipment for their eyes. I am going into work every day petrified. In my role I have to go all over the hospital to both people with and without the virus and worry I am spreading it to other patients."

She had just treated sixteen patients in two hours. At one point she had direct face to face contact with a patient, and as she was leaving the room two other staff came in wearing hazard suits. The patient had already tested positive for coronavirus and was now been taken to a specialist ward.

The woman was furious that she had been allowed to speak to and touch a patient with suspected Covid, without proper PPE. "I would have thought we would have a supply of masks," she told me. "The ones we do have, there are no tests to make sure it has been fitted right. I have been contemplating leaving because I don't want to expose my children to this."

This was a recurring theme with all the staff I spoke to. No PPE. It was not just the lack of PPE that was the issue for many but the way the problem was not fully acknowledged by the Welsh Government. One Cardiff surgeon told me that the lack of PPE "represents a failure at a local level and at the Welsh Government level" and that there had "been a lack of honesty and transparency over these shortages, with rationing disguised as policy".

On March 25, we saw the very real risks that staff were exposing themselves to when Dr Habib Zaid, 74, died at Southend Hospital in Essex. He is believed to be the first practicing doctor to die from the virus[8].

So PPE is essential. With a deadly virus the public must be careful, act prudently and most importantly, be responsible. Contracting the virus was a risk to the individual, and to those who might become infected through contact. It was also a pressure on the NHS, where resources, including care beds and ventilators were like gold dust in the first week of lockdown.

And yet the Prime Minister didn't seem to get the memo (or apparently the dozens of scientific papers prepared for him for the last three months). At 11.15am Boris Johnson posted on Twitter a video in which he said he'd tested positive for coronavirus. I saw it pop up immediately while I was in an interview with hospital workers. I'd have felt like such a swine to end an interview while someone was pouring their heart out, so I scrambled to send it to newsdesk while also trying to shorthand what the interviewee was saying.

Some of the predictable disasters resulting from coronavirus take a bit of digging and analysis to unpick. However the fact the PM would contract coronavirus was an event that was obviously going to happen. Earlier in the month he had excitedly, in the blasé style of a Big Brother contestant turning on the Christmas lights in Neath, told a press conference that he 'shook hands with everybody' at a hospital including coronavirus patients.

It worth remembering that a sub-group of the UK Government's Scientific Advisory Group for Emergencies (SAGE)
recommended that the government should "advise against greetings
such as shaking hands and hugging, given existing evidence about
the importance of hand hygiene"[9]. This advice was issued on the
very day that Johnson was shaking hands more than a candidate on
The Apprentice.

At the same time England's Chief Medical Officer Chris Whitty
was self-isolating because he also had symptoms, as was health secretary Matt Hancock who'd tested positive. Obviously news
organizations descended on Downing Street at these revelations.
The cameras picked up Dominic Cummings running out of the
famous black door and scuttling off in great haste. I remember discussing with colleagues whether we should do a light hearted piece
about how, in my opinion, he was running like a mixture of
Smeagol from Lord of the Rings and Mr Bean, but decided it
wasn't worth it as most members of the public didn't have a clue
who he was. Give it a few weeks.

The first week of lockdown was utterly bizarre. It was daunting
and scary for everyone but there was something surreal about it.
Everyone knew you were living through (and reporting on) his-
toric events but it didn't quite feel real. Each day seemed to blur
into one. It was just like freshers week at university but instead of
getting drunk and discovering new friends you were thinking of
team names for the first of 80,000 Zoom quizzes you would take
part in (Professor Quiz Whitty is a personal favourite).

The country was experiencing a collective novelty of discovering walks you never knew existed thirty minutes from your home
and working out why your back was hurting after working at your
dining room table for eight hours.

Facebook was full of funny videos featuring nurses dancing in A&E with a 'stay home' banner behind them.

As the supermarkets remained lacking in hand wash and loo paper you cursed the fact that you hadn't stolen toilet roll during your last day in the office.

It wouldn't take long for the novelty to wear off.

3. A Death Warrant from the Grim Reaper

March 30 to April 5
Wales' confirmed Covid-19 cases – 1,241
Wales deaths – 48
UK confirmed cases – 19,522
UK deaths – 1,228

After week one of the lockdown the country was trying to catch its collective breath, and not just because of the Joe Wicks exercise videos.

As the initial shock of the lockdown wore off the key issues of the crisis were starting to crystalise, with testing becoming the major talking point of the next month. 'Test, test, test' was the advice from the WHO. The need for testing was enormous. The UK and Wales were flying blind. The Government and the scientists advising them, simply didn't know where a lot of the cases were. By the time people showed up in intensive care units the disease would have been circling in a community for three weeks. There were global shortages in the materials needed to create the tests. I have never used the word 'reagent' so much in my life.

Testing wasn't just needed so that resources could be correctly directed. It was also needed to keep the NHS staffed. The advice was that a temperature or a persistent cough meant self-isolation for seven days. Just emerging from winter, many NHS staff had a cough for a multitude of reasons that were not actually Covid-related. Yet because they were unable to be tested they had to sit on the bench when they were most needed. This was not just an issue in hospitals. In care homes many staff were told to isolate under the UK Government guidelines. But people needing care always need that care. This meant that care homes, which were already struggling for staff before the crisis, were often forced to use agency staff. This completely predictable turn of events would condemn many of Wales' most vulnerable to die, alone, surrounded by strangers. This will be explored in depth in the chapter on care homes.

In response to the testing shortage First Minister Mark Drakeford announced that there would be 5,000 tests a day by the middle of April and 9,000 a day by the end of the month. Considering that Wales was languishing at under 1,000 a day at the start of the month this was an ambitious target. At the same time UK health secretary Matt Hancock announced (in what I am sure he felt was a statement oozing Churchillian statesmanship) that England would be doing 100,000 tests a day by the end of the month.

In Wales, the Welsh Government and Public Health Wales ended up coming nowhere near and the target was abandoned. They were not helped by the fact that an enormous order for 5,000 tests a day from the pharmaceutical company Roche was being commandeered by NHS England at the end of March[1]. Wales would not get close to 5,000 tests a day until September 1. On the English side of the border the test target was not abandoned. Matt 'give myself a big Hand'cock would be in bullish mood when he announced that NHS England had hit its target of 100,000 tests a day[2]. Yet just a cursory glance at what they had actually done showed that their 'achievement' involved as much misinformation and misdirection as a Moscow internet café.

The issue of testing threads its way through the entire crisis and deserves full analysis and assessment. Shortcomings in our testing strategy meant that there were more avoidable deaths in Wales. The issue is explored in full detail in the chapter 'Testing Times'.

On Monday and Tuesday of this week the issues beyond just the deadly effect of the virus were starting to emerge. Wales had suspended all 'non-urgent' outpatient and surgical care in mid-March[3]. The move, designed to free up health workers to focus on the avalanche of Covid-19 cases about to crash into hospitals, was widely seen as prudent and decisive at the time. But now the reality of what a 'non-urgent' procedure is began to hit home.

Non-urgent includes many cancer treatments. Tenovus Cancer Care chief executive Judi Rhys said hundreds of people could die because of the lack of treatment[4]. The outlook for patients was grim. Even services not suspended were delayed because specialist staff had to self-isolate as they had symptoms but were unable to take a test to allow them a return to work. At the end of April I would interview a cancer patient who spoke about the terror of knowing that a cancer was growing inside them with no date for when it would be treated.

The situation is another example of a completely predictable disaster. The NHS was struggling before the pandemic. This was not a smoothly functioning machine that became unstuck by coronavirus. Our NHS was already a prime example of a system with an underlying health condition.

In the summer of 2018 I had written a piece on the enormous number of operations cancelled in Wales[5]. A freedom of information request to the Welsh Government found that almost 75,000 operations in Wales were cancelled for 'non-clinical' reasons in 2017 and 2018. Operations in the Welsh NHS can be cancelled for three different reasons: clinical, non-clinical and patient. A clinical cancellation happens when it is unsafe to proceed due to the patient's health and fitness. A non-clinical cancellation occurs when the hospital itself decides to cancel. This can be due to a number of reasons, including staff sickness or a lack of available beds. Patient cancellation is, obviously, when a patient cancels the operation, for whatever reason.

Clearly clinical and patient reasons are perfectly justifiable and a part of the unpredictability of treating human beings. However, 75,000 cancellations is not a symptom of a healthy system. Many procedures were cancelled on the day of the operation with the person already having gone without food or water ahead of the procedure. I interviewed a man called Stephen Eddy from Gwaun-Cae-Gurwen, near Port Talbot for that story. He'd had an operation on an infected knee cancelled four times. On the fourth occasion he found out only on the morning of the op because he called the hospital to double check. I relate this story to both hammer home again that this is individual human beings who are suffering, not merely numbers on a spreadsheet, and to show how much the NHS in Wales was already struggling before Covid.

This also needs to be remembered when considering the cancellation of non-urgent appointments. Though the word 'cancer' naturally creates really powerful reactions in people and the idea of cancer patients not receiving the treatment they need is awful, there are many other people who also needed attention. The NHS does not perform operations on you unless you need one. Every person who has had an operation cancelled because of this crisis will be worse off for the experience. It could be mild discomfort but may also have condemned people to an indefinite period of living in pain, possibly disabled and needing assistance too, with no end in sight. And all too often, the people hit by this will be the worst off and most vulnerable.

Elsewhere many people seemed to have found a way to adjust to lockdown as supermarket sales of alcohol jumped £125 million in just three weeks, with the pubs all closed. This week corresponded with my remembering how much I enjoy Brewdog's Dead Pony ale. Judging by my skin, waistline and bank account, by the end of April I was certainly a contributing factor to this spike in sales. People's growing thirst produced a story I heard from one of my colleagues during this time which made me laugh in spite of myself, because what these people were doing was irresponsible and technically illegal.

In one Valleys pub, which shall remain nameless, some of the patrons were clearly pretty devastated at the loss of the local. As pubs were shut but essential building and repair work was allowed these, erm, enterprising individuals decided on a 'work around'. They would all go to a lock-in at the pub but would only be admitted if they had paint brushes or rollers. The idea was that if the police were to turn up they would all say they were just painting. Though one suspects that their devastation at losing their boozer would be significantly less than their devastation at losing their lives (or passing the virus to their loved ones). However, in spite of my disapproval I chuckled at the idea of thirty pissed-up blokes stinking of Carling trying to explain to a copper why they had all had to carry out essential maintenance work at 11pm.

Throughout the week the burden being shouldered by NHS staff was becoming more and more stark. I covered the April 3 Welsh Government press conference where Mark Drakeford confirmed that at least 450 healthcare workers in Wales had tested positive for the disease. With 2,466 cases of coronavirus in Wales at the time almost 20% of cases were healthcare workers[6]. The anecdotes we were hearing backed up those figures. We ran stories featuring Libby Nolan, a senior nurse in a south Wales ITU, who said that she and her colleagues were writing letters in case they died in service. In a letter to the *Guardian* she added her voice to the hundreds calling for more PPE[7]. She wrote: "You just wouldn't send firemen into a burning fire without apparatus, would you?" No of course you wouldn't, because they would die.

That Mark Drakeford press conference (aka presser) was an absolute gold mine of stories. He revealed temporary morgues were being created to deal with increased demand and that the field hospitals that were being set up would be for people who didn't have, or had recovered from, the disease to free up hospital places for Covid-19 cases. He also announced that the rules around funerals would be relaxed. Previous guidance restricted who could attend; now families would be given a number and would decide among themselves who would go. I come from a very large family and can't even begin to imagine having to have those conversations. Funerals are such an essential part of the grieving process and not being able to give loved ones the send-off they deserve must be emotionally crippling.

The First Minister also announced that the Welsh Government would be introducing regulations that employers would now be required by law to keep a 2 metre distance between staff, the only UK nation to take that step. This was also the beginning of what became mainstays of Drakeford pressers: telling people not to break rules because it was sunny, and telling people not to drive from their houses to exercise elsewhere.

At this point, journalists were not allowed to attend the press conferences in person, and Zoom was used instead to ask questions. The difficulty with this is that it makes it hard to follow up a question. There is also the lingering anxiety that you will forget to change your Zoom name from when you were doing a quiz with your family the night before and your face will be broadcast with

'Will the Winner' written underneath.

Asking Mark Drakeford a question is a bit of an art form. The First Minister is a trained social worker and teacher, and worked as a lecturer for two decades. He likes to explain. Unlike many politicians who may give you a more comprehensive answer to a question when you annoy them or put them off balance, Drakeford is very different. He tends to be less forthcoming when you adopt a confrontational style. The best option is to ask for insight into decision making, then he will talk, and talk, and talk. You can almost feel the press officers on the other side of the camera signalling to him to stop.

Many think that 'holding politicians to account' is being aggressive, calling them out and overtly challenging them. These people usually have similar traits in common. They are often keyboard warriors on Twitter who wouldn't have the courage or the faculties make these challenges face to face. They also monumentally miss one of the key roles of a reporter.

It is absolutely true to say that the role of a journalist is to hold power to account. However, holding someone to account can take many forms. Just shouting someone else's political agenda at a politician rarely makes any meaningful change. If all you do is loudly challenge, make overblown statements and be aggressive, that becomes the base level of noise. You can't increase it from there. When something really bad happens or the Government makes a monumental cock up, all you can do is keep ranting in the same old tone. This is exactly why some of the speeches by Emily Maitlis at the start of *Newsnight* where she absolutely unloads on a political event carry so much weight. They are the exception and not the rule.

Asking the 'killer question' or getting a really good sound bite might get you a lot of retweets but often that does very little to enhance the lives of your readers. Being able to ask a question in a press conference is a real privilege. The vast majority of people do not get to directly question the people who make decisions that affect their lives. Questioning politicians, especially on such an important and developing issue as coronavirus, means asking the questions that people want answered. It is not about being seen to ask the clever or the witty question. It is about your reader leaving this conference more informed about the virus that is killing them and the lockdown that is making them poorer.

Getting politicians to commit to something, confirm things on the record and describe the current state of play is actually a far more effective way of holding them to account long term than finger pointing vitriol (social media has loads of bots that do that for free).

Of course when politicians are inept, corrupt and in the wrong they should be challenged. But in the main this is done far more effectively by shining a light on their errors than by being seen to tell them off for it.

Drakeford's press conference that day gave enough lines for half a dozen spin-off stories. Many would become flash points throughout the next few months of the crisis. The issue of healthcare workers catching the virus; a call by the First Minister to Westminster politicians to be careful to check whether their announcements apply to Wales (they won't); asking people not to travel; a refusal to answer questions on the collapsed Roche tests deal and NHS capacity.

Political messaging around the lockdown showed that it was here to stay and figures released on April 4 showed why. The number of people who had died from coronavirus in the UK had risen by 708 to 4,313 – the highest rise since the start of the outbreak. Even those parts of the NHS not under direct pressure were having to make tough ethical decisions. Even the toughest ethical decision should be handled with tact and compassion, with basic human warmth probably more essential in those times. Yet it seems that tact was in very short supply at one GP surgery in the Llynfi Valley[8]. A letter sent to many of their sickest patients seen by WalesOnline, asked them to sign a 'do not attempt CPR' form if they get Covid-19. At first I was sure it must be a mistake, joke or spoof.

The letter started by outlining the underlying conditions that mean someone is at a higher risk from the virus. After a long list of serious conditions the letter said: "People with these conditions are also unlikely to be offered hospital admission should they become unwell and certainly will not be offered a ventilator bed". It then said that it wanted patients with these conditions to sign a do not resuscitate form meaning that "the emergency services will not be called and resuscitation attempts to restart your heart or breathing will not be attempted". If this didn't sound appealing they added that signing the form would have 'several benefits'. They were: "Your GP and more importantly your friends and family will know not to call 999"; "Scarce ambulance resources can be targeted to the young and fit who have a chance of surviving the infection", and "The risk of transmitting the virus to friends, family and emergency responders from CPR (even chest compression alone) is very high. By having a DNACPR form in place you protect your family and emergency responders from this additional risk."

This left patients at the practice, including the woman who contacted us who had been living with cancer for eight years, pretty crushed. The practice attempted to put them at ease by saying (in bold, underlined font) we "will not abandon you" but ruined the effect by adding straight after "but we need to be frank and realistic about what the next few months holds for us". The woman who contacted us said "it was like having my death warrant being sent by the grim reaper" and that "I'm not digging my grave yet." The black humour in this miserable story sums up why the Llynfi Valley is my favourite of the South Wales Valleys. Not only is it one of the widest, but the people there have a unique sense of humour and character. They are very welcoming (just don't slag off Maesteg).

Clearly this letter is just awful. Older People's Commissioner for Wales, Heléna Herklots said she was "shocked that it was even written, let alone sent out." An apology letter was dispatched afterwards saying the letter was "poorly worded and did not properly articulate the care and commitment we have for our patients". This really shows the pressure that medical professionals were under to prepare for the coming storm. On April 2, the UK death toll was higher than Italy's was at the same stage (though they were about three weeks ahead). People in the medical profession do not make requests like what we saw in the Llynfi Valley without good reason (though the handling was disgusting). They knew something was coming down the pipe.

It was in this week that the risks healthcare workers were taking were starting to become all too apparent, as was the impact a lack of proper PPE was having. Following Mark Drakeford's announcement that a significant proportion of the people testing positive for the virus were healthcare workers, and the deaths of some these staff was announced, it was becoming evident that there were a disproportionate amount of people from black, Asian and minority ethnic (BAME) backgrounds. Sadly this trend would continue and it is addressed in Chapter 17.

Usually Saturdays are one of the quietest days on our website in terms of traffic. With the exception of sport, there is a bit of a lull between about 10am and 6pm. Numbers are often particularly low if the weather is good. Saturday April 4 was a bit different.

First, Sir Keir Starmer was elected as the new Labour leader. There will be far more to say on Starmer later, especially as he began to demolish Johnson at Prime Minister's Questions. This is not to be over-dramatic. I live blogged PMQs regularly throughout the lockdown and at times it was hard to write the exchanges without appearing biased, such was the degree that Starmer out-matched the PM. It was almost like he is a trained barrister.

Next came the news that up to 4,000 prisoners in Wales and across the UK were to be temporarily released from prison in an attempt to control the spread of the disease[9]. Those released were low risk, all to be electronically tagged and temporarily released on licence. It would soon become clear that these people were not just gaining their freedom, they were leaving an environment that would become an absolute hotbed for the virus.

Thirdly came the growing weight of evidence that this was not just the disease of the old. This warning came from critical care consultant Dr David Hepburn who was running the ICU at the Royal Gwent Hospital in Newport which was at that time the heart of the epidemic in Wales. He had contracted the disease himself and had previously gone viral (excuse the pun) online when he spoke about his experience. A few weeks later I would conduct an in-depth interview with David but at this point I had not met him. Speaking to Channel 4 he said that all the patients in his intensive care unit were either in their fifties or younger. The youngest was a young woman in her early twenties. As if to back up this point came the news from NHS England that a five-year-old child had died after testing positive for coronavirus[10].

The following day Boris Johnson was admitted to hospital ten days after he had tested positive for the disease. According to Downing

Street he was still carrying a high temperature, and they were very keen to paint the move as a 'precautionary step'. At the time my instinct was that there wasn't much in this. Clearly the PM going to hospital is a big deal but I really thought that this would just be for check-ups. Other members of the Government had contracted the virus and were starting to come out the other side. However, over the following week it became increasingly clear that this was a very serious situation.

That Sunday finished, with an address from the Queen. Channelling a bit of Blitz Spirit and Vera Lynn she rounded off her speech with "we will meet again".

4. Please, Take My Liberty

April 6 to April 12
Wales' confirmed Covid-19 cases – 3,499
Wales deaths – 193
UK confirmed cases – 47,806
UK deaths – 5,373

My first diary note at the beginning of the third week shows how confusing this week felt. Despite only being in lockdown for a fortnight, a certain sense of normality had arrived. It was just accepted. If you had told me in 2019 that the Government would order me to stay home and only go out once a day for thirty minutes I would have probably scoffed. The idea that we wouldn't be allowed to go where we wanted when we wanted, would have been completely unbelievable. I don't think I would have believed that people would accept it – but they did. As the deaths and the horror stories from clinicians piled up many people were not resenting the lockdown – they were grateful for it. I would absolutely include myself in that.

It is amazing how happy we are to trade away our liberty in the interests of safety. You realise how easy it is, given the right set of circumstances, for dictatorships to start. Our history books are crammed full of men who have convinced nations of people to forego freedom for the sake of safety. Sometimes the threats that face them are real, sometimes they are manufactured, and sometimes the threat is real but fear is misdirected. I recall walking along a path and seeing the panic in another person's face at the realisation we were going to have to pass close to each other. I felt the same fear and yet just three weeks ago had stood in a three deep queue for a pint at the Tiny Rebel bar in Cardiff. Shoulder to shoulder with people and hardly giving it a thought. The difference three weeks makes is surprising. Fear is such a big driver of human action and now, I cannot judge the human beings throughout history who sat back and allowed their countries to slip into tyranny in exchange for security.

Monday started with a press conference from the First Minister as a routine started to develop around them. Drakeford would do Monday and Friday, Vaughan Gething the health minister would do Tuesday and the other two would be made up of a combination of Ken Skates (economy, transport and North Wales), Rebecca Evans (finance), Julie James (housing and local government) and Lesley Griffiths (environment, energy and rural affairs). There was also the appearance of Kirsty Williams (education), who is one of the rarest of all Cardiff Bay species – a lesser spotted Liberal Democrat.

Since the Prime Minister had been admitted to London's St Thomas's Hospital, the lobby reporters had been pushing Downing Street daily for updates on his health. Listening to his chief spokesman, the impression given was that Johnson was doing well. "He is in good spirits" was all he would tell journalists on the midday lobby call. This 'all is rosy' illusion was comprehensively shattered when it was announced that he had been admitted to intensive care. According to Downing Street this now meant that Dominic Raab would fulfill the PM's duties and it felt important to me to clarify the position here in Wales. Though the virus affects everyone, we knew it was more likely to be severe in older people and the First Minister was two years off drawing his state pension. It is a strange question to ask someone: 'what do we do if you contract the virus?' There was a plan in place.

If the First Minister was taken ill with the virus, Julie James would take up his responsibilities and if health secretary Vaughan Gething was ill, Drakeford would take over. To be fair to him, the First Minister didn't seem perturbed by the question or that fact his opposite number in Westminster was now quite seriously ill. He delivered his answer in his usual style – like a kindly librarian reading the shipping forecast.

Drakeford also announced that a testing centre would open at the Cardiff City Stadium the next day. People in the Leckwith area of Cardiff had for days watched equipment arriving along with people in high visibility jackets and masks (lucky buggers). They did not know what was going on but assumed it was to do with the virus. What we didn't realise at the time was that the Welsh Government was just as uninformed on what was going on as the people of Leckwith. Despite health being a completely devolved competency under our devolution settlement, the UK Government had totally blindsided the administration at Cardiff Bay. There will be more about this in the chapter on testing. Once the Welsh Government took over this facility, tests would be initially focussed on healthcare, prison, police and care workers from the Gwent area – still at this point the centre of the outbreak in Wales.

On the same day it was announced that for the next three months the Welsh Government's existing childcare scheme (providing thirty hours of early education and childcare to the working parents of three and four-year olds for forty-eight weeks of the year) would be suspended. Instead childcare would be offered for just the preschool children of critical workers. Importantly, it would also be available for children classed as vulnerable. A necessary addition.

As Drakeford was wrapping up his shipping forecast ('Humber, southwest 5 to 7, occasionally gale 8. Moderate or rough. Occasional rain. Good, occasionally moderate'), the Foreign and Commonwealth Office were issuing guidance advising against non-essential travel abroad 'indefinitely'. This was a significant step because it allowed people with holidays booked in the next couple of months to claim a refund. Before this advice, holiday companies were under no obligation to provide a refund for people booked on flights because it was the choice of the holiday maker if they opted to cancel their trip. This long overdue advice meant that travellers were now guaranteed a refund. Though it was supposed to be made within seven days, many were still chasing their payments well into the summer (giving Martin Lewis many a radio rant).

Later in that day Sir Keir Starmer announced his new shadow cabinet. Whereas for most journalists this is a case of picking out the interesting appointment and working out who has been snubbed, for Welsh political journalists it is a test of how well you know the forty Welsh MPs (who had quite inconveniently changed in December of 2019).

There were three Welshies in the new shadow cabinet and they clearly showed a shift in selection policy – overwhelming loyalty to Jeremy Corbyn was no longer a prerequisite. The three new members were: Nick Thomas-Symonds (Torfaen) who was made shadow home secretary; Jo Stevens (Cardiff Central) shadow culture, media and sport secretary; and Nia Griffith (Llanelli) the new shadow Welsh secretary. All three had served in one of Corbyn's shadow cabinets but had at some point resigned, with all three supporting the failed 2016 leadership bid of Pontypridd MP Owen Smith.

Stevens was particularly handy for me as I have known her in passing for several years and happen to drink in the same pub in Roath (The Four Elms, an establishment which is the perfect combination of rough but charming). Like Griffith, she had actually served in the shadow cabinet after Owen Smith's leadership bid. She had resigned again to vote against the three line whip obliging Labour MPs to vote in favour of Article 50, which would be politically suicidal in the overwhelming pro-remain Cardiff Central seat.

On a non-political note it was about this time that, after two weeks of just walking the same route during my once-a-day mandatory thirty minute exercise, I began to get itchy feet. I wasn't alone as conversations with others revealed that people everywhere were suddenly discovering the parks and nature reserves they never knew existed just a short walk from their homes. I was sure this spring the birds were getting louder.

However there were some people who were told not to leave their houses – those that were shielding. These were people considered so vulnerable to coronavirus that it was believed unsafe for them to even leave their front doors. They included people with certain cancers, those who'd had organ transplants, cystic fibrosis, severe asthma, severe COPD and those receiving immunosuppression therapies. There were originally 85,000 of these people identified in Wales though the figure rose above 130,000 as more information about the virus became available. In a country of only three million, this is not a small number.

These people were in for a rough time. Not only did they have serious underlying health conditions and face months of isolation, but a series of poor decisions, implemented glacially slowly by the Welsh Government exacerbated their problems. This was brought to my attention in my favourite of ways: a random phone call by a random member of the public. Life as a political journalist, especially when you are busy, can be a world of press releases, self-titled 'politicos' (give me strength), media officers and Twitter. All of whom are telling you what people want to read and what is relevant to your readers. Nothing brightens your day and makes you better at your job than when a member of the public calls you to say they have a problem. There is no bull crap. No email starting 'Happy Monday! I wanted to reach out to you about blah blah bland'. They tell you that they have a problem, why they have a problem, why that is a problem and want you to tell their story. They are real human beings and it reminds you what is great about the job.

On Wednesday, April 8 that real human being was Richard Mathias, from Merthyr Tydfil. Both he and his wife were in their eighties and were both shielding. "I go to Waitrose because my wife likes the spaghetti bolognese," was the first thing he said when I picked up the phone. "Since self isolating, I have had an enormous problem. We are both in our 80s and I received a letter saying I am particularly at risk."

Richard was one of the lucky ones because he had actually received a letter. In these early weeks 13,000 letters that were supposed to have been sent to the most of the most vulnerable people were sent to the wrong address[1]. The Welsh Government 'sincerely apologised' for the mistake blaming a 'processing error'. It took two weeks for everyone affected by the error to be contacted. It is easy, especially after some time has passed, to shrug and say mistakes happen but it is worth taking a moment to appreciate the serious-ness of this. For a fortnight, at the height of the virus circulating in Wales, the most vulnerable in society (who we had already identi-fied), were unknowingly putting themselves at risk because their government cocked up telling them how much danger they were in.

This is not the problem Richard had. His issue was the fact he was not able to secure an online supermarket delivery slot. Since the lockdown these slots had been as coveted as diamonds (and almost as much as toilet paper) as everyone scrambled to avoid risking their health queuing in the local supermarket. Many people would wait until midnight (when the next slots were released) in order to do this. This was a nightmare for people who were shielding. It wasn't the fact they didn't want to go to the shop, they had been explicitly told that they must not and their lives were perhaps dependent on following that advice. In England the UK Government and supermarkets had arranged a scheme whereby those who were shielding received priority in booking online slots. However, two weeks after this was introduced east of Offa's Dyke, there was no sign of a similar strategy for Wales.

Fair play to Richard, he really had tried to fool the system. He told me: "If you go to the supermarkets' websites they will ask you whether you are on the list of people who are at risk. It then asks if you live in England. If you click Wales it takes you to advice about self-isolating! I thought I would try putting in that I am English. Then after I had gone through all the rigmarole of registering it asked for my postcode. As soon as I put in CF48 they realised I was in Wales! I got sent back to the advice again."

When pressed about this issue the Welsh Government initially responded by referring to its own weekly free food box for people without family support networks. It is to be congratulated that any person who was shielding in Wales who didn't have a support network to shop for them were able to have some essentials dropped off for free.

But Richard didn't want this charity, he simply wanted to be able to buy the food and products he wanted. He told me: "We are entitled to a free food parcel but we don't need it, we want to do our normal shopping. The lists are out there because we had a call from the council offering us a free food parcel. If you want to buy your own food you have to take the risk to do a shop unless you have someone who can drop it on your doorstep. All I want is someone to open the list of vulnerable people up to the supermarkets as they do in England. Someone who is in Hereford on just the other side of the border would be able to access this."

Richard didn't need taxpayers' money to go towards giving him food, he just needed to be able to safely spend his own money on essentials. For many shielding people it was not just a matter of wanting choice as a consumer. The same day I spoke to Richard I also talked to 39-year-old Alex Collins who was shielding because he has cystic fibrosis. Due to his CF Alex is pancreatic insufficient, meaning he absorbs far less of his food than a normal adult and has very specific high fat and high sugar dietary requirements to maintain a healthy weight. This simply wouldn't be catered for with a generic food box.

So why hadn't the Welsh Government got its act together and arranged the priority slots with the supermarkets like they had in England? This is something of a mystery. Minister for environment, energy and rural affairs Lesley Griffiths was questioned about it in the Senedd and said that the delay was because of her personal concerns about data protection issues. She told the chamber: "I wasn't prepared to just release data without going through all the hoops that we had to do". This is weak given that England had acted far quicker, and reeked of excuses for slow action[2]. It was futher undermined when the Welsh Government contradicted itself just two weeks later. On April 22, when questioned by Leanne Wood in Plenary, First Minister Mark Drakeford then said: "Let me just be clear: there was no delay in getting supermarkets the information. There was a considerable delay in some supermarkets taking down off their websites the notice that said they were waiting for the information. They'd had that information for several days, many days in some cases, before they managed to take that notice down."[3]

The only weapon journalists have is to ask questions. Some may think that we go through bins or hack into databases (some of the reporters I have met can hardly turn their laptop on). Two seemingly contradictory statements by members of the same Government needed to be queried. We went to all the major supermarkets. The respective press offices of supermarkets were exactly how you would imagine. Asda were friendly but wanted to rush you through as quickly as possible to deal with the next query and Waitrose greeted you like you'd just walked into the business class departure lounge, giving you plenty of space and profusely apologising for having to put you on hold.

Waitrose said it had not received the required information from Welsh Government until the week before and Asda said they did not get the information until April 8. Other supermarkets said April 7. This was after the England scheme had been up and running for weeks. This is one of several occasions where the Welsh Government could have acted quicker.

Towards the end of the week the familiar story of care homes, testing and PPE rumbled on. WalesOnline[4] published a leaked letter from the Royal College of Nursing in Wales to Drakeford regarding the frustration of many of its members. The letter from RCN Wales director Helen Whyley painted a picture of a disjointed and confused care system. The letter said: "Our members deserve to know how the Welsh Government plans to protect people and have their anxiety and stress reduced by being able to access the latest guidance and plans."

These letters (and their subsequent leaks) don't just happen. The media are not the first port of call for an organisation or group that is having problems. Going public is usually the method of last resort for an organisation that simply wants answers. At the same time the Swansea branch of the union UNISON were complaining that many staff in private care homes were not able to access PPE. The

PPE saga took on a whole new dimension when some care owners started reporting that many of the wholesalers they used to source PPE from were now saying that much of the stock was 'reserved for England'-based care homes. Though this was technically true and Plaid Cymru made a great deal of fuss about this there was actually much more to this than meets the eye as we will see later.

As the week drew to a close it appeared that the worst was over for the Prime Minister as he was released from intensive care.

The weekend of the 11-12 of April was forecast to be the most beautiful of the year so far. Politicians fell over themselves to appeal to people to stay inside and be responsible. With three weeks of lockdown done, many were starting to ask when it would end. In what would turn out to be somewhat of an understatement health secretary Vaughan Gething told BBC Radio 5 Live that "We're in for several more weeks at the very least."

This had already been confirmed by an announcement by Mark Drakeford on Wednesday, April 8. Though Mr Drakeford was under no legal obligation to announce the lockdown until Monday the following week he opted to go ahead days before the same announcement was made by the UK Government in Westminster. It was the first example of Wales flexing its muscles over the lockdown restrictions and moving independently of the UK Government. Drakeford justified jumping the gun on the other devolved nations. He said he had intended to announce it at Plenary later the same day but didn't want people to make plans for the next week when he already knew full well that restrictions would be in place. On the Downing Street lobby call earlier in the day the Prime Minister's spokesman categorically refused to say whether the lockdown would be extended, though it was obvious it would need to be.

Amongst the seemingly endless misery of the first lockdown week was some good news. In the daily briefings we got used to seeing regular daily charts. There were so many at times it felt like that if Covid-19 didn't get us, death by Powerpoint would. In these charts the Government would show new cases, the amount of deaths, the amount of people on the roads and using public transport.

On April 9 deputy chief scientific adviser Professor Dame Angela McLean said that though deaths were continuing to increase, daily cases had started to plateau. This was significant because it showed both that lockdown was starting to have an effect but also the value of the three week cycle. It takes up to three weeks for any changes to the lockdown rules to have an impact. Over the coming months Drakeford and the Welsh Government would be loath to make more than one change every three weeks because they would not know the impact until twenty-one days in the future.

5. Thank You, Key Workers

April 13 to April 19
Wales' confirmed Covid-19 cases – 5,610
Wales deaths – 384
UK confirmed cases – 85,206
UK deaths – 11,282

The UK entered the second period of lockdown with the creeping realisation that, despite our hopes, the restrictions were not going away soon.

Even though the constraints were unheard of in a democracy, and right wing commentators must have written the word 'draconian' more times than their own name, there was still a general acceptance of the impositions. In many cases, people were glad to have the lockdown, with some vocal that it was not going far enough and needed to be more rigidly enforced.

One of the most read stories on Wales Online on Monday April 13 was of four men caught travelling from Cardiff to the Mumbles to go fishing. The interest this provoked highlighted the strength of feeling, made all the more intense by the fact they were travelling from Cardiff, which had large amounts of Covid in the community, to a rural area which was fairly untouched.

On the subject of website traffic I should add that we hit 70 million views on the site over a four week period – pretty astonishing for a news provider that caters to a country of three million. A reporter wants their journalism to matter to people. At a time when they are scared, confused and want to understand what is happening to them, people turn to the news sites they trust and, crucially, will provide information that is relevant to them. That people came to WalesOnline for answers and kept returning, was a real motivation to me and my colleagues. I hesitate to say things were really hard for us in the newsroom over this period. We were not risking our lives nor were we sweating our skin into oblivion covered in PPE, we were just telling stories. If you are not excited and motivated to cover massive stories in creative ways under pressure why would you want to be part of our industry? That said, that first month was the most intense and tiring I can remember.

The novelty of the lockdown had well and truly worn off by the start of the second period. Speaking to your granny through their patio window was not the same as being able to physically hold a loved one in your arms. A few exchanged words as you dropped off the shopping to a vulnerable family member (they probably hadn't been able to get an online delivery slot yet) paled in comparison to sitting around a kitchen table with a brew. Yet there was a growing acceptance among people that it was here to stay – the 'new normal'. There was also a new normal in the apparently relentless shortcomings in our response to it. PPE issues had not gone away and there was an incredible story of how more than 1,200 face shields sat in boxes unable to be given to frontline staff as they had not been assessed for safety standards. The visors were made by a web designer, Richard Blackwell, from Pentyrch in Cardiff using 3D printers and brought together a group of volunteers to assemble and distribute them. They had already supplied over 1,500 free visors to desperate care home staff, hospital workers and paramedics but were told to stop while they could be tested properly.[1]

Clearly PPE needs to be tested to make sure it is up to standard and 1,200 face shields is a drop in the ocean in terms of a nationwide health service but this exemplified the chaos reigning in the system at this time. The problem was not the willingness of people in Wales to step up to the challenge, they wanted to and they were, but there were simply not the organisation and the systems to manage this mass mobilisation.

Tuesday, April 14 was an especially busy day for news. It began with a report from the independent Office for Budget Responsibility (OBR) which forecast a bleak few months for the economy. It predicted that two million more people would be unemployed and UK GDP could fall by as much as 35%. According to the OBR, which was set up by the coalition government in 2010 to provide independent analysis of the UK Government's finances, up to 10% of the working population could end up without a job[2].

This seemed about right. During your thirty minutes of exercise a day you couldn't help but notice everything was closed. The only people you would see working were police, rubbish collectors and Deliveroo drivers. Of course, there was going to be a huge hit to the economy despite the successes of the furlough scheme. The part of the announcement that seemed less credible was their predictions for recovery, that despite the rapid drop, there would also be a very quick bounce back. This so-called 'V shaped' recovery (as opposed to a U shaped recovery) seemed a little far fetched. In this rapidly changing situation I had moved from being excited to watch a rugby match with 70,000 others to being at risk if I exercised for more than thirty minutes on my own. Now, the idea of the economy roaring back within six months seemed too good to be true. As a journalist (though admittedly not an economist), when something seems too good be true tiny little alarms sound. This happened in a big way when I heard this, though admittedly instead of the sirens it was just Boris Johnson's voice going 'fwoah fwoah fwoah'.

I was not the only one who was suspicious. On the daily Downing Street telephone lobby briefing the Prime Minister's spokesman (James Slack CBE, a former *Daily Mail* journalist who wrote the infamous 'Enemies of the People' front page story about judges, at the height of the Brexit debate) was joined by the representative from the Treasury to talk about the economic implications of the virus. All of the lobby reporters were of one mind, had the UK Government leant on the OBR regarding the report? The answer from the both Government representatives was a consistent 'no'. Getting anything he doesn't want to expand on from the PM's spokesman is like pulling teeth. He played it with such a straight bat that Geoffrey Boycott would have nodded appreciatively. "All I can do is point you to the fact that the OBR is an independent body," he would say again and again. This is another example of where journalism is more than simply asking one killer question that gets a big clap and cheer on *Question Time*. You cannot make someone answer a question, you are not the Spanish Inquisition. But you can try and elicit a commitment on something and then use good journalism practices afterwards to ascertain if what they are saying is the full truth.

On that same Tuesday some trends became apparent in the data the Welsh Government had begun publishing on a daily basis – the demographic that was contracting the disease most often was working age women[3]. According to Public Health Wales (PHW) the five gender age groups who were most affected were:

- Women aged 50-59: 13.3% of cases
- Women aged 40-49: 11.7%
- Women aged 30-39: 8.9%
- Men aged 50-59: 7.6%
- Women aged 20-29: 7.2%

This was not a slight anomaly or explicable by being within a margin for error: there was clearly something going on. What was most strange, was that it seemed to contradict the prevailing coronavirus narrative to this point – that the disease disproportionately impacted men. The data at the time from China's Centre for Disease Control found that for every 100 women who had the disease there were 106 men. A study published in the *New England Medical Journal* of 1099 patients in Wuhan found only 41% were women. This was supported by WHO data finding 51% of cases were men. There was a lot of debate about the rationale behind this. Suggestions included genetics: men are far more likely to smoke in China, men are more likely to be in occupations and environments to catch the virus, men are less likely to wash their hands.

So why was Wales different? News providers live and die on their ability to provide information that is entertaining/helpful/relevant to their readers and what could be more relevant than why the women of Wales were more likely to catch this deadly virus? The journalistic challenge was to report on a fast-moving situation involving a virus that did not even exist six months before. The smartest people in the world didn't know everything about this virus and only long term, peer reviewed research would be able to definitively answer the question of why Covid-19 was disproportionately infecting working age women in Wales.

But that question still needed to be addressed and it would be disingenuous not to try. Across the world issues affecting women are consistently under reported. Though progress has been made, and the very fact we even acknowledge the issue is a step in the right direction, but it is only the first step on a long journey we must undertake.

In order to try to explain the story I spoke to leading academics, physicians and women's groups to produce some hypotheses. The

issue that came up again and again (and that I personally am convinced is the explanation for the data) was that the occupations
which expose people to the highest risk of catching coronavirus
are dominated by women. Many of the key worker roles such as
nursing, care work and working on a supermarket checkout are
dominated by women. The Kings Fund reported that 80% of all
jobs in adult social care are undertaken by women with this figure
up to a possible 95% in direct care and support-providing jobs. The
Royal College of Nursing published figures in 2018 showing that
89.3% of all registrants are female.

The more you consider the higher proportion of working age
women catching the virus, the more apparent becomes the back
to front values system held by our society. Fundamentally, women
in Wales are putting themselves at risk because they care. They are
our front line. When the lockdown happened people were not
dying for lack of merchant bankers; policy makers were not kept
up late for fear that we would run out of chief executives. The point
is in the name – 'key workers'. Much like in the First and Second
World Wars, it was women who picked up a lot of day to day occupations that were essential to keeping the country going. In the
coronavirus crisis it was again women on the front line that saw us
through and the very least we as a society should have done is
ensure they were properly equipped for the battle against the virus
with the right PPE. Alongside the fairly pitiful wages paid to care
staff, this truly challenges society's values.

April 14 also saw Wales miss a substantial testing milestone. Back
on April 3, Mark Drakeford said there would be 5,000 tests a day
by the middle of the month and 9,000 a day by the end of the
month[4]. As the halfway point was reached PHW announced that
only 770 tests had been carried out the day before. health secretary
Vaughan Gething pointed the finger of blame at lack of referrals

for frontline workers. This was not really a full explanation as at the time the maximum testing capacity in Wales was just 1300 tests.

So it was double failure, not only had the Welsh Government failed to increase its testing capacity to the levels promised only eleven days before, it had also failed to utilise over 40% of that available capacity. This is perhaps a harsh assessment as the preceding weekend had been Easter and across the world countries were seeing drops in capacity after a weekend but it still remains a fairly damning set of stats.

Mr Gething himself said that it was "really frustrating for me that we haven't maximised that capacity" and that ten of Wales' twenty-two local authorities had not referred any social care workers for tests. This frustration was mirrored across all public services fighting the virus, not just in healthcare. On the same day I also broke the story that over two hundred firefighters, who felt physically able to work, were self-isolating because they'd had some mild coronavirus symptoms or had been near someone who'd had the virus[6]. The tests were available to allow these people to return to work, we simply were not using them.

There was some potentially positive news when it was announced that University Hospital of Wales (UHW) had become the first in the UK to conduct an antibody transfusion, which involved taking blood plasma from patients who had recovered from the virus and transferring it into a patient suffering from Covid-19. It was anticipated that this would result in a faster recovery.

In the middle of the week events took a bizarre turn, even by 2020 standards. With an autumn election and his poll ratings sliding, Donald Trump did what all children and bullies do when they are being blamed for things that are their fault. He tried to deflect the criticism, this time on the World Health Organization (WHO). In a series of accusations that built up over the next few months Mr

Trump claimed the WHO had opposed his travel restrictions imposed on China: it hadn't. He also claimed that the WHO had said no human to human transmission had taken during mid January. This was an 'interpretation' of a WHO Tweet saying that there was no clear evidence of it, though leading WHO staff confirmed human to human transmission on 22 January. Finally, Trump claimed that WHO had ignored credible reports on the virus in *The Lancet*. Richard Horton, the editor of this medical journal, debunked this by pointing out that its first article on the virus hadn't appeared until 24 January.

Despite this the President suspended the United States' contribution to the WHO. To do this during a global pandemic is about as advisable as chucking your Imodium in the bin when you are halfway through a vindaloo.

Such craziness appeared contagious, on Wednesday mobile phone networks reported a surge in attacks on 5G masts, with twenty cases of suspected arson reported. This stemmed from disinformation (aka lies) circulating online propagating the conspiracy theory that coronavirus was caused by the new 5G network currently being installed across the UK. I can't even bring myself to explain why this theory is utter tripe, and it can be filed in the same drawer as 'vaccines cause autism', 'the Earth is flat' and 'the EU has banned straight bananas'. It is easy to laugh at these claims as just crackpot but there are reasons why they cannot be shrugged off, such as the fact that one of the masts attacked provided mobile connectivity to the new Nightingale hospital in Birmingham. Bogus Facebook and Twitter accounts (often originating in Russia) churn out this garbage in accessible and shareable ways designed to achieve traction online. You may think what you are watching is rubbish but it is produced in the same studio that contributed to the blockbusters 'Brexit' and 'Trump'.

On Thursday, April 16 my emails and voicemails were full of just one story. Apparently care homes in Wales were unable to purchase PPE from English wholesalers because it had been reserved by Public Health England. If this was true it was a big deal as all new PPE procurement was undertaken through the joint four nations group which, though headed by Public Health England, was supposed to allow all four nations an equitable share of PPE. It was a way of maximising the purchasing power of the UK as a whole at a time when there was a global shortage. Put simply, this should mean that all PPE in the UK was coming out of the same pot and therefore there should be not 'English only' personal protective equipment.

Despite this the website of the England-based specialist wholesaler Gompels had a note on one of its face mask products that said:

> You must be registered and operating in England – apologies to Wales and Scotland, we are told you have a different process for getting emergency supplies.
> These restrictions are not something we have decided, they are criteria given to us by Public Health England.
> We have been told that there are alternative arrangements in place for Welsh and Scotland but we have not been able to discover what they are. Please don't think it is us discriminating against our lovely and loyal Welsh and Scottish customers.

People in Wales were outraged. I had about a dozen emails from care homes and several missed calls from Plaid Cymru. This really was leapt on by the Welsh nationalists as it ticked all their boxes – an English plot to prioritise care homes over the border despite a prearranged agreement. Plaid Cymru Leader Adam Price wrote to the President of the European Commission, Ursula von der Leyen, to lodge a formal complaint saying that: "EU regulations relating to Personal Protective Equipment, which still apply to the UK in the transition period, clearly state that Member States shall not prohibit, restrict or hinder the placing on the market of PPE or PPE components which satisfy the provisions of this directive."

As a reporter my initial instinct was 'wow what a great story' and the temptation was just get it out into the world and watch the hits roll in. It is important however to establish the facts, after all as the phrase goes 'a lie can travel halfway around the world while the truth is still putting on its shoes'. I should add that I love this phrase all the more because it is commonly credited to both Mark Twain and Winston Churchill but hilariously and fittingly was in all likelihood said by neither thereby proving its point.

In order to establish exactly what was going on I rang Gompels directly and had a conversation with a rather put-upon Sam Gompel who had clearly been bombarded with calls from angry Welsh journalists all morning. This was followed by a series of emails and a conversation with the Department for Health before another call to Mr Gompel again (poor bloke).

We were right to check as there was far more to this story than met the eye. In the first week of April, 20 million items of PPE were distributed to the devolved nations from the UK procurement process, with weekly meetings by a four-nations oversight board to check this was working. Once each nation received its share of the PPE it was the responsibility of each devolved administration to decide how it was distributed. Wales opted not to distribute through wholesalers and instead sent it directly to care settings through local authorities and other bodies. Across the border, Public Health England instead used the private sector such as Gompels to distribute its share. For this specific PPE, Gompels was not acting as a wholesaler but as a distributor for English supplies to English care homes. So their inability to supply Welsh care homes was as justifiable as if the Welsh Government refused to supply English care homes.

Some of the stock they were distributing also came from NHS England's 'pandemic flu stocks', which were built up before the crisis. Each devolved nation has stocks built up for a flu pandemic which they can choose to distribute how they wish; again England opted to go through wholesalers whereas Wales sent directly to care homes[6].

So unfortunately for me (and Adam Price), this was not the story it initially appeared to be, though it is a useful demonstration of how complicated the system is and the importance of properly researched journalism before simply accepting the press release at face value.

Towards the end of the week there came the good news that 99-year-old Captain Tom Moore had raised over £20 million for the NHS after completing the last of 100 laps of his garden on Thursday. Despite the rather miserable realisation that our health service needed charity as opposed to taxes in order to keep going, Captain Tom was an inspirational figure for so many.

A less uplifting milestone came on April 17 when Wales passed 500 deaths from the disease but there were some signs for optimism as the First Minister announced encouraging new NHS data that showed that the three-week lockdown appeared to have reduced the number of Covid-19-related admissions to hospitals. This began to reinforce the view of the First Minister that all changes to the lockdown must continue to be based on that three weekly cycle to allow full evaluation of the impact of any changes to lockdown measures.

With every day that went by it felt like we were starting to understand the virus even more, though the conclusions from that understanding were not always heartening. Research from the

Bevan Foundation found that Wales was more at risk from coronavirus than any other part of the UK. The reasons it cited included the fact that nearly 15% of the Welsh population is aged over 70, which is the highest proportion in the UK. Not only that but 8.3% of the Welsh population has a heart condition, which is also higher than the rest of the UK. In addition one in twelve people in Wales has a respiratory illness, including chronic obstructive pulmonary disease (COPD) and asthma — with Wales having the highest prevalence of asthma in Europe. This is partly down to some respiratory conditions being much more common in deprived areas due to higher pollution levels, higher rates of smoking, and greater exposure to pollutants in some industries. To top it off, Wales has higher rates of smoking than the UK average.

This was clear evidence that Covid-19 was a predictable disaster. Nearly a quarter of people in Wales live in what is officially considered poverty. The virus was new but the faultlines in our society that it exposed were deep and entrenched.

6. 'What the F___ is the Matter with Her?'

April 20 to April 26
Wales' confirmed Covid-19 cases — 7,546
Wales deaths — 584
UK confirmed cases — 124,743
UK deaths — 16,509

As the total deaths figure reached 16,500 at the start of the week it was eminently clear that the UK was not handling the crisis well. Appearing before the Health Select Committee just before lockdown, the UK Government's Chief Scientific Officer Sir Patrick Vallance had said that keeping the coronavirus death toll below 20,000 would be 'a good outcome'. The chances of staying under Sir Patrick Vallance's 'good outcome' of 20,000 deaths looked slim with 429 deaths reported on just April 19. At the current rate that grim milestone would be reached in just over a week.

Monday April 20 was a day of openings.

First came the Dragon's Heart Hospital opening in the Principality Stadium. In an arena that just thirty days before was supposed to have hosted the Six Nations match with Scotland, the Ysbyty Calon Y Ddraig had 300 beds (with more to follow), a mobile x-ray, CT scanners, a pharmacy and an end-of-life pathway of care for people in the last weeks or days of their lives. Just next door in the Cardiff Blues Stadium there was a rest area for staff and a reception area for relatives. It was opened by Prince Charles (who had recently recovered from the virus himself) via video, with former Wales centre and qualified doctor Jamie Roberts hosting the ceremony. Putting the hospital together in just thirty days was a mammoth task and a significant achievement that is well worthy of praise.

The second big opening was B&Q. With the weather unseasonably gorgeous, people queued outside Cardiff's Culverhouse Cross branch – one of fourteen stores across the UK opened for a social distancing trial. This created a run on garden furniture much like the run on the bank in Mary Poppins as swarms of Cardiffians desperately tried to secure themselves a sun lounger for their garden, banned as they were from lying down in a park. More importantly this activity gave an insight into the retail future we would all need to get used to until there was a vaccine. Limited numbers inside the store, perspex screens at checkouts, card payments only at tills and floor markings showing what a 2 metre distance really looks like.

The final and most significant opening was the UK Government's job retention scheme (popularly known as furlough) meaning that employers could claim cash grants worth up to 80% of wages, capped at £2,500 a month per worker. A team of 5000 HMRC staff were operating the scheme, which saw a huge uptake across the whole of the UK and particularly in Wales where 378,400 employees were furloughed – a higher proportion of the workforce than in any other UK nation[1]. The reasons for the scheme's popularity in Wales are obvious. Wales has a higher number of manufacturing jobs than many parts of the UK and these tend not to be conducive to home working – production lines struggle to go through living rooms.

However Welsh dependence on the furlough scheme immediately limited the degree to which Mark Drakeford's government could deviate from the UK Government when it came to lifting lockdown because Wales lacks the financial firepower to sustain the furlough scheme alone.

Even with the furlough scheme the pressure of the lockdown was too much for some businesses with home furnishing shop Cath Kidston announcing the closure of all sixty of its stores along with hundreds of job losses. Elsewhere many parents were in dire straits as they attempted to combine home schooling and home working, with many praying to be furloughed in order to take care of their kids. With children going 'back to school' after the Easter break (which in reality meant staying at the kitchen table) the BBC released a series of virtual lessons from famous names. In some ways this was great: who wouldn't want to be taught about the oceans by Sir David Attenborough? I am less convinced that my passion for history would have been quite as well developed if I had been subjected to Danny Dyer (though for me no one will ever beat my secondary school teacher Mr Todd, RIP).

Beyond this, parents of children with autism and certain learning difficulties were desperate to be able to leave the house more than once a day, with Mark Drakeford announcing they were considering allowing such families to have multiple daily trips out to exercise.

Though it was hard for all parents during this period we must not forget that it is children who can be the hardest hit during times like this – especially as, without schools, there is often no one to witness what they can be suffering at home. For many children who are victims of abuse, school is a place of sanctuary. This abuse can take many forms: sexual, physical, emotional, verbal or neglect. Even children not in direct danger from a parent often rely on school as the one time of the day they are guaranteed a hot meal.

I could barely read a piece our education correspondent wrote on the calls Childline in Wales had been receiving. Children in abusive households often rely on friends and grandparents for support. Now those networks had been removed and they were condemned to spend their time in the company of their abusers, not allowed to see friends, unable to risk a conversation with grandad because that contact could infect them. The worst thing is that the number of children who suffered at this point is unknown, they will have suffered in silence and carry emotional wounds long after a coronavirus vaccine has been found.

On Tuesday there was hope that a vaccine developed in Oxford would be on the way with health secretary Matt Hancock announcing that trials would begin on Thursday, April 23[2].

The same day, Vaughan Gething confirmed at the daily Welsh Government lunchtime briefing something that had been becoming clear from anecdotal evidence for some time – the virus was disproportionately killing people from black, Asian and minority ethnic (BAME) backgrounds. Mr Gething said a report had found more than a third of people critically ill with coronavirus in English, Welsh and Northern Irish hospitals were from BAME backgrounds, compared with 18% of the UK population. An urgent investigation was to establish the reasons why this was, and what could be done to stop it.

As already stated, the temptation to see deaths as merely numbers when cases are increasing sharply needs to be resisted. One death is a tragedy, a life ended before it should, a family distraught, parents losing children and children losing parents. When the number is 3,000 and not one, there is 3,000 times the hurt, pain and grief. If, as with many coronavirus cases, that death was avoidable, collective anger should also be 3,000 times greater. To fight against their slide into analysis by numbers I keep drawing attention to the human beings behind these figures. Like Brian Mfula, a lecturer in mental health nursing at Swansea University and a father. Professor Ceri Phillips, head of the College of Human and Health Sciences at Swansea University, called him "An inspiring teacher and role model who taught from the heart." Brian was also described as having a generous spirit and a "highly infectious laugh". He left behind a wife and four children, one of whom, Kato, posted on Twitter: "I never even got to say goodbye to my hero, my dad Brian Mwila Mfula. I'm so broken right now I don't know what we're going to do without you. I love you so so so much." When we read the figures for coronavirus deaths, every single one is a Brian with a Kato.

As we move on to Wednesday, April 22 it is probably worth outlining what an average day looks like working as a political journalist in Wales. In 'normal' times, the daily work of a political reporter has a greater degree of consistency than in general reporting. On a Monday you can look at your diary and see when the committees, speeches, interviews and key announcements are going to be. Clearly these are nothing like normal times and, if politicians are flying by the seat of their pants, by necessity so are you. For four years our elected representatives have nearly worn out their idiomatic pants much to the detriment to the social life and sleep patterns of the poor political reporter (and err... the detriment of the entire country).

Despite this there were still regular events through the crisis and a typical week looked like this:

- Senedd/Westminster committees: These tend to happen every day except Friday..
- Plenary (Wednesday either at 11.30am or 1.30pm): This is a chance for MSs to grill the First Minister and Welsh Government.
- Prime Minister's Questions (Wednesday 12pm): In principle a

chance for the Opposition to hold the PM to account in a verbal sparring of oratory and intelligence but more often than not descending into a series of dodged answers and soundbites for Facebook while our representatives bellow and bleat like horny walruses on a block of (probably melting) Arctic ice.

- Daily lobby briefing with the Prime Minister's spokesman (12pm every day except Wednesday, when it is at 11am).

- Downing Street TV briefing (5pm daily): the daily briefing on coronavirus where a Government minister is flanked by two (increasingly uncomfortable looking) scientific/medical experts. Could be dynamite with loads of news lines or dull as dishwater, leaving the public with nothing to do except speculate on whether Dominic Raab and Matt Hancock are actually the same person/political robot.

- Labour Party huddle (Wednesday straight after PMQs) – Similar to the lobby briefing, this is a chance for journalists to question Labour policy and seek clarification for comments made in PMQs.

- Daily Welsh Government press conference at 12.30pm every day

On top of this is the day to day madness of announcements, u-turns and long road trips to test eyesight. The challenge of reporting these events is that the two governmental structures run simultaneously with no attention to overlap. This means it is hard to cover all of it live. This was not a problem in the days before news websites when all that was required was for the stories to be written before the print run, and there were also more reporters available than Boris Johnson has had dismissals from employment. With news websites there is a hunger from readers to consume news as it happens, meaning priorities have to be considered.

Wednesday is by far the busiest day with the lobby briefing at 11am, PMQs 12pm, Welsh Government press conference 12.30pm (and if you are asking a question you need to be logged on to Zoom at 12.15 to do a sound check), Labour huddle at 1pm then

Plenary at 1.30pm. There is no set way of covering it all and quite often a decision is made by myself and my news editors on the day as to where the strongest news lines will be and what is most relevant to our readers. We will of course be monitoring everything but it is not possible to report it all live.

As the Welsh Government press conference is usually the one most likely to create spin off stories relevant to Welsh readers, I would often watch Plenary on Senedd TV (not the busiest stream on the internet) but thirty minutes behind the live stream. This gave the opportunity to write spin-off stories from the earlier conferences and worked well. Plenary is a decent source of stories and, though never compelling enough viewing to justify live coverage of it, it is important journalists go through proceedings with a fine tooth comb as part of our duty to be the eyes and ears of the public and hold the Welsh Government to account.

Wednesday 22 however was a watershed moment in the history of Plenary as something dramatic happened. During the proceedings health secretary Vaughan Gething was routinely taking questions from Members on the handling of the crisis so far. The final question came from fellow Labour MS Jenny Rathbone who really pressed him on the lack of PPE being produced domestically and talked about care home workers who were unable to get tested because they didn't have a car − perfectly legitimate and worthwhile lines of enquiry.

Mr Gething replied calmly enough and then turned off his camera as his part in proceedings had finished. Unfortunately for Mr Gething he simultaneously took deep exception to what Jenny Rathbone had said but had forgotten to turn his microphone off.

He was heard to say: "I tell you what, I know Jenny is regularly [inaudible] but... what the f★★★ is the matter with her?". The presiding officer desperately tried to speak over him which (much to the disappointment of social media) made the rest of his comments inaudible except for a few words. The session was then delayed while the 'technical problems' were 'solved'.

The fact the comments were made on a Zoom call when all the other Members were visible meant viewers were able to get everyone's live reaction. Non-Labour MSs reactions ranged from unsuppressed laughter to holding their heads in their hands. Labour MSs mainly just stared stoically into their camera as though nothing had happened. Ms Rathbone hardly reacted except to adopt a look of simmering fury akin to Miss Trunchbull from Roald Dahl's *Matilda*.

Mr Gething, presumably after managing to extradite his foot from deep in his throat, tweeted: "I'm obviously embarrassed about my comments at the end of questions today. I've sent a message apologising and offered to speak to Jenny Rathbone if she wishes to do so. It is an unwelcome distraction at a time of unprecedented challenge."

Opposition parties obviously smelt blood in the water with Plaid Cymru Leader Adam Price calling on Mark Drakeford to sack him "with immediate effect" while the Welsh Conservative leader Paul Davies said "For a health minister to show such unpro-fessionalism and disdain at this time is completely unacceptable and he should be sacked." However, this was not the consensus of all opposition Members with former Welsh Conservative Leader Andrew R.T. Davies saying he would have concerns over a Labour backbencher coming into post during the midst of the Covid-19 crisis. Jenny Rathbone would not reply to any requests for comment.

The issue with Vaughan Gething's reaction to Jenny Rathbone was not his bad language. Most people will swear to themselves, especially with the immense pressure he was under at the time. The real concern was his reaction to perfectly legitimate and fair scrutiny. Ms Rathbone was fulfilling her role as a back bencher and holding the government to account. His furious reaction to anyone having the audacity to question him during a crisis where he had made obvious errors is far more concerning than any overheard dropping of the F-bomb. This is not the first (or the last) time Mr Gething would be prickly during questioning. In 2017 he walked out of an ITV interview after the journalist asked him a question he did not like[3].

Outside the glass walls of the Senedd the reality of the day to day decisions physicians were having to make was starting to bite. It is almost taken as gospel that doctors will always try to save everyone's life. If there are multiple people who need to be treated at the same time, there is an acknowledgement that the sickest will be treated first. If you arrive in A&E with a broken finger you assume that if someone else is having a stroke, they will take precedence. However, the pressure put on our health service by the crisis meant that ethical red lines were being re-evaluated.

On Wednesday, April 24 a number of contacts in the medical profession alerted me to a paper published on the British Orthopedic Association website by a group of surgeons from Swansea Bay University Health Board[4]. They all specialised in treating people with broken hips and, with the coronavirus crisis sucking up healthcare resources, had been asked to plan how to manage the dwindling capacity for other treatments and procedures. In the paper, which had the full approval of the health board's ethical committee, the group suggested "giving up our normal model of 'Sickest First' to a new model of 'Fittest first'". They added: "We as clinicians are no longer able to do what is in the best interest of a single patient in front of us. We have to do what is in the best interest of the whole population we serve" adding "if we cannot treat all, should we treat those most likely to survive and those likely to regain most quality of life?"

This shift from sickest first to fittest first would ultimately mean that patients who are the most sick, most frail and oldest would be at the back of the queue for surgery. If implemented, the plans meant the most frail and elderly patients would be the last to get treatment and could potentially be left at home untreated when they break their hip.

The system proposed by the doctors involved giving a patient a score based on certain indicators, the higher the score – the sooner the patient would likely die after surgery and the further down the list the patient would drop. The surgeons admitted that under the new system "patients with higher scores may never get to the top of the list depending on the number of cases presenting and capacity available". If after seven days of waiting the patient had still not been treated they would be removed from the waiting list. The physicians suggested that this model could be rolled out across the Welsh NHS and wider UK in areas struggling to keep up with demand.

The reaction to this story was horror and a huge outcry with one clinician telling me he thought the plans 'unethical'. This is not to point the finger of blame at the authors or shame them but to be an illustration of the incredible pressure the crisis was exerting on our health service. All non-essential procedures had already been cancelled, yet health boards still felt the need to plan for a time when they were so stretched that an old person with a broken hip was not worth the scarce resources it would take to fix them.

No doctor goes into medicine wanting to leave the most vulnerable at the back of the queue or treat the 'fittest first' but the position these clinicians were in was entirely predictable. Years of austerity policy meant that the NHS was already under-resourced, that social care was the ugly sister of policy making, that it was a case of when, not if, a pandemic was coming – we knew. The idea of fittest first health care is reprehensible, but revulsion should not be directed at the doctors forced into proposing such a policy by necessity. It should be reserved for the policy makers who year after year allowed these wounds to fester and multiply.

As the week drew to a close it could have been assumed that, given that the health secretary had publicly sworn at a member of his own party, nothing more bizarre would happen. Luckily for Vaughan Gething, the 45th President stumbled back on to the news agenda with the poise and finesse of a toddler running towards a ball pit. In a press conference the President (let that sink in) suggested that it would be 'interesting to check' whether disinfectant injections could help combat the virus. Mr Trump said researchers were looking at the effects of disinfectants (like bleach) on Covid-19, saying coronavirus "does a tremendous number on the lungs, so it would be interesting to check that". The makers of Dettol released a statement telling people that under no circumstance should they put bleach into the human body whether through "injection, ingestion or any other route". When the First Minister was asked about this in his press conference that day he responded: "I thought it was an extraordinary thing for anybody in that position to say, just looking through the internet and finding stray ideas with no scientific basis and no medical science behind them and then suggesting [it] in a press conference."

We need now to talk about domestic abuse. Not being able to leave your house is hard for everyone, but mostly home is a place of safety, and shelter: home territory. This is not the case for everyone.

Throughout my career this has been one of the topics on which I have focused the most, being privileged to tell the stories of survivors, and delivered talks and training to other journalists on ethical reporting of this important issue. As a journalist you want to cover the biggest stories and the stories that matter and, alongside the environment, I believe that violence and abuse of women is one of the single biggest issues facing the UK (and the world). Forget Brexit, forget terrorism, violence and abuse of women and girls is a disease which reaches into the very fabric of our society. It is an epidemic that was here long before coronavirus and will sadly still be here long after Covid-19 has gone the same way as smallpox. We simply do not know the true scale of domestic abuse because so much goes unreported, but the available figures are disgusting. Almost one in three women aged 16-59 will experience domestic abuse in her lifetime. Two women a week are killed by a former or current partner in England and Wales. Last year 1.6 million women experienced domestic abuse.

These murdered women have names. Natasha Bradbury[5], Alison Farr-Davies[6] and Zoe Morgan[7] are all women killed in Wales by partners or ex-partners. I say again, this is an epidemic. If terrorism or a natural disaster inflicted the damage and misery of domestic abuse there would be round the clock media coverage, COBRA meetings and it would top of every election campaign leaflet – but it isn't. Part of the reason for this is that it happens behind closed doors, but the real reason it does not get the money and attention it deserves is because, frankly, this crime is against women.

If you need any evidence the UK in the 2020s is not an equal place for literally half of all the human beings that live here, look no further than how we deal with domestic violence. Like every other pothole in Welsh society, coronavirus did not create the issue of domestic abuse, but because we did not do enough to fix the problem when the sun was shining the virus has turned the cracks into fissures which add to human misery and loss of life. Much like the children who were no longer able to find sanctuary at school, the lockdown also cut off women suffering abuse from their support networks. These poor women are shut in a house, often with only their abuser for company, an abuser no longer scared of leaving a mark because no-one was going to see it.

In order to combat the upsurge in domestic abuse the Welsh Government proudly announced it was offering £1.2m to fund community accommodation as well as another £200,000 for furnishings – an amount of money which would be a welcome boost for beleaguered services. Disappointingly this was not all it seemed as Welsh Women's Aid pointed out that these funds had already been allocated. The £1.2 million was originally announced in December 2019 and the £200,000 being a 2019/20 capital underspend which had already been promised last quarter. These services had just been hit with a triple whammy of being unable to fundraise because of the lockdown, increased demand on the services, and increased cost in delivering those services because they had to employ social distancing in their shelters. For the Welsh Government to expect plaudits for simply giving them money they had already promised them does not constitute an adequate response.

Only a month previously deputy minister and chief whip Jane Hutt wrote in an open letter published in the *Western Mail* that "Victims of domestic abuse and sexual violence across Wales need our support now, more than ever. I am working with specialist domestic abuse services to make sure help is available for anyone who needs it, and to make sure there is a safe place for victims and survivors to stay."

Service providers on the ground were telling me that none of the promised cash had reached the front line and some of it was not expected for over a week. England and Scotland had both allocated new money to the issue during the crisis but providers told me Wales had not.

In a letter to Jane Hutt on April 22, Welsh Women's Aid CEO Sara Kirkpatrick accused the Welsh Government of "giving false hope to survivors". She said: "While the Welsh Government continues to allude to funds in its announcements, there appears to be a clear disconnect between this and the process of money being allocated to front line VAWDASV (violence against women, domestic abuse and sexual violence) services. This gives false hope to survivors that services will continue to have the capacity to meet their needs, when in reality, we know that even before this crisis 512 survivors were unable to be supported in refuges because of a lack of service space, capacity or resources."[8]

To think that even when this money reaches the front line that it is job done is a fallacy. The cash is the equivalent of putting a plaster on a shotgun wound. Even before coronavirus, refuges were having to turn women away. What is really needed is long term, reliable and sustainable funding if these services are going to have any hope of properly supporting all the women who need their help.

This was the point in the first wave of the virus that the impact domestic violence services was most prominent. However just because it slipped off the news agenda doesn't mean the issue went away. Throughout the crisis the virus made an already difficult situation for women even harder.

7. Lies, Damn Lies, and 100,000 Tests by the End of April

April 27 to May 3
Wales' confirmed Covid-19 cases – 9,280
Wales deaths – 796
UK confirmed cases – 142,373
UK deaths – 21,092

After just under a month out of action from contracting coronavirus Boris Johnson was back at the helm of the UK Government and was 'raring to go' following what was a near death experience. Speaking to the *Sun on Sunday* Mr Johnson said it was "50-50 whether they were going to have to put a tube down my windpipe" and that his doctors had actually planned how they were going to announce his death. Though back in work Mr Johnson did not take on Sir Keir Starmer at PMQs this week while he got his feet back under the desk, leaving it to Dominic Raab.

The grim news continued to pour in, and as the death toll continued to climb a cold storage facility at the Queen Alexandra Dock in Cardiff was converted into a temporary morgue to hold bodies from across the Welsh capital[1]. The Welsh Government also announced the introduction of a new 'death in service scheme' of £60,000 paid to the families of NHS workers who died of coronavirus. It was also bleak on the jobs front as Airbus announced a cut to production at Broughton, and the First Minister said that the Welsh steel industry could not be supported by the Welsh Government and required UK Government support.

There were some reasons for cheer though. A contact informed WalesOnline that the Welsh Government were preparing for a delivery of an enormous shipment of PPE on a flight from Cambodia. When we contacted the Welsh Government they were determinedly tight lipped about publicising its arrival. This was strange, given the devastating shortages in PPE over the last two months the shipment looked like a remarkable and welcome coup. The reason for the hesitancy was an embarrassing incident involving the UK government a few days previously. The RAF had sent a plane to Istanbul to pick up twenty tonnes of PPE to replenish UK stockpiles. This had transformed from success to debacle when the plane had, for reasons unknown, spent four days sitting on the runway. According to reports the supplier had contacted the NHS on April 16 claiming it could make the 400,000 gowns and the UK Government had paid a deposit the next day. However, the supplier subsequently announced an unexpected manufacturing delay which reduced the amount of gowns that could be collected. On arrival in the UK many of the gowns had to be returned as they were subsequently found not to be up to UK safety standards. Fortunately for the Welsh Government both its flights from Cambodia (containing 200,000 fluid resistant gowns) did arrive as planned as did a delivery of ten million masks from China. These deliveries went a long way to take some of the immediate strain off Welsh PPE stocks[2].

When you look at Wales and think of the places most at risk from coronavirus, you don't need to be an epidemiologist to pick out the likely candidates – care homes, hospitals, crowded accommodation. These facilities all have certain traits in common: human beings in close proximity to each other, people having no choice but to frequently interact with each other, and chronic underfunding. Welsh prisons provide a similar scenario. Underfunded and full to bursting, prisons in Wales are such perfect conditions for coronavirus they could have been designed by the virus itself.

Welsh prisons are in such a poor state that people who enter them without addictions often leave hooked on narcotics like spice. Analysis of data by think tank Reform shows one in seven prisoners are becoming addicted to illicit substances, with the figure increasing from 6% to 15% between 2014 and 2019[3]. This is part of what has become a seamless transition from sleeping in a cell to sleeping on the streets – and was the case before the coronavirus crisis. Combined with a privatised and equally overwhelmed probation service a costly merry-go-round has been created for those who transgress in our society that does little to deter, provides no sense of justice for victims, cuts off petty criminal offenders from support and serves as a criminality finishing school. So the depressing, monotonous, misery never ends for victim or perpetrator. And this is not to mention the underfunding of our courts. So our prisons were another hole in our society's underbelly ready to be carved open by Covid. Like many of the others there were two reasons that our elected officials never got round to filling it. First (and most importantly), it was not politically expedient to do so. Elections are not won on the back of prison reform, in the same way that they are not won on tackling domestic violence, climate change or inadequate social care. The political system rewards short term headlines over long term success. It shifts the focus of our politicians away from successful, sustainable governance, to simply staying in power. So social ulcers such as a failing justice system go untreated, if they are even acknowledged.

The second reason is that they are really hard to fix. They are complex problems and people who come bearing simple solutions to complicated problems should be treated with the utmost suspicion. Crime rising? Increase sentences! Planet warming? Just plant some trees! Welfare state expensive? Work shy benefit scroungers!

On April 28, in a 'shocking' turn of events, the predictable disaster made its way into Welsh prisons. Despite having only 6% of England and Wales' prison population, a quarter of positive Covid-19 cases within prison settings were in Wales as the virus swept through the system. This was significantly higher than areas of England with both London and the West Midlands, the next highest places, seeing 16% of confirmed cases each. Up until April 24 there were 398 'probable' cases of coronavirus in Welsh prisons, with six of these resulting in hospital treatment and one death.[4]

Why was Wales so badly affected? Cardiff University's Welsh Governance Centre is a reliable source for Welsh specific policy and their previous research has shown that Wales has the highest imprisonment rate in western Europe. Add this to the fact that at the end of March 2020, HMP Swansea was the most overcrowded prison in England and Wales and it is unsurprising that the virus managed to take hold.

The outbreak in prisons does more than lay bare the shortcomings in the prison system, it also shows the half-finished dog's dinner that is our constitutional settlement. Justice is not devolved area so Welsh prisons are run by the Ministry of Justice (MoJ), but it is the Welsh Government and Public Health Wales who are responsible for healthcare in prisons, except HMP Parc in Bridgend which is privately run by G4S. Therefore the provision of healthcare in public sector prisons in Wales is the responsibility of the relevant health board (are you keeping up?). Despite this an MoJ assessment of the coronavirus situation in England and Wales' prisons made no reference to Welsh Government in their management of healthcare in Welsh prisons with a prison service spokesman telling me that they make their plans on the back of 'the latest advice from Public Health England'.

Beyond Wales' Victorian prisons it seemed the sudden drop in human activity had been a bit of a wake-up call for spring. Around the world there were hilarious images of animals having a lovely old time on our abandoned streets. In Buenos Aires a massive sea lion took a stroll past some abandoned industrial units. In Corsica people living in a residential estate could see wild boar chowing down on grass embankments from their balconies. Venice, which would normally be rammed with tourists queueing for gondolas on the filthy waters of the canal, had instead clear waters where seabirds merrily tootled along.

It was no different in Wales, though the news was distinctly more...err...Welsh. In Ebbw Vale a locked up Mcdonald's restaurant, which normally would have backed up traffic in its drive-thru instead had some lovely woolly sheep and lambs (though it would have been more fitting if they had been bullocks). It seemed that sheep across Wales were enjoying some peace and quiet as in Monmouthshire a flock were seen hanging out in a closed off children's playground, slowly spinning on the roundabout. Perhaps the most famous animal incursion was some Kashmiri goats who ventured into Llandudno from the Great Orme to eat people's flowers and hedges. The goats became such a sensation that St David's Hospice got novelty t-shirts made with them on and raised £120,000 in funds selling them.

All the seagulls and pigeons in our city centres probably thought humans had become extinct. I can empathise with them, livelihoods destroyed overnight, no contingency plans, hungry chicks furious there were no fallen kebabs anymore to be lovingly regurgitated – poor things. Joking aside there was a real feeling that, free from humans and their associated noise and pollution, nature was rejoicing. It may simply have been that we all had more time to stop and listen, but there really did seem to be more bird song..

Unfortunately, though the sheep were living their best life, the spread of the virus in Wales started to change. Aneurin Bevan Health Board was the epicentre of the Welsh outbreak from the very start. However, as the unseasonably warm April ended and May began the growth of the virus in those areas began to wane. The latest data suggested that the areas of Swansea, Neath, Rhondda Cynon Taff (RCT) and Merthyr Tydfil had more cases per head of population. There were also a few spikes in cases in the north west of Wales though at this point it was hard to be sure if this was something more substantial or just an aberration over a few days. When questioned PHW health experts said that all the evidence suggested that the virus was moving south to north and east to west. Thankfully rural areas of Ceredigion, Pembrokeshire and Powys, which were uniquely vulnerable because of an older population and less developed healthcare infrastructure were yet to be greatly affected.

Though the movements of the virus were very concerning in the areas affected there were some glimmers of hope that it was possible to come out of the other side. Doctors at the Royal Gwent Hospital reported that many of the other indicators of high coronavirus levels such as ICU capacity, deaths and hospital admittance were heading in the right direction.

This week I was lucky enough to interview Dr David Hepburn, who works at the Royal Gwent Hospital in Newport. The 43-year-old was the acting clinical director for intensive care so was on the front line of the front line, in the battle against virus in the early days of the crisis. He had become something of a household name after he spoke publicly about contracting coronavirus himself. As well as the revelation that at one point all of the patients in intensive care in his hospital were in their fifties or younger.

There is something wonderful about speaking directly to people on the frontline. Free from the press officers, PR consultants and politicians, you are able to ask real people, doing an important job, questions that readers want answered. There is no 'we really want to thank our strategic, multi-agency partners', just real insight into what it is like to treat the virus that is killing us.

The insights he offered were fascinating. With so much attention placed on issues like ventilator numbers there had been an absence of focus on the best of resources – staff. Normally an intensive care ward would have one nurse for every patient. In the Gwent at the busiest times they had to move to a 1:2 ratio. Dr Hepburn explained that once ratios increase to one member of staff for every three patients it is almost not worth bringing the patient in. This again demonstrates shortcomings in our health service. Whereas you can shift your economy to suddenly build loads of ventilators, a highly trained and knowledgeable intensive care nurse is not made in a factory, they are trained in university and they are forged over years of experience.

If you want to look at why Matt Hancock and the gang were concerned about the NHS being overwhelmed look no further than capacity in critical care. In the UK we have about 6.6 ICU beds for every 100,000 of our population. Germany has 29.2, USA 29.4, Austria 21.8, Belgium 15.9[5]. Even Italy, a country whose health service was overwhelmed has almost twice the UK capacity at 12.5.

Dr Hepburn also talked about how the crisis had forced the NHS to cut through the layers of red tape in the health service. He said: "We have seen clinicians of all disciplines come and help. The estates guys are amazing as well, when we have had to put new air pipelines in as well as new doors and new walls. Everyone has just said 'yes we can do that'. That is quite different to the normal levels of bureaucracy you see in the NHS. Normally to get a new set of doors will take you months. It has been good to cut all that red tape out and see what we can do when everyone pulls together."

One of the most striking of Dr Hepburn's comments was about PPE. He'd had no trouble getting hold of personal protective equipment because as he put it "we are in a privileged position because we are top of the tree in terms of priority". Early data would suggest that ICU workers caught the virus less than other colleagues in hospital[6] (though there is still research to be done on this). If this shows one thing, it is that PPE works. The people working in Wales' ICUs were exposed to more coronavirus than anyone, but because they were properly equipped and enabled to carry out their roles safely, they were less likely to die. This makes the total failure to provide adequate PPE, especially at the start of the pandemic, all the more scandalous.

Scandalous can also be applied to the treatment of care homes. For months the Welsh Government had refused to test asymptomatic residents entering care homes after being discharged from hospital. Right through April the First Minister Mark Drakeford said the expert advice said there was 'no value' in asymptomatic testing. The same rules applied to staff. This meant that many staff, who had provided direct care to covid patients, were not allowed to be tested because they didn't have symptoms. Even though we know that the majority of Covid cases have no symptoms or mild symptoms the Welsh Government would not relent on its policy. Even though there was evidence that people could be infectious during the incubation phase of the disease, before the onset of symptoms, the Welsh Government would not approve the testing of asymptomatic patients and staff.

This was the uniform policy across the UK but in the middle of April the UK Government changed the rule in England. At the end of April, as evidence mounted that the virus was decimating parts of Wales' care system, the Welsh government changed its policy.

You can read the full details of this in the chapter on care homes.

With this terrible policy blunder hanging around its neck and the care sector apoplectic with rage, the Welsh Government wanted to make a big gesture to redirect the headlines (and of course to show their heartfelt gratitude). On April 30, two days after the UK death toll became the third highest in the world, Mark Drakeford announced that all care home and domiciliary workers would receive a £500 gift from the Welsh Government. The First Minister told the press conference: "I want our social care workforce to know their hard work is both appreciated and recognised. This payment is designed to provide some further recognition of the value we attach to everything they are doing to – it recognises this group of people are providing the invisible scaffolding of services, which support both our NHS and our wider society."

Apart from the fact it was a blatant attempt to appease a sector that felt totally let down by the Welsh Government's handling of the crisis, there were elements in this policy to be commended. Care workers as a rule are very poorly paid, are often women and from minority backgrounds, they also look after our most vulnerable and were taking huge personal risks throughout the crisis. It is hard to make an argument that they are a group undeserving of extra cash. And the Welsh Government also said that this money would not be pro-rated so part time workers, most likely to need this cash injection, would take home the full amount. This was a progressive step.

However there were a series of screw ups in the planning and implementation of this policy that deserve attention. First is planning, the issue being there didn't seem to have been any. The policy looked like a 'back of a fag packet' job, though the First Minister is a vocal opponent of smoking having attempted when he was Health Minister to ban e-cigarettes in enclosed spaces. Perhaps it is better described as 'back of cheddar wrapper' (the First Minister would later become a viral video for his love of cheese).

The lack of planning was clear straight away as dozens of people filled up my inbox seeking clarification of who the payment applied to. Did it include chefs, cleaners and agency staff? I immediately tried to find out and was told that the details of the policy were still being fleshed out. Within a few days the Welsh Government clarified what 'all care home and domiciliary workers' actually meant saying that the payment would only apply to people 'providing personal care'. This meant the cleaners and cooks were not included. However a month later on June 5 this would change again with the First Minister announcing that kitchen and domestic staff working in care homes would receive the £500 extra payment meaning it now applied to 64,000 people.

The lack of planning did not end there. In his initial announcement Mark Drakeford appealed to the UK Government not to tax the payment or to penalise people by paying out less in working tax credits or other benefits. This request was ignored.

So on-the-fly was the Welsh Government's policy as it attempted to claw back some favour within the care sector, that they had evidently not consulted the Treasury on any of it. A spokesman for the Treasury told ITV that they were "working with the Welsh Government to determine the exact scope of the proposed bonus" but that "payments made in connection with employment are chargeable to income tax and NICS unless explicitly exempt."

In reality this meant that some workers would only receive £125 of the £500 payment. According to calculations from Unison Cymru Wales, if a person was earning over £12,500 a year (well below the full-time living wage) they would have £100 of the payment taken in income tax, £60 in National Insurance contributions and lose a further £214.20 in cuts to their universal credit payment. Even people earning under £9,000 a year would only see £185 of their £500 after a brutal £315 cut to their Universal Credit. Ultimately the Welsh Government's policy did help some of the poorest working people in Wales – this is to be applauded. However it also sent loads of money allocated to Wales by the UK Government straight back to London. Perhaps many of the workers would rather have had PPE and tests?

The last day of April was judgement day for UK Government health secretary Matt Hancock. At the start of the month he had set the bold target to be conducting 100,000 tests a day by the end of April. As the month rolled on it seemed highly unlikely that Mr Hancock would get even close to the target with just 19,316 tests on April 19. The sharks were circling for the health secretary with friends of mine at the nationals telling me they had prepared huge spreads and analysis pieces assessing his impending failure. Rumours were that his own Government was ready to throw him under the bus in the event of missing the target.

But then the seemingly impossible happened. On May 1 Matt Hancock walked up the lectern like both the proverbial dog having its day and the dog with two appendages. With his tail wagging vigorously he described 'an incredible achievement' as the UK had conducted a fairly astonishing 122,347 tests in the 24 hours leading up to 9am Monday 1. This is a remarkable increase in capacity – almost too good to be true. Over the next week it would become clear that Mr Hancock should not have been looking like the dog having its day but instead, to quote George in *Blackadder*, as guilty as a puppy sitting next to a pile of poo.

It turns out there was more sleight of hand than in a Dynamo show, with the *Health Service Journal*¹ revealing that the government also included tests that had been posted or delivered in its figures before the test had been returned to the lab. Of the 122,347 tests, 27,497 were home tests and 12,872 were sent out to satellite sites. Thus as few as 81,978 of the tests were actually processed. This is the equivalent of saying twenty people have completed my questionnaire the second after I put my twenty questionnaires in the post box. In the same vein I have not finished my GCSEs when I turn over my paper. On top of this it is also important to consider that only 73,191 people were tested that day which means that some individuals will have been tested multiple times.

If more proof was needed that the UK Government had fudged the numbers to get over the line it is in the testing figures for the subsequent weeks. In the seventeen days after the target was reached, the total tests only passed the 100,000 mark six times. The effect of these skewed numbers was to further polarise debate. On one side you had people who could quite reasonably argue 'they hit the target' who were then vilified. On the other side you had people who could quite reasonably argue that there were clear shortcuts and problems with the methodology, who were also vilified. It contributed further to the toxic dialogue around the issue. You cannot ignore that it was impressive to increase testing capacity to over 70,000 in a month from such a low base and that the target did have a galvanising impact on increasing test capacity (though you can severely criticise that the base was so low in the first place).

More important than the arguments of whether the target was 'technically' hit is what this incident indicates about the mentality of the UK Government at the time. It was not about hitting the 100,00 tests because it would save lives, it was about being seen to achieve. The *New York Times* reported that in the 48 hours before the deadline some UK hospitals were told to rapidly expand tests to thousands of workers and patients even if there were no symptoms. This was problematic for labs which had to burn through supplies of chemical reagents with some reporting that two weeks later they had been unable to restock and so had to reduce the number of tests they conducted. One junior doctor at St Mary's Hospital in London said that after two days where they were told they needed to urgently ramp up testing they then heard nothing for two weeks after the target had been hit. This suggests that these tests were done not because the patients needed them, but because Mr Hancock did.

Back on the Wales side of the border the criticism of the Welsh Government was also based around testing. Just a month before, Mark Drakeford and Vaughan Gething had set the target (now abandoned) of 9,000 tests a day by the end of April but on the 30th Wales conducted just 1,090. Unperturbed Vaughan Gething took a pot shot at the UK Government on BBC Radio Wales saying their plan lacked 'scientific underpinning'. He said: "England have gone out and created lots of capacity very quickly and they have then gone out and used that capacity. The challenge from a policy point of view is that there is clearly a difference but that is partly because England decided that having set a big target they needed to go out and use all the tests. Now other people will tell you about how many of those tests are actual tests or tests that have been sent out. But part of the difficulty we've had is that the scientific underpinning of how and why you extend that policy isn't something where there has been a fully informed debate and we don't see that the science supports all of the differences in policy and the testing reach in England."

On Sunday May 3, beleaguered parents, who for six weeks had pretended to know how to solve simultaneous equations and the difference between sedimentary and igneous rocks, were given the first glimpse of a road map by the First Minister. Speaking on the *Andrew Marr Show* Mr Drakeford said that it would be the start of June at the earliest when schools would be able to reopen. To maintain social distancing certain children would be prioritised for returning. They would be children with special educational needs whose specialist support was difficult to provide in a home setting despite the incredible efforts of parents. The second group was year six children, who needed to catch up with friends and prepare to head for secondary school. Finally, children who learn in Welsh but don't have a Welsh-speaker at home, which made home schooling even more difficult.

Unfortunately for both Mr Drakeford and the parents who immediately opened the prosecco, the unions did not seem to be on the same page. Within hours Laura Doel, the director at NAHT Cymru, the union for head teachers, commented furiously that the announcement was 'confusing and unhelpful', that there had been a lack of consultation with schools and that there wasn't enough evidence about how the virus was transferred in relation to schools.

"We need to know about infection rates between the young, and transmission rates between the young and adults. Only when these questions have been answered can we begin to understand the conditions necessary to support a safe return," she said. "We have been clear in our discussions with the Welsh Government that the profession must be at the heart of any plans and not merely part of a consultation once plans have already been drawn up."[8]

Does anyone know how long prosecco lasts once opened?

8. The Virus Can't Get You As Long As You Stay Alert

May 4 to May 10
Wales' confirmed Covid-19 cases – 10,524
Wales deaths – 997
UK confirmed cases – 172,664
UK deaths – 28,734

As Wales approached the wretched figure of 1,000 confirmed coronavirus deaths it is worth considering what the number of deaths actually means. The number used at the start of each chapter comes from the Public Health Wales data published every day and only includes deaths that occur after a positive test. Anyone who died in a care home or their own home but hadn't been tested for the virus was not included in this figure.

Another figure that was often quoted by politicians, analysts and the media is the death figures from the Office for National Statistics which was consistently considerably higher than the figure given by PHW. There is nothing sinister or untoward in this, it is simply a different way of counting because the ONS includes every death where coronavirus is mentioned on the death certificate.

There is a further way of measuring the deaths caused by the pandemic which offers a different insight into the true impact the virus and lockdown had – excess deaths. This figure takes the total number of people who have died for any reason and compares it to the average for that time of year. Although this figure means we cannot say 'X amount of people died of coronavirus' it is very useful because it gives an insight into indirect deaths from coronavirus. So this will be more likely to factor in all of the people who lost their lives because their operation was delayed, they were scared to go into hospital when they had chest pains because of Covid-19 or were killed by a partner during lockdown. As of July 14 there had been 2,058 (11.3%) more deaths in Wales than the five-year average since the start of the pandemic with the figure not going back to normal until June.

At the beginning while people were still in a heavy lockdown and, particularly in rural areas, were worried about rule breakers seeding their community with the virus. Between March 27 and April 27 Welsh police forces issued 299 fines for breaking the lockdown which, when you think about it, is not a very high figure at just ten a day. Some of the excuses were quite impressive and straight out of the 'dog ate my homework' repertoire. Among rule breakers that particularly stand-out were the campers who drove to Tenby from Hereford, removed obstructions at the entrance to the car park at the beach and then got stuck in the sand[1].

As the weeks passed and more research was conducted into the virus, the importance of social distancing became clearer. Giving evidence to the Health and Social Care Committee on May 5 the UK Government's Chief Scientific Adviser, Sir Patrick Vallance said: "A minute at 2 metre contact is about the same risk as six seconds of 1 metre. The risk at 1 metre is about 10-30 times higher than the risk at 2 metre. So the distancing is an important part of this."[2]

May 5 was an interesting day for me personally as I was contacted by the *Mirror's* political editor Pippa Crerar (who in a matter of weeks would break the Dominic Cummings/Durham story) saying it was my turn to ask a question at the daily Downing Street briefing. All lobby reporters were on a rotation to ask a question at the briefing and it is a nightmare for the lobby chairs to facilitate.

The Downing Street press conferences had a regular routine where a UK Government minister would appear flanked by two experts. In the beginning it was usually the Prime Minister accompanied by Professor Chris Whitty, the Chief Medical Officer, and Chief Scientific Adviser Sir Patrick Vallance.

As time went by the PM attended fewer and fewer briefings, in part because of his ill health but also because he was obviously considered a bit of a liability in front of a live mic and camera (a tactic that Conservative strategist Cummings and co employed throughout the 2019 General Election when Johnson was considered an unacceptable variable outside strictly controlled campaign videos). Dominic Raab and Matt Hancock tended to pick up the slack. Both Whitty and Vallance were also seen more sporadically though this was less to do with their competence than to give other people with different expertise a chance to offer insight, such as NHS bigwigs or Deputy Chief Medical Officer Jonathan Van-Tam, who gained quite a cult following for his authoritative, concise and no-nonsense style (which was a mixture of a tough PE teacher and Gandalf). Incidentally, the later increased absence of people like Van-Tam was also allegedly because they refused to fully endorse UK Government advice (or certain advisors) as it deviated from scientific opinion.

I don't normally get nervous and had by this point appeared dozens of times on the Welsh Government televised briefings, but I was fairly apprehensive ahead of the Downing Street Briefing. Welsh media does not always get a voice in UK-wide events and I felt a real sense of responsibility to ask questions that would directly benefit our readers and leave them better informed. There is also a pressure to be a strong voice speaking up for Welsh interests. I am so lucky at WalesOnline to have a really strong and supportive newsdesk. Journalism is not conducted in a bubble and there have been thousands of times my colleagues have made me a stronger reporter, supported me, and made my journalism more informed. The Head of News David James is my direct line manager and friend – together we puzzled out what questions to ask.

Luckily for me this was before the Dominic Cummings affair, after which Downing Street stopped journalists from coming back with a second question. Nothing says 'healthy democracy' and a Government that accepts scrutiny like cutting journalists off and muting them before they can ask a second question. We decided on two questions:

Watching these press conferences for the past six weeks has been very confusing for many people in Wales, as some of the language used makes it very unclear if what is said applies to them because of devolution.

Clearly foreign affairs such as repatriating people from abroad does apply.

However commonly mentioned issues around schools, local government, support for vulnerable people, healthcare and even the rules on lockdown itself do not apply to people in Wales.

Do you concede that the Government could have been clearer up till now and will your ministerial colleagues and yourself commit to making a distinction, as to what issues apply just to England in the future?

The First Minister of Wales has stated his desire for Wales and England to come out of lockdown together in order to keep the message simple and ensure the restrictions can be enforced.

How is Wales able to input into the announcements about the lockdown that we are expecting this weekend and next week? And to Professor McLean if I may, does Sage take into account Welsh data and the impact on Wales when offering advice for NHS England and have we seen marked differences in Wales and England?

The first question tackled a frustration for many people in Wales that when announcements were made by Westminster, they apparently paid no attention to the realities of devolution. When you live in Merthyr Tydfil and hear the Prime Minister you voted for say 'UK schools/pubs/businesses' are opening next week you quite naturally assume that information applies to you. Throughout the coronavirus crisis there was a consistent misrepresentation by the UK Government where they portrayed announcements for England as announcements for the UK. This was then compounded by a London centric print media which also often failed to make the distinctions. If someone in Wales simply consumes their news by watching the Downing Street briefing, putting on the *10 O'Clock News* to see the headlines and buying a *Daily Mail* it is only natural that they are going to assume that England-only policies apply to Wales.

The second question was actually two questions. Simply bolting on a third question with a polite 'if I may' is a great way of getting more bang from your buck because there is not really a way that a politician can say on live TV, 'no you may not'.

About two hours before the briefing I received a call from the press office at Number 10 enquiring what questions I was going to ask. As a reporter, when someone asks to see your questions in advance it sets alarm bells ringing. It gives them a chance to prepare an evasive answer or get all their ducks in a row – there is no chance of catching people out, and it is not considered good practice. There are occasions when I think it is useful to do this however and it very much depends on the individual situation. There have been (rare) occasions where I have told the Welsh Government one of the questions I am going to ask in advance because I want a specific detail. There is no point in me requesting a figure out of the blue in the press conference and the minister saying they don't have it to hand. This leaves you with one less question to ask and your readers are no more informed than they were before you asked it.

The reason Number 10 gave for requesting the questions in advance was 'because Wales is a devolved nation' and they may need to gather some information first. I decided to give some indication of what I was asking but not verbatim. I said that I would be asking questions about UK Government communication with regard to Wales. When I asked Dominic Raab the first question he answered a completely different question where he talked about co-operation between the UK and Welsh administrations which didn't really apply at all to what I had asked him. What had clearly happened is when I said I "would be asking questions about UK Government communication with regard to Wales" they took it that I would be asking about Cardiff Bay/Westminster relations and just answered that without actually listening to the question put to them.

This is not a one off. It is a well-polished and rehearsed tactic for politicians (and anyone with media training) to just simply answer the question you want to answer, not the one you were asked. It is an absolute fungus in our politics and is part of the reason why the public is so disengaged with the political system and elected representatives. Of course, no politician is going to say 'oh you got me, yeah we screwed up, don't vote for me', but the amount of evasion is just vomit-inducing. It is part of the reason why politicians like Boris Johnson and Nigel Farage are able to resonate with normal people despite the fact they are a blustering Etonian and a former commodities broker respectively. They are different, they say controversial things, they are not immaculately presented. Even though many people don't agree with everything they say at least they feel they know where they stand. Many politicians are so cultivated into oblivion that people are not able to relate to them and find themselves warming to all sorts of, err, characters as at least they sound vaguely like a human being. Take Gordon Brown, who was widely ridiculed for putting on a fake smile when he was PM because focus groups told him that 'smiling is good', but when he had loads of misspellings in a hand written note and was mocked for it by the tabloids there was a groundswell of support for him – people respond to people.

Wednesday May 6 was the day that the UK ceased to be, as politicians used to say, 'about three weeks behind' our neighbours on the continent as the UK death toll became the highest in Europe – despite having more notice of the approaching virus than many of them. By way of contrast, Germany, which adopted mass testing early on in a policy more akin to the Asian countries which handled the virus most effectively, announced a slow lifting of some lockdown measures with shops and Bundesliga football being given the go ahead to reopen.

The same day the Welsh Assembly officially changed its name to the Welsh Parliament which I imagine was pretty frustrating news for the 'Abolish the Assembly' party who opted to keep their original name to 'avoid confusion'. Over in the other parliament in Westminster, Boris Johnson was taking on Keir Starmer in their first PMQs. With the vast majority of MPs only able to dial in through Zoom it was a far quieter Prime Minister's Questions than normal, and this was to only benefit one of the men. Starmer and Johnson have two very contrasting styles of oratory. Starmer, a trained barrister, is methodical, forensic and focussed on detail. Johnson, a showman, is all about energy, quips and feeding off his audience. The courtroom quiet of the lockdown Commons played far more into the Labour leader's hands as he challenged the PM on why the contact tracing was abandoned in mid-March and why 40% of doctors had had to buy their own PPE or rely on donations (it actually seemed like Johnson relied on Matt Hancock to feed him information at this point). In previous PMQs when he had floundered Boris Johnson had been able to quickly reel off a slogan or a generic phrase and rely on the noise generated from his back benchers to make it seem like he just scored a point; in the quiet he seemed to wilt. This was a running theme in their early exchanges and was a key reason the Leader of the House Jacob Rees-Mogg was keen to get the chamber full again.

It wasn't just in Westminster where Boris Johnson was having issues. With the next lockdown period drawing to an end after the weekend there were increasing rumours that the UK Government could end the motto of the lockdown so far – 'Stay home, protect the NHS, save lives'. This was a cause of deep concern for Nicola Sturgeon and Mark Drakeford with Wales' First Minister being a long-time vocal backer of the 'four nations approach'. However following these rumours, and seemingly little consultation from Westminster, cracks started to show.

Ms Sturgeon said she would not "be pressured into lifting measures prematurely" and that dropping the "clear, well understood" stay at home message could be a "potentially catastrophic mistake". She added that the evidence in Scotland made her believe that: "the lockdown must be extended at this stage. The decisions we take now are a matter of life and death and that is why they weigh so heavily."[3] What is interesting about the remarks about evidence is that, though Scotland has its own chief medical officer, both administrations were drawing from the same evidence pool from SAGE – they were just reaching different conclusions from the science (or one/both of them simply was not following it). Drakeford also called for more communication from the UK Government rolling out his favourite phrase 'a regular, reliable rhythm' for the first of very, very many times also adding that working with Downing

Street was a 'bit of a fits and starts experience'.[4]

In a break from the norm (whatever that was anymore) the Prime Minister then announced that he would reveal the planned changes to lockdown in a pre-recorded television address on Sunday, May 10 – leaving no chance for journalist questions or parliamentary scrutiny. As I said before, nothing like a healthy democracy right? With Boris not appearing until Sunday, the First Minister went ahead and announced what the next three weeks of lockdown would look like for people in Wales. He began his statement talking about the R rate (which was greater than 2.0 at the start of the crisis) saying it was now between 0.7 and 0.9.

According to the First Minister the current modelling in Wales suggested that 800 people would die of coronavirus in Wales in the following three months if the R rate remained at 0.8. An increase to 0.9 would result in 1400 deaths, and a rate of 1.1 would cause 7200 deaths in the same period, with a predicted 47,600 infections and 25,700 hospital admissions. Mr Drakeford said: "We must not lose the progress we have made. All of us must continue to work from home wherever they can. All of us must only travel when absolutely necessary. All of us must continue to observe the 2 metre social distancing and to wash our hands often."

He announced three modest changes to the lockdown from Monday 11. Exercise would be allowed more than once a day (a great relief to many). Councils could decide to open libraries and recycling centres if they wished. There were good reasons to open libraries again: social distancing in them is fairly simple to maintain and the people who would benefit most were those on low incomes, and young people struggling to work in a crowded home environment. Finally, garden centres could re-open if social distancing could be maintained.

None of these changes applied to the 120,000 people in the

shielding group who were still condemned to sit in their houses, isolated from loved ones and hoping they could book a supermarket delivery slot.

That weekend saw the 75th anniversary of victory in Europe and unfortunately all of the ceremonies planned for it had to be postponed because of the coronavirus. However, in many ways this did not hold people back and it gave everyone a reason to celebrate after two months of misery for many. Across Wales and the UK the bunting was thrown up and people sat in their front gardens (where they had one) and had a socially distanced street party. Music, sing-a-longs of 'We'll Meet Again', and fancy dress were on display and it was hard to know how to feel about it. It felt in many ways so right to be smiling and talking with your neighbour. However, there was also a feeling of fear, that somehow you were not allowed to have fun or that you were doing something naughty. The weather, thankfully, got on board with the programme and it was a day that everyone needed. Walking around Cardiff people were smiling again. It felt like the London 2012 Olympics when it became acceptable for a few weeks to chat with a stranger (though of course you couldn't actually do that this time around).

Obviously there were the odd muppets who took it too far with a few people after one (or by looks of it six) too many ending up in scraps with the police who told them to social distance. But there was also a video which went viral of a group of revellers who had tied knots in a rope every 2 metres and then were using it to do a long conga round the street. You couldn't help but feel that if the person at the front had had the virus the conga would probably have been more like an infection train. Though it is impressive that they were even able to hold the rope considering the whole country seemed to have dry, sore hands from two months of relentlessly washing in soapy water and anti-bac.

On Sunday, May 10 it was time for Boris Johnson's announcement. People in England waited with bated breath to find out what was to come and political reporters in Wales waited by their keyboards to explain how none of this would apply to Wales.

Compared to Wales' modest changes, the lifting of restrictions was substantial – far in excess of some of the speculation from earlier in the week. The Prime Minister said: "From this Wednesday we want to encourage people to take more and even unlimited amounts of outdoor exercise. You can sit in the sun in your local park, you can drive to other destinations, you can even play sports but only with members of your own household. Anyone who can't work from home, for instance those in construction and manufacturing, should be actively encouraged to go to work. We want it to be safe for you to get to work. So you should avoid public transport if at all possible, because we must and will maintain social distancing, and capacity will therefore be limited." It marked the end of the 'stay at home' period in England and the start of the 'stay alert' period.

There was very little in the speech to suggest that these measures only applied to England, with Welsh Government Minister Jeremy Miles going straight on to BBC Wales to make it clear to people that Wales was not open to business: "I want to be really clear about this. The position in Wales is very different from the position in England in relation to that. Our regulations do not permit people to get in their cars and drive to destinations in Wales and this includes people getting in their cars in England. We are not permitting that in Wales." Though one does wonder what the point of saying that was on a station almost exclusively listened to by people already in Wales.

The lack of consideration or clarification was so brazen it

seemed almost deliberately misleading. If you are being really cynical you could make a case that it was politically expedient for the UK Government to be deliberately misleading. It would both undercut the devolved administrations and there is simply more gravitas to addressing 'the nation' as opposed to England – it couldn't be suggested that there was another way of doing things after all! That theory should be filed under C for cynical and also P as there is no substantiated proof to back it up.

Whether deliberate or not is frankly irrelevant. Either way the result of this lack of clarity was to make it harder for the Welsh Government and police to keep people in Wales safe – hardly a signal of respect and concern for their partners (and in many cases constituents) across the border.

The other thing to note is that England had now diverted significantly in policy from the other home nations despite all sides drawing from a very similar scientific base. It could be argued that the countries are different with separately run health services and so is perfectly natural for there to be divergence. But there was such a gulf in the messages coming from the respective administrations that you couldn't help but feel that either one side was being reckless or the other overly cautious (or both).

9. 'Too Fast, Too Confusing and Too Risky'

May 11 to May 17
Wales' confirmed Covid-19 cases – 11,344
Wales deaths – 1,111
UK confirmed cases – 202,085
UK deaths – 31,571

The effect of Boris Johnson's televised address was the last thing needed in a pandemic – confusion. Not only did very little in the Prime Minister of the UK's address apply to anywhere other than England, it posed more questions than it answered. The road map he outlined was less A to Z and Ordnance Survey and more one of those mazes on a child's placemat with some crayons in a restaurant. Whereas 'stay home' was a clear, easy to understand message, 'stay alert' was open to interpretation and begged the question of how to be alert for a virus you cannot see? Those unable to work from home were now encouraged to return to work while avoiding public transport, which for many was simply impossible. Released on a Sunday evening, business owners scrambled to tell employees not to come into work the next morning as they simply were not prepared.[1]

Many police chiefs went public over what the announcement would mean for them. Police and Crime Commissioner for Gwent Jeff Cuthbert said the PM's statement had "muddied the water!" He added: "I worried about my colleagues in England and how they will police the idea of 'staying alert' – I'm not sure how that is going to happen. Undoubtedly, because of the strength of the English media there is going to be confusion in the minds of many people. It could well be because the Prime Minister didn't mention the situation in Wales."

North Wales Police and Crime Commissioner Arfon Jones, whose force now had the unenviable task of policing the populated and porous border with England, said: "I have real concerns about the number of people who will be tempted to head to North Wales, particularly as there is no restriction in England on how far people can travel in their cars to take exercise. The danger is that people will be travelling to places like Snowdonia and the Llyn Peninsula from cities like Liverpool, Manchester and Birmingham because they will believe they have been given the green light to do so. It's made our work here in Wales so much harder and it is so unnecessary." This fear was justified when Welsh holiday parks were suddenly inundated with calls as people attempted to make bookings.

That the Prime Minister, who is as much the Prime Minister for people in Wales as he is England, made the jobs of Welsh police 'so much harder' in a way that was 'so unnecessary', by being too vague is quite appalling. These rules were in place because they were literally saving lives of people in Wales; to make them harder to police therefore risked costing lives. This whole affair again exposes the total mess of our constitution. Boris Johnson doubles as the Prime Minister of both the UK and England, and yet there is no formal role of an English PM. This is a completely intolerable situation on both sides of the border which resulted in Wales receiving confusing messages and often being overlooked and people in England having even less formal representation than Wales and Scotland because there is no 'English government'.

It wasn't just police who were concerned about the new messaging. Doctors felt there were serious risks that it would lead to a spike in cases and a resurgence in the virus which had only just come under a semblance of control. Dr Chaand Nagpaul, chairman of the British Medical Association, said the measures were "too fast, too confusing and too risky".[2]

Dr Nagpaul told BBC Breakfast the next morning: "We have seen about 4,000 new cases every day over the weekend, and that is just a fraction of the real number of cases. There is still a considerable amount of community circulation of the virus. If we now allow the public to go to parks in an unlimited sense, we have not heard how the government is going to enforce social distancing. I am really concerned there is clarity. There are a lot of unanswered questions and we are very concerned."

The afternoon of Monday, May 11, First Minister Mark Drakeford made an error in the Welsh Government's press conference. For most people the hardest part of the lockdown was not being able to see their closest family, with parents, children, grannies, grandads separated – many for the longest time they had experienced. All they wanted to do was be able to see their nearest and dearest face to face and talk. People understood that they couldn't go in for a cwtch or meet family indoors but there was a growing frustration that they could not arrange to meet even one member of their family for a socially distanced walk in a park. After all, when going for their thirty minutes daily exercise in parks people were seeing dozens of strangers – why couldn't they just be socially distanced with their grandad rather than a random person?

I was on the Zoom call for this press conference and one of the questioners before me asked the First Minister directly about the new changes in England. Mr Drakeford responded: "I am not sure that I fully understand what is being proposed in England. It has been the case throughout coronavirus in Wales that if you as an individual are out taking exercise you can, at a social distance, have contact with one other person. We always said that two people can interact in that way and if you did as I did go on my bicycle to my allotment through one of the major fields in Cardiff then you see people doing that all the time."

This hit me for six. For the last two months my colleagues and I had covered all the intricate details of the lockdown rules in Wales and at no point was it made clear that it was OK to arrange to meet up with someone at a social distance in a park! Did he really mean to say that I could have been meeting my family all this time?

This was such a significant story, the headline 'you can meet a family member in park' would be the most welcome sentence many people in Wales had read in a very long time. It was almost too good to be true, and when you have that feeling, you have to clarify: these are literally questions of life and death.

On my turn I pressed the First Minister on this point. Mr Drakeford repeated: "The rules in Wales are that two people can meet providing they observe social distancing, so if one person from a household is going out and meeting another member of their family then under our rules that would be permitted." He then went into further detail, emphasising members of the public could not meet more than one person from another household at the same time adding: "You can't go above two, once you go above two, in our definition it is a gathering and gatherings are not allowed."

This left me in no doubt about what the situation was in Wales. When you hear things from health officials, or junior ministers there can be a lingering doubt in your mind that they may have made a mistake or got the facts muddled. But this was the First Minister, the man who not only had the final say on all lockdown measures in Wales but was also one of the most detail orientated politicians I have ever come across. We therefore published what the First Minister had said.

The story was read by tens of thousands but after several hours the Welsh Government contacted us telling us the story was wrong. They issued a follow up statement saying: "Our overarching advice is to stay at home. You need a reasonable excuse to go out, and arranging to meet friends and family is not a reasonable excuse." By the time the Welsh Government had issued their second statement over 50,000 people had read the story. There is no other way of framing it – the First Minister of Wales had given the wrong advice. This really matters for several reasons.

First, the perception that the First Minister was not fully informed on one of the biggest public health threats is not good for public confidence. For weeks people in Wales, many desperately lonely or with mental health problems, had not been able to meet their support networks face to face because of these rules but the bloke responsible for setting these rules does not seem to know what they are.

Secondly, and most importantly, incorrect advice kills people. If these rules exist, they exist because they are necessary to keep people alive. People had been desperate to see their family or close friends and may quite naturally have made plans immediately after reading the article to meet people in their local park. Yet because of this error by the First Minister they took an unnecessary risk to their health and those of a loved one. Not to mention the fine they could have received for doing so.

When we had amended the content of the original article a colleague and I had a serious conversation about what to do next. There were multiple things to consider. First, there were 50,000 people who were now living under the false assumption that they could arrange to meet their loved ones in a park. They were not likely to come back and re-read the amended story (why would they?). Secondly, the First Minister had made a mistake that could cost the lives of people in Wales. If Boris Johnson had done that he would have been absolutely slaughtered in the media. The First Minister had obviously just misspoke and thought he was being clear. Everyone makes mistakes, we know that. But in running for public office, politicians are accepting that they can and should be held to a higher standard – especially as leader. Mistakes cost lives and Mr Drakeford had made one.

I therefore put together an opinion piece that same evening called 'Wales' First Minister has made a massive mistake' which was one of our most read stories for the next two months[3]. A part of me hoped this wouldn't make Drakeford less inclined to be as forthcoming with answers in press conferences as he does seem genuinely to try to give insight into policy-making and endeavour to help people understand the reason behind decisions. As I wrote at the time, of course he is a politician, and should come served with a dollop of critical thinking and anti-spin, but at least you usually left briefings with him feeling more informed than when you entered. The piece didn't change his style in press conferences, though in Plenary two days later he was challenged by opposition party leaders on the mistake and attempted to dismiss it as stirred up by people "willing to cause mischief".

It was also not a good start to the week for the Health Minister Vaughan Gething after a picture appeared of him in the *Sun* sitting on a bench in Cardiff Bay eating chips with his wife and five-year-old son[4]. Critics immediately jumped on this as picnics had been explicitly forbidden under Welsh Government guidance that warned against using exercises as an excuse to undertake other activity like picnicking or spending a prolonged period on a park bench. Pre-empting the publication of the story Mr Gething tweeted: "Really disappointing that @TheSun are planning to print a photo of me on a walk with my wife and young son on the weekend. Our 5 year-old was hungry and we bought some chips – all within the rules."

In a virtual Senedd session Conservative Members challenged the First Minister on Mr Gething's behaviour. Former Welsh Conservative leader Andrew R.T. Davies asked: "If any individual purchased food, eat it on a public bench, they would clearly be breaking the rules – should they apologise?"

To which Mr Drakeford responded that he wasn't "going to get drawn into this sort of personality bashing" and that Mr Gething was entitled to privacy and could "speak for himself". He said the question was "simply designed to attack an individual out with their family entitled, I would say, to some privacy in the way they were going about things and who will speak for himself". Another Conservative, Clwyd West MS Darren Millar, added that "It looks to the public it's one rule for the health minister and another rule for them" to which Mr Drakeford responded a "brief stop to allow a child to eat is not a picnic in anybody's language". Luckily the First Minister managed to resist an explicit fuelled tirade after the session as his health minister had previously done in the Senedd.[5]

Mr Gething was vociferous in his defence that nothing he did amounted to a breaking of the rules. Several opposition politicians went on to suggest that the fact the Welsh Government subsequently changed its exercise guidance to say that activities that are 'good for people's health or wellbeing' are also 'considered to be reasonable' was a cynical attempt to absolve the health secretary retrospectively – a claim the Welsh Government strenuously denied.[6]

Elsewhere the economy was under more pressure than Vaughan Gething. For weeks there had been concerns that the widely successful furlough scheme would be brought to an end because it was, well, too successful. With Chancellor Rishi Sunak suggesting that by the end of June the £40 billion scheme would be costing the same amount to run as the NHS, the 7.5 million people in the UK who relied on it to pay some of their wages and the businesses who needed it to stay afloat were nervous about any changes. These fears were increased when Sunak described the scheme as "clearly not a sustainable situation".

There were multiple possibilities for what might be done to the scheme. The most extreme was the 'cliff edge', simply ending the scheme. With many businesses still closed this was called 'unthinkable' by Wales' finance minister, Rebecca Evans. Or it could be scaled down, reducing the government contribution from 80% to 60%. Another option was to reserve furloughing for those most at risk. People renting, and likely to be living more hand to mouth; people in the twenties and thirties, similarly. However, it would be difficult to justify criteria for omission, and large numbers of workers might fall through the net. A fourth option was to limit the scheme to certain industries and professions most at risk. Workers in hospitality or aviation, for example, were unlikely to see an upturn in their sectors for some time. Finally, the possibility of all workers taking part time employment, so that everyone was employed but for fewer working hours. The idea being instead of having 40% of your staff off you instead have all your staff working 40% less.

On May 12 the Chancellor opted simply to extend the scheme in its current form until the end of October. Even the success of the furlough scheme was not enough to save many businesses, with 122,160 individual claims for Universal Credit in Wales between the start of March and May 12. These were not all people coming from low paid roles in the shut down hospitality industry. Many of these jobs were highly skilled: jobs that drive the economy and often never come back.

Giving evidence to the Welsh Affairs Committee on May 12, John Whalley, chief executive of Aerospace Wales, the trade association for all companies operating in the aerospace and defence sector in the country, said that Wales could see 8,000 job losses from which it "may never recover to the levels we had". In a depressing prognosis of the future he said: "If we look at the industry, not just in Wales, but in the UK, people are talking about 30% cuts. If you think about it, we had a 10-year backlog, aviation is going to be depressed now for a number of years. It's going to take at least three years to recover, and possibly a lot longer. We may never recover to the levels we had, there are all sorts of scenarios. So, 30% is my best guess if you factor that across Wales, 23,000 people, that's probably 7,000 or 8,000 jobs are going to go – that's the stark bottom line."

Meanwhile in Westminster a more personal politics was in play. At the daily lobby briefing with the Prime Minister's spokesman almost everyday the same questions were put to him by journalists: "Where is Dominic Cummings and where did he self-isolate when he was suspected of having the virus?" and "When are you going to release the report into Home Secretary Priti Patel's bullying allegations?" Week after week, these same questions were asked. The answer to the Cummings question was always the same: that he was self-isolating at home.

The Priti Patel report was a little more complicated. At the end of February the top civil servant in the Home Office Sir Philip Rutnam resigned and began a claim for constructive dismissal against the government. He well and truly pointed the finger at Priti Patel for creating a campaign against him. He said: "In the last 10 days, I have been the target of a vicious and orchestrated briefing campaign. It has been alleged that I have briefed the media against the home secretary. This – along with many other claims – is completely false. The home secretary categorically denied any involvement in this campaign to the Cabinet Office. I regret I do not believe her."

Following these accusations of bullying, which Priti Patel strenuously denied, an investigation had been ordered. That report was asked for almost every day by journalists and every day the spokesman for the Prime Minister said it was not finished or ready to be released. When asked how long it would be, the spokesman for the PM would only add: "it will take as long as it takes". Though not directly coronavirus related it is worthwhile remembering that behind all the craziness of fighting the virus, the rest of government was still having to function. The virus was the biggest story in the country for months, but it was not the only story, and the day to day running of the country and decisions that affect people's lives were still being made – only with less scrutiny and oversight.

It wasn't just the journalists that the Westminster Government were not answering, the 'four nation approach' to tackling the virus of which Drakeford had been such a vocal proponent, seemed to be floundering as well. The First Minister told a press conference on Friday, May 15 there had now been no communication from the UK Government over lockdown since last week. Mr Drakeford said: "This week has been one of the stops in the stop-start process. Last week in the run-up to the announcements [on lockdown changes] we had good meetings on four out of five days. But now a whole week has gone by without any meeting of that sort. One out of three weeks has now gone by without any contact of that sort. We don't want to see a sudden splurge of contact in the days before a decision has got to be made."

Drakeford continued, "When we had the last COBRA meeting I felt there was a commitment there to have these discussions on a more regular and predictable basis. I immediately followed that up by communicating with the UK Government, hoping to see that in place this week. It is a disappointment to me that that rhythm has not been established. The reason I am disappointed is simply because I am committed to a four-nation approach. Getting a four-nation approach becomes more complicated and challenging as we move out of lockdown. Therefore you need more conversations, more opportunities to share information, share perspectives, share ideas and hammer out a common way ahead. Without the opportunities to have those conversations, I think that becomes more difficult."

There were starting to be regular positive signs that the lockdown in Wales was having an effect on the virus with the number of patients in hospital with Covid-19 at its lowest level since early April. While Mark Drakeford was looking longingly at the phone waiting for Boris to call ("he has seen my messages, do you think he is seeing other ministers?") he may have been better served having an in-depth chat with his own Health Minister. Vaughan Gething's week had got even worse after he and the First Minister had seemingly conflicting accounts of Wales' PPE stocks. Speaking at a press conference way back in March, Mr Gething was asked: "Can you tell us what the Welsh Government had in terms of gowns, visors, swabs and body bags in its pandemic stockpiles when Covid-19 reached the UK?"

Mr Gething had responded that "all of those items were available in our pandemic stock". However, this was seemingly contradicted by a letter Mark Drakeford sent to Plaid leader Adam Price when he said gowns were not included in the pandemic stockpile, with Mr Price concluding: "They do not seem to be on top of this crucial detail on the pandemic stock." After some enquiries WalesOnline managed to establish that the reason for the inconsistency was around the phrase 'pandemic stock' which technically is back-up PPE ahead of flu outbreak and is not the entirety of PPE the Welsh Government has available to it . At the same time WalesOnline also revealed that, a month after the Welsh Government had apologised for sending around 13,000 letters telling people to shield to the wrong address, letters were still being sent out in error, though not on the same scale as in April. One mum in Swansea was shocked to discover that she was in fact at high risk from the virus despite no underlying health conditions[8].

Though this would not have an impact on this woman, who was able to quickly establish that it had been sent in error, there was the potential for much more serious consequences from these continual mistakes on shielding letters. If someone isolated themselves when it was not necessary, it could seriously affect their well-being and mental health. Even worse, a letter might not reach a person who needed it and they were risking their lives by continuing to visit the supermarket when they had a higher likelihood of death if they caught the virus.

With thousands dead across the UK it is hard to believe that anyone could be opposed to the lockdown, especially in the early stages when the virus was absolutely running rampant. And yet this is 2020, a time when people do not vaccinate their children against deadly diseases and well-known public figures think the earth is flat. Misinformation is false or inaccurate information though not necessarily created deliberately. Disinformation is when false information is created with the intention of misleading, and there were huge amounts of disinformation circulating on social media regarding the virus. These lies (for that is what they are) had contributed to the vandalising of 5G masts earlier in the crisis and now fake accounts on Twitter and Facebook inflamed protests against the lockdown itself, suggesting it was a con. These accounts are not new, they have been used in the past to help both the leave side of the Brexit argument and on the side of President Trump in the

2016 US election. These shady disinformation factories (which often align with Russian geopolitical aims) went into overdrive blaming the EU for failing to protect its citizens and stoking resentment with measures put in place to protect the public.

This culminated in a series of protests in the UK against the lockdown, with protesters waving placards against the lockdown, 5G, the wearing of masks and Bill Gates (a long-time proponent of action to prevent pandemics). As the UK death toll neared 36,000 people, 19 people were arrested in London for breaking the lockdown rules. In Cardiff, rather hilariously, only a couple of people attended the rally there, with a similar story across other advertised protests in Swansea and Newport. It is easy to laugh at conspiracy theorists (and this is certainly what they deserve) but they have such potential to become something much worse. This was the case in America where in states totally overwhelmed by the virus, people would still refuse to wear masks because it was part of some deep state plot. If these people were only hurting themselves they could be left to it, but as with the growing 'anti vax' movement, it is just as likely to harm others.

With England having announced a route out of lockdown, pressure was mounting on the Labour Government in Cardiff Bay to do the same. People needed to know the way out. Not just those trying to plan for businesses and jobs, but everyone. Parents were desperate to know at what point schools could reopen, families when they might be reunited, people of faith when they could return to worship, and when someone could have a kick about with their friends.

On Friday May, 15 Mark Drakeford unveiled the new traffic light system for Wales. With four levels (lockdown, red, amber and green) it applied to eight areas of life affected by lockdown: reopening schools and childcare facilities, seeing family and friends, getting around, playing sport games and relaxing, working or running a business, going shopping, using public services and practising faith and special occasions.

It is not necessary to explain every single one but by way of example the sport section was:

Lockdown
Exercise once a day outside of the house on your own or with your household.
Red
Exercise more than once a day and incidental activity locally.
Outdoor sports courts to open.
Elite athletes resume some activity.
Amber
Team and individual sports, non-contact sport and games in small groups indoors and outdoors.
Some outdoor events with limited capacity and events behind closed doors for broadcast.
Green
All sports, leisure and cultural activities open, with physical distancing.
All events resume with limited capacity.

When Wales moved to a different colour in one group it didn't necessarily have to move in the others. So for instance in sport Wales was in the red zone but for 'relaxing and special occasions' it was still in the lockdown section. Even when a section moved from one colour to another all those bullet points were not entered into at once. In sport, Wales was in the red zone but only "exercise more than once a day and incidental activity locally" was allowed, outdoor sport courts did not.

A week on from Boris Johnson's announcement, how did the

England and Wales lockdowns compare? In terms of timescale the Welsh Government released no dates at all for when restrictions would change, with Mark Drakeford saying it will be "when the scientific and medical advice tells us it is safe to do so". In England there were timeframes given with pubs, restaurants, hairdressers, beauty salons, places of worship and cinemas all to be allowed open by July 4.

Whereas in Wales there was the traffic light system, in England there were 'the three steps' underpinned by the 'Covid alert system' which had five levels which would dictate how quickly the amended the lockdown.

England and Wales were now on different paths to tackling the virus and lifting the lockdown. Something that would have been fairly surprising at the start of the crisis.

10. 'Welcome to the opticians, if you would please start your engine we can begin'

May 18 to May 24
Wales' confirmed Covid-19 cases – 12,404
Wales deaths – 1,207
UK confirmed cases – 223,236
UK deaths – 33,958

May 18 and the new week started with a technical briefing from the darling of Twitter, deputy chief medical officer Jonathan Van-Tam[1]. Since the start of the crisis people who suspected they may have coronavirus had been given the same advice. If you had either a high temperature (it was not needed to actually take your temperature, just that you feel hot to touch on the chest or back) or a new, continuous cough (coughing a lot for more than an hour, or three or more coughing episodes in twenty-four hours) you were supposed to isolate for seven days. If you lived with someone who had these symptoms you were supposed to self-isolate for fourteen days from the day their symptoms started. This could mean isolating for longer than two weeks if you developed the symptoms on your 13th day you had to begin another seven days from scratch. Though fatigue, sore throat, runny nose, diarrhoea, vomiting, loss of taste or smell and headache had also been found to be symptoms in some people – only temperature or a cough had been signs that the advice said you should self-isolate.

At the technical briefing JVT announced that loss of smell or taste was being added as the third symptom that triggered immediate isolation. Deciding this list was a fine balancing act. It was in the public interest that people with possible coronavirus shouldn't leave their house, but some of the symptoms are so vague and generic they can apply to a long list of other ailments. Who doesn't feel fatigued at least once a week for example? To include fatigue as a symptom would therefore be counter-productive.

Someone who was probably wishing he hadn't had a sense of taste a few weeks ago was Vaughan Gething who was still taking criticism for the chips incident. Over the weekend passers-by didn't fail to notice that the seating area in Cardiff Bay where the Health Minister had chowed down had been fenced off. Many playgrounds, benches and exercise equipment in public places had been fenced off since the start of the lockdown to prevent the spread of the virus. Many people now asked if Mr Gething had been doing nothing wrong – why was it fenced off?

WalesOnline approached the Welsh Government to find out why the land, which it owned and ran, was closed off. It responded: "The area has seen a significant amount of littering over the past week and has been temporarily closed off until additional recycling bins are installed." It seems after seeing the Minister's chips many others hankered for some salt and vinegar slathered potatoes by the sea and followed suit. However, fencing off an entire area within days of an apparent spike in litter stretched credulity.[2]

I think probably Vaughan Gething did break the lockdown rules when he stopped to have chips on a bench. However, I don't for a minute pretend that I wouldn't do exactly the same in his position with a hungry five-year-old away from home. The public's anger about this was understandable though. For months the vast, vast majority of people in Wales stuck to both the letter and spirit of the rules, often to their own personal detriment. I personally know people who were spoken to by the police for doing something similar to Vaughan Gething and I think for the Welsh Government to pretend his actions fitted the letter and spirit of the rules at the time is quite comical. Should he have done it? No. Would most people have done it given the circumstances? Yes. A reason to be sacked (or should we say had his chips)? Get a grip.

The same day I published a story from the Senedd's Health, Social Care and Sport Committee where members of both the Royal College of Nursing (RCN) and Royal College of General Practitioners (RCGP) were scathing of the Welsh Government's initial response to the pandemic. Director of RCN Wales Helen Whyley identified six 'areas of concern' from their members. They were: PPE; testing for health and social care workers; arrangements for student nurses; guidance for BAME staff; staffing levels staying in legal limits; communication from the Welsh Government.[3]

Slamming the Welsh Government on the latter she said: "When we started out on this journey some months ago now, we were asking, on a daily basis, for information, which was not always forthcoming." This assessment was echoed by Dr Peter Saul from the RCGP who also added that 'glitches' in technology delayed many staff working remotely.

While both said that many of the communication issues from Welsh Government had been resolved they painted a very confusing picture across the seven health boards. Dr Saul told the committee: "There have been inconsistent messages across the country. We've had members in one part of a health board saying, 'Well, we're being told to do this', and in another area being told to do something differently. So, [we need] a more consistent and better distributed message. Also with messaging we've had, I get lots and lots of emails, they're almost too much to keep up with."

Ms Whyley said that the Welsh Government needed to learn

lessons so that this didn't happen again labelling some of the systems 'slow and clunky'. She said: "So, I believe there is a lesson to learn there to be able to follow that in a more succinct and quick manner if – and hopefully never – we're in a position like this again. But similarly, things like answering letters, et cetera, has been slow and clunky and letters have only been sent because we haven't been able to get the information to seek those assurances for our members."

The criticism of the Welsh NHS as 'slow and clunky' zeros in on challenges in our health service which had taken root a long time before coronavirus. Two years previously I conducted a six month investigation into the systems and shortcomings of the Welsh NHS. Titled 'The great mystery of Wales' missing nurses' I tried to answer the simple question of how many nurses the NHS had gained and lost over the period of a year[4]. This is a basic question of workforce management yet it was a complete nightmare to try and find out. After six months all I had been able to properly establish is that the Welsh Government did not really know how many nurses were employed on a day to day basis. The response to the piece was huge with several frustrated people working in the health service contacting me to say that it encapsulated the daily struggle they have as they attempt to swim butterfly stroke through treacle because of the convoluted and confused system in which they work. The piece ended up winning me the award of Welsh Journalist of the Year for 2019 and was actually nominated for several UK prizes.

It showed that the Welsh NHS is organised in such a way that it is only by the outstanding efforts of many of its employees it actually manages to function at all. In Wales there are seven health boards. Seven! In an area only slightly larger in population than Greater Manchester. If that is clunky, only a decade ago one of the health boards, Betsi Cadwaladr University Health Board, absorbed all the six health boards and two trusts across north Wales and Anglesey. Contacts within that health board say that even now certain departments still divide themselves up along those lines.

In addition to the health boards there are also four NHS Trusts in Wales which cover the whole country: Welsh Ambulance Services, for emergency services; Velindre NHS Trust, offering specialist services in cancer care and a range of national support services; Public Health Wales, the national public health agency in Wales; and Health Education and Improvement Wales (HEIW), which brings together the Wales Deanery, NHS Wales's Workforce Education and Development Services and the Wales Centre for Pharmacy Professional Education. This arrangement doesn't include care homes, which also have input from local councils, the Care Inspectorate for Wales and the Older Persons Commissioner.

All of the health boards have different systems, processes and ways of collecting and measuring data. There have been attempts to bring the many systems under a centralised support system called Shared Services but there remain huge discrepancies in how different health boards operate. For example, each health board has its own finance team, who all work in slightly different ways which make it harder to invoice in a uniform way. It is also a complicated process for staff to move from one health board to another despite they're all being employed by the Welsh NHS.

For example, moving an IT worker from the Royal Gwent Hospital in Newport just fourteen miles along the M4 to UHW in Cardiff requires completion of a payroll new starter form with bank details, a new holiday year etc, just to go from Aneurin Bevan to Cardiff and Vale. They are, for all intents and purposes different organisations: it's like trying to move someone from Tesco to Sainsburys. This is particularly ineffective if there was to be... I don't know... a global pandemic which required speedy mobilisation of staff to the areas that most needed it.

Shared Services carries out some recruitment but ultimately medical recruitment is retained by each individual health board and therefore checks and compliance for staff differ across the country. This is not criticism for criticism sake. There are perfectly legitimate reasons that it is optimal for patients that decisions are made as closely as possible to where they will be enacted, but the disjointed and confused system is not fit for the twenty-first century in normal times let alone during a public health emergency.

The issues underlying this convoluted and 'clunky' system should be easily apparent. An example arose early in the crisis. Betsi Cadwaladr and Hywel Dda university health boards failed to report 85 and 31 Covid-19 deaths respectively because they were not using the correct IT system[5]. Large amounts of public money had been spent on an 'all-Wales' IT system created specifically to tackle these sorts of issues. Chair of the Senedd's Public Accounts Committee, Nick Ramsay, said: "The misreporting of coronavirus deaths this spring has highlighted that the problems highlighted by the Public Accounts Committee still exist. A lack of consistent electronic reporting has led to an undercount of Covid-19 related deaths over the period of the pandemic. This has serious consequences in terms of monitoring the pandemic and informing the actions needed to overcome the virus."

None of this is to cast aspersions on NHS workers and managers who do a really tough job, under really difficult circumstances – they really are heroes. All the more reason to simplify this crazily complicated system so they no longer have to do their job with one hand tied behind their back. It can be argued that all large organisations have a degree of duplication and inefficiency, especially (but by no means exclusively) in the public sector. But this doesn't mean we can't expect a higher standard and simplify systems when they self-evidently are not fit for purpose. What can be measured can be managed', but if it isn't possible to measure basic data across your health board how can you possibly manage?

To reinforce the point about heroes, a fundraising page for a nurse who died after contracting coronavirus raised over £8,000[6]. Lalaine Lopez Pesario, who worked at a care home in Swansea, was described as "a loving wife, mother, sister, auntie and a friend" and a "warrior who bravely fought and risked her life in the name of service and dedication to her profession." We must not forget that every person who died in this pandemic was a person, not a number.

On May 19 I did a sit-down interview with First Minister Mark Drakeford over Zoom. It was a wide-ranging interview and I adopted the tactic outlined earlier of not being overtly confrontational[7]. I only had twenty minutes with him and when someone used to work as a university lecturer their answers can often eat up a lot of time. Of all the questions I asked the one that received the best answer (and best response from our readers) was the most simple: 'Can you just paint us a picture of what Wales may look like in January 2021?'

He told me: "I think there are two very different destinations. On the hopeful path, we will have continued the journey through our traffic light system to a point where there are a lot of things that people wanted to do before they are able to do again in January next year. That may be in terms of public services being available in a different way, travel being available in different way, or shopping being available in different way but still with some things that we are unlikely to see back in place. Mass gatherings, I think, are at the very end of the spectrum. Places where people are packed tightly together in conditions for the virus to thrive in are, I think, unlikely to be happening in January next year. On a pessimistic path, despite every precaution we are taking, and the monitoring of every step we take, the virus begins to take off again in the autumn – when some light begins to disappear and nights begin to get darker and there is more damp – the things we know the virus likes are more prevalent. We then could see a repeat of the experience we have had in March and April. I don't think you can rule either of those things out. I think those are the two ends of the spectrum."

This week the ONS released their latest stats for deaths which showed that, tragically 1,852 people had so far died in Wales from the virus. This coincided with the First Minister agreeing in the Senedd to a future public inquiry into the handling of the pandemic. The PM would make a similar commitment, but not until the middle of July.

With England and Wales now having significantly different lockdown rules the police had the thankless task of enforcement. Until this point their main weapon was fines which started at £60 (reduced to £30 if paid quickly) and could rise to a maximum of £120 for further offences. Up to May 21 a total of 1,300 fixed penalty notices had been issued and forces across Wales, particularly those policing rural tourist areas, wanted fines to be significantly increased to act as a deterrent. On Wednesday, May 20 the First Minister announced that the top fine for people caught repeatedly flouting lockdown rules in Wales would increase to £1,920. Dramatic, but not really.

The initial fine was still £60, which would double with every new offence, so £60, £120, £240, £480, £960 before hitting the big scary £1,920. Although declaring 'fines of nearly £2,000' may grab headlines, in reality the new measures did little to help. The problem the fines were designed to stop was people breaking the rules and spreading Covid-19. The virus was not going to take off again because five mavericks went to Barry Island and got caught for the sixth time. The issue came from a far larger number of people nipping twenty miles away when they shouldn't, or gathering with too many people in close proximity in their local area. For these people the deterrent was still as little as £30. When you haven't seen your nearest and dearest for two months, it might be a risk you would be willing to take.

Police and Crime Commissioner for Dyfed Powys Police, Dafydd Llewelyn, said: "I'm personally disappointed that the first fine hasn't been altered as a deterrent. What I was calling on was for the deterrent of the first offence to be higher because what we're seeing, particularly in the Dyfed Powys area that I am responsible for, is people travelling vast vast distances coming to the beauty spots, coming into our area. I feel this sends the wrong message to the public. We saw a group of off road bikers who had returned to DP over the weekend following some intervention from the police about a fortnight ago. They've been fined two weeks ago. The £60 fine is reduced to £30 if it's paid within a certain time – that obviously wasn't much of a deterrent. If they had been slapped with a higher fine in the first instance, I'm pretty sure that they wouldn't have returned."

The overwhelming majority of people were keeping to both the letter and spirit of the rules. It is frankly a miracle that two months into the pandemic, the levels of compliance were still astonishing. It wasn't £30 fines that was keeping people in their homes – often to great personal detriment and suffering. What was keeping people inside was a social contract, a collective agreement that we all needed to follow these rules for the protection of our most vulnerable, ourselves and our country. We followed the rules out of gratitude to the people who were risking their lives to treat those with the virus – to not make their difficult jobs harder than they needed to be.

This message came from the very top of Government and several prominent people had fallen on their sword for flouting the rules. At the start of April, Scotland's chief medical officer Catherine Calderwood, who had been a prominent and visible figure in the efforts to tackle the outbreak in Scotland, quit after breaking her own rules and twice visiting her second home during the lockdown. Though not an immediate resignation, the pressure became too intense and she stepped down. First Minister Nicola Sturgeon said at the time that though "she has apologised sincerely and honourably" the whole affair risked distracting from and undermining confidence in the government's public health message at this crucial time". She added that "is not a risk either of us is willing to take".

Just a month later, on May 5, there was another resignation when epidemiologist Professor Neil Ferguson, whose modelling and advice to the Prime Minister had led to lockdown, quit as a UK Government advisor. It had been reported that Prof Ferguson's lover had visited him at his home. In a statement he said that he "made an error of judgement" and "took the wrong course of action". He added that he believed he was immune having previously tested positive for the virus and isolated for over a week. But despite this statement he stepped down from his role in Sage (Scientific Advisory Group for Emergencies) because he had "undermined the clear messages around the continued need for social distancing."

Tough but fair treatment, right? The UK Government certainly thought so. Calling his behaviour 'extraordinary' Matt Hancock told Sky News that he 'took the right decision to resign' as it was 'just not possible' for Neil Ferguson to continue advising the government. He added that social distancing rules 'are there for everyone' and are 'deadly serious'. On the lobby correspondents' call, the Prime Minister's spokesman said that the PM had not asked Prof Ferguson to resign but Mr Johnson agreed with the decision, adding that: "Social distancing regulations are there for a very clear purpose."

This leads to the Saga of Durham Dom. Dominic Cummings, the man with a passion for Russia, Brexit, wide ranging reform and high-speed optometry. The bonkers series of events where Prime Minister Boris Johnson put his top advisor above the health of the entire country. To look at this we need to look at four questions: What happened? What was Dominic Cummings' justification? Why it was complete bollocks? Why does this really matter?

What happened? On March 30 Downing Street confirmed that Mr Cummings was suffering from coronavirus symptoms and was self-isolating. This was shortly after he had been seen scuttling out of Downing Street. Time and again the PM's spokesman was asked in the telephone lobby briefing 'where is Dominic Cummings?' and we were told 'he is isolating at home'. However, on May 22, the *Guardian* and the *Mirror* broke the story that he had broken the lockdown rules and driven to Durham with his wife and child on March 27[8]. Not only had he stayed with his family, he was also spotted during a 60-mile round trip to the picturesque town of Barnard Castle.

This immediately sparked an eruption of condemnation. On Sunday May 23 Johnson stood by his man after a statement was issued saying: "Owing to his wife being infected with suspected coronavirus and the high likelihood that he would himself become unwell, it was essential for Dominic Cummings to ensure his young child could be properly cared for. At no stage was he or his family spoken to by the police about this matter, as is being reported."

There were unsavory scenes outside his London home with a huge pack of photographers, reporters and even protesters. Footage showed Mr Cummings tell the assembled: "I behaved reasonably and legally", adding "Who cares about good looks? It's a question of doing the right thing. It's not about what you guys think."

Through this early stage the PM was nowhere to be seen. Instead transport secretary Grant Shapps was sent out like a baby-faced sacrificial lamb to defend the indefensible. Mr Shapps may have been well-equipped to re-writing history as he was accused by the *Guardian* in 2012 of editing out unfavourable parts of his own Wikipedia page (though he claimed to have been changing it for accuracy)[9]. Mr Shapps said Mr Cummings has the PM's 'full support' and that the PM "knew that he was unwell and that he was in lockdown". Shapps also stated that it had always been allowed that families could travel to be closer to relatives as long as they "go to that location and stay in that location".

In a statement the same evening, Durham police said they were made aware on March 31 that Mr Cummings was present at an address in the city and that an officer spoke with Mr Cummings' father at his own request, and he confirmed his son had travelled with his family and was "self-isolating in part of the property".

On Monday, May 24 the public finally got to see the Prime Minister face the camera and answer questions on the incident. They also got to see why Government spin doctors and strategists were so keen to keep him out of the spotlight. In a weak, doddery and somewhat pathetic performance, Mr Johnson said his aide had acted in the best interests of his child, in a way "any parent would frankly understand" and that Mr Cummings "acted responsibly, legally and with integrity".

When it came to the questions from journalists he completely ignored a request from the BBC to confirm if Mr Cummings had travelled to Barnard Castle. This press conference was the point at which Downing Street cut off the second question from journalists and refused a follow-up. From the start of the crisis every reporter had been allowed to ask a question and then follow up. In this press conference they were muted before they could come back, though hilariously the camera still cut back to them. This led to one clip of Robert Peston rolling his eyes and throwing his hands up in exasperation upon realising that these questions were simply too hard and on-the-money to be allowed. It was time for our democracy to self-isolate: it was very sick.

Everyone was convinced that Cummings would have to go. How could he possibly remain? Unsurprisingly, the PM's lacklustre performance did nothing to reduce the pressure. On the contrary, watching the Prime Minister throw away any goodwill and political capital he had in order to protect his advisor seemed to be the last straw to many. Tory MPs, the opposition parties, scientists and even members of the clergy called for Cummings' head. The Rt Revd Nick Baines, Bishop of Leeds, tweeted: "The question now is: do we accept being lied to, patronised and treated by a PM as mugs?"

Members of a Sage subcommittee spoke out, with Prof Stephen Reicher, of St Andrews University, tweeting: "I can say that in a few short minutes tonight, Boris Johnson has trashed all the advice we have given on how to build trust and secure adherence to the measures necessary to control Covid-19. Be open and honest, we said. Trashed. Respect the public, we said. Trashed. Ensure equity, so everyone is treated the same, we said. Trashed. Be consistent we said. Trashed. Make clear 'we are all in it together'. Trashed. It is very hard to provide scientific advice to a government which doesn't want to listen to science. I hope, however, that the public will read our papers ... and continue to make up for this bad government with their own good sense."[10]

Even the legally impartial Civil Service tweeted (and swiftly deleted): "Arrogant and offensive. Can you imagine having to work with these truth twisters?" MPs from across the Conservative Party went public saying that Cummings had to go. In Wales, former Welsh Conservative Leader and Member of the Senedd Andrew R.T. Davies stated that Mr Cummings should apologise: "In my own view I think he took the wrong decision to travel 250 miles."

With pressure still building and the story not going away, it was announced that Mr Cummings would give a public statement in the Rose Garden of 10 Downing Street

To answer my second question: what was Dominic Cummings' justification?

The whole Durham Dom incident had quickly become a national scandal, and obsession. Millions watched on television as he sat in the Rose Garden to read a pre-prepared statement. 'Pre-prepared' did not only mean he wrote it down in advance. On this occasion it meant a group of top lawyers (likely at the public's expense) poring over the document to check it against every piece of evidence against Mr Cummings to ensure it was water-tight. In the view of many, what he read out reeked of a narrative constructed around what was known by the public, not a truthful telling of events.

Cummings made several points, the main one being that he had done nothing wrong and would not apologise. He had driven to Durham because his wife was ill with suspected Covid-19 and he was worried that he would become infected and their child would be left without proper care. The rules, he said, allowed travel to safeguard a vulnerable child. And he had a full tank of petrol so hadn't needed to break his journey. He also claimed that the virus had affected his eyesight and a trip to Barnard Castle had been necessary to test his eyesight before driving back to London. Cummings had also claimed that 'for years' he had been warning about the threat of coronaviruses, and as recently as the previous year had written about this and the urgent need to plan for them.'

Did I mention he did nothing wrong, has no regrets and won't apologise?

Now I don't want to insult your intelligence by pointing out why this is utter dross. However, it is important to do this because, as Mr Cummings was talking, what he said seemed eminently plausible and reasonable. While explaining his behaviour he attempted to project such an aura of a responsible, reasonable, moral man that it was perfectly possible to be swept along by it – he is after all an outstandingly effective communicator. If you have ever read *Lord of the Rings* you will know that the traitorous wizard Saruman's greatest power is that of his voice. With it he can make you believe almost anything, even if totally contradictory evidence is right under your nose. Right now, Cummings was attempting to pull a Saruman on the public.

According to Mr Cummings the justification for his sixty mile round trip to Barnard Castle was that he and his wife "agreed that we should go for a short drive to see if I could drive safely". If you decide that the best way to test your eyesight is by operating a huge, fast moving box of metal and driving 60 miles (not a quick tootle round the block) you must surely realise that taking your young son and wife along as crash test dummies is hardly the action of a responsible man. We must remember that the rationale for the entire trip was to safeguard the wellbeing of his son. What Mr Cummings neglected to mention was that the day of the trip was also his wife's birthday: she must have been furious that she had to spend her special day taking part in an eye test....

Even if we accept that driving is an acceptable way to test whether your eyes are fit for driving there is still the question of why Barnard Castle? If the purpose of the drive is to see if you are able to drive back to London, why not simply start driving back to London and then turn around if you are not fit to drive (though surely pulling over at that point is safest)?

The act of writing about why this is bollocks demonstrates the farcical nature of the situation. We know he broke the rules, he knows he broke the rules, but in 2020 Britain that no longer matters. It is best summed up by the title of Peter Pomerantsev's book on Russia (a country that Mr Cummings is apparently somewhat obsessed with): *Nothing Is True and Everything Is Possible.*

It is also worth questioning the premise of the entire trip to begin with. The justification was that there was no one in London who could look after their child if they both became sick and therefore had to go to Durham to be near family. Let us be absolutely clear on this again – bollocks. To suggest that a man as wealthy, connected and resourceful as Dominic Cummings could not source childcare in the capital of the UK isn't credible.

There is further evidence we are being spoon-fed a great dollop of deception in article that Dominic Cummings' wife wrote in the April 25 issue of the Spectator. In it she described her and her husband's symptoms in detail but at no point feels it important to mention that the family travelled more than 260 miles to Durham during that time. She also said they came out of quarantine in London.

On Cummings' claim that he had been a long-time advocate for tackling the threat posed by coronavirus' and pandemics. Indeed, Mr Cummings had written a blog the previous year which spoke about coronaviruses. What he didn't mention in the Rose Garden is that the article was edited sometime between 8 April 2020 and 15 April 2020, with additional information about coronavirus added.

Why does this really matter? Why does one government advisor breaking the lockdown rules matter so much? After all it is unlikely that he personally transmitted the virus to many people at all. Yet there are several important reasons why this is a big deal. First and foremost is that it led to a plummeting in public respect for compliance with the lockdown rules.

Before the Cummings' affair there was a real sense that obeying the lockdown rules mattered. Obeying them was as important as not stealing, breaking and entering or assault. Some people would break them but they were widely considered to be 'bad people'. They were lawbreakers, a minority, worthy of scorn and contempt. Following Cummings breaking the rules (and crucially the most senior politicians in the Government coming out to defend him), the laws around lockdown ceased to matter as much. They were now seen on the same level as speeding on a motorway or jaywalking. Yes, they are technically illegal, but they are seen by many as open to discretion. If you go 80mph on an empty motorway are you really being unethical? The speed limit is in place for public safety but few would consider someone a bad person for doing it. The second the Prime Minister defended Cummings, the lockdown rules became, to many, a matter of interpretation.

Whereas just a month before it had been 'the right decision' for Neil Ferguson to resign and it was 'just not possible' for him to advise the government, Mr Cummings was now 'just doing what any father would'. From this point there was a marked difference in how people in England in particular regarded the rules, which had already been diluted by the move from 'stay at home' to 'stay alert'. To quote Captain Barbossa in *Pirates of the Caribbean*: "They are more like guidelines anyway".

This is to say nothing of the gross unfairness of the entire situation. For months people had not seen their loved ones. Parents and grandparents had been left to die alone to keep to the rules. Single parents, who were ill themselves and would have loved to have some help from others, had been forced to look after their kids alone because of the rules. But now they were told not only did they not have to go through this alone, in fact they were not doing 'what any parent would do'.

The credibility of the Westminster Government was at a new low. In an attempt to justify Cummings' actions cabinet ministers like Michael Gove claimed that he had previously driven 'on occasion' to test his eyesight?! The blame for this is not really with Dominic Cummings, it lies ultimately squarely at the feet of Boris Johnson. Cummings existed at the centre of government at the behest of Johnson. He is not elected and his position is completely on the approval of the Prime Minister. If Boris Johnson didn't want him there, he would not be there. It is as simple as that. This begs the question of why Johnson, a man who has pursued power and position with such zeal, would risk his own position and political capital for Cummings.

The answer is simple: he needed him to maintain his position. Cummings is a superb campaigner and will happily intervene into every facet of how the government runs in an attempt to mould it into what he perceives to be a better way. For Johnson, who is defined by both his desire to have the prestige of being the top dog and also an aversion for looking at things in too much detail, this is all he could want from an advisor.

Some have said the relationship between the two of them is symbiotic. That like a clownfish and sea anemone, they are together for mutual support. But this is not a fair reflection as this suggests that the relationship is conducive to the long-term health of both parties and their environment. But that analogy falls down because the utter dependence is so one sided. On both Covid and Brexit,

Dominic Cummings has guided Johnson and this administration down a blind alley which, in all likelihood, only he has the ability to guide them out of politically intact. Johnson is utterly dependent upon Dominic Cummings. That is why the erosion of the rules was worthwhile collateral damage in pursuit of the real goal of keeping Durham Dom and thereby staying in power.

11. A Five Mile World

May 25 to- May 31
Wales' confirmed Covid-19 cases – 13,415
Wales deaths – 1,274
UK confirmed cases – 238,472
UK deaths – 36,050

There was nothing unusual about Monday, May 25. At 8.20 pm in the US city of Minneapolis, police officer Derek Chauvin knelt on the back of the neck of a man named George Floyd for over eight minutes until he was dead. During that time Floyd had said "I can't breathe" at least 16 times. There was nothing unusual about this because George Floyd was black and Derek Chauvin is a police officer. There is overwhelming evidence that people of colour are disproportionately victimised, targeted, discriminated against and killed by police in America.

The situation is not so different here in the UK where evidence[1] suggests that dangerous restraint techniques and excessive force are disproportionately used on Black, Asian and minority ethnic (BAME) people. Police use of restraint against detainees was identified as a cause of death by post mortem reports in 10% of deaths in police custody between 2004/05 and 2014/15. Use of restraint was found to be more prevalent in cases of BAME individuals who have died in police custody than in deaths of white people.

The institutionalised and deep-rooted prejudice against non-whites in our police forces and wider society is not a matter for debate – it is a matter of fact. On becoming Prime Minister the former Home Secretary Theresa May she said: "If you're Black, you're treated more harshly by the criminal justice system than if you're white." If you don't think there is institutionalised racism in the UK you are either willfully ignoring the overwhelming evidence or you are simply not looking hard enough.

Videos of Floyd's killing were widely shared online. No one knew at the time that this one pebble would create ripples that would form a tidal wave which crashed into shores around the world.

The impact George Floyd's death and the rise of the Black Lives Matter movement are considered in more detail in the chapter which looks at how the virus impacted people of colour, but this terrible murder brought an enormous issue into the mainstream and put minority issues firmly on the agenda.

An issue that wasn't on the agenda was climate change. Climate change is the issue. Despite the damage coronavirus is doing to human life and the world economy, it is simply the canapes before the seven course feast that is global heating. The list of risks associated with allowing our planet to become more than 1.5C warmer than pre-industrial times are so significant it makes the lockdown look like a minor inconvenience. Flooding, rising sea levels, water shortages, increased risks of droughts, disease and famine. Add to this the associated population migrations that it will cause. Looking at the chaos that the war in the relatively small country of Syria caused in terms of migration and scaling that up to include whole nations being underwater or without water the problem is huge.

The parallels between the climate crisis and the Covid crisis are stark. Both have been predicted by the smartest minds humanity has for decades. The solutions to preventing them are also well known. In the case of Covid they are implementing robust worldwide systems that can identify and isolate new outbreaks quickly, as well as national stockpiles of PPE and well-rehearsed local systems to protect people in the case of a pandemic. For climate change the solution is the rapid and sustained decarbonisation of our lives and economy. Sadly the parallels don't end there. In both cases our elected government has been woefully slow in recognising the threat. In the case of climate change they are still not going far enough or fast enough. Despite their clear and obvious failings, in both Covid and climate change they publicly profess the opposite, that they are 'leading the world'. Even if this was true, the world is so far off the pace when it comes to tackling global heating that 'leading the world' is simply claiming to be the country that is failing the least.

The initial public reaction to the two crises are similar too. As late as the beginning of March people who are otherwise well edu-cated and informed messaged me after every coronavirus article with accusations of 'scaremongering'. Even today stories on climate change produce a barrage of people calling it a hoax.

But can people be blamed for being sceptical when there is so much misinformation about both topics spread by those who find it either economically or politically beneficial to mislead? Car use was a daily topic the UK Government's press conference where a scientist would talk viewers through a graph showing that car use had absolutely plummeted. In the first week of lockdown research by the AA suggested an 80% fall[2]. This was the case globally in all areas that went into lockdown, with satellite images revealing dra-matic reductions in concentrations of the pollutant nitrogen dioxide in China and northern Italy as soon as restrictions were introduced.

When combined with an apparent blossoming in nature many people had the impression that the natural world was enjoying something of a comeback. Unfortunately for those in favour of a sustainable planet, CO2 emissions figures quickly put pay to that hope, and to the idea that climate change could be prevented solely by the action of individuals.

Air travel down by 95% and car use by 80% would surely significantly reduce our collective carbon footprint, alas no. The amount of emissions produced over the lockdown period had only fallen by, drum roll,...8%. To put that into context we need to cut global emissions by 7.6% every year to keep global temperatures from rising 1.5C (which is when scientists say the really serious damage will be done). Gulp.

So the world only just hit its annual target by the vast majority completely stopping driving further than the supermarket once a week. This is the scale of the task and the reason to be sceptical when politicians say that the UK is "setting the standard for tackling climate change' when they are promising to plant some trees, install some electric car charging points and give your nan loft insulation.

The reason that CO2 emissions fell so little during the first months of lockdown is that transport is the source of 20% of global emissions whereas electricity and heating make up 40%. Though we were not in our offices or schools as much, we still used electricity, the internet and needed to keep warm or cool. The situation is worse in rural Wales, where people rely on oil for heating as well as wood burners. Even those using electricity are contributing to emissions as less than half of UK electricity comes from renewable sources[3].

While it is true that the UK emissions have dropped hugely in recent years much of this is because we have outsourced production to places like China and India. We have exported our emissions and added the associated CO2 cost of transporting products to us. This is not to mention the pressure of producing enough meat to satisfy our carnivorous obsession with beef and the associated deforestation which in turn means less carbon is being absorbed by trees.

It is important to point this out, not to virtue signal or shame, but because Covid-19 has provided an early warning of the cost of inaction. The lessons to learn from coronavirus aren't just that we need to properly fund our health service. They also include the stark reality that climate change needs to be tackled right now, as our number one priority. When we were caught short of PPE during Covid we were able to quickly change our economy. By the time the impacts of climate change are forced upon us and people in Wales and the UK are dying it will be far too late to do anything about it.

With Wales and England following different lockdown procedures the Welsh Secretary Simon Hart appeared to make murky waters even more opaque after a meeting with top police officers in Wales. Mr Hart tweeted: "Fascinating to hear from Wales' four police chiefs today, and the commissioners too, especially on what's permissible under lockdown. Consensus was that travelling 10-15 miles from home to fish, play golf, surf or exercise is fine, subject to all other distancing requirements." However, Mr Hart's advice contradicted the the latest guidelines set out by Welsh Government. The guidance in Wales stated that exercising outside the home was allowed and could be multiple times a day but that "exercise should be undertaken locally, as close as possible to the home – in general this should not involve people driving to a location away from home for this purpose."

This led to a huge amount of confusion with the chief constable of Dyfed-Powys Police, Mark Collins, having to clarify that the UK Government politician was not correct, saying that "people should not drive outside their local area to undertake these forms of exercise." It seems the confusion came when Mr Hart was told that it might be appropriate to drive 'around 10 miles' to exercise if a person lived in a particularly rural area. However, as the majority of people in Wales live in urban areas the Welsh Secretary was widely condemned for issuing misleading advice. However, he declined to remove the offending tweet.[4]

It was a tough time for another Welsh Conservative MP when the *Mirror* reported that the police had been called to the house of Rob Roberts, the MP for Delyn in north Wales, after reports of an illegal lockdown birthday party. It seems Mr Roberts' wife had turned 40 on Monday, May 25. The MP, who has one of the smallest majorities in Wales, had recently separated from his wife when he came out as gay six weeks previously and was not in the house at the time. Though clearly in no way responsible this particular incident these were not the only negative headlines associated with him over the lockdown. In July the Conservative Party would be forced to launch an investigation after Mr Roberts allegedly made inappropriate advances on a young female intern asking if she wanted 'fun times', as well as causing a male colleague to move jobs after Mr Roberts invited him for dinner.[5]

On May 27, after the previous bank holiday weekend had seen English beaches packed and Welsh ones deserted (nothing to do with Cummings obviously), another phrase was added to the coronavirus lexicon: 'local lockdown', where a specific area of the country is locked down due to a localised outbreak. At the UK Government daily briefing Matt Hancock suggested the measures could be used in England, the logic being that it made no sense to impose a lockdown in Norwich because there was a spike in cases in Truro. In Wales Drakeford had already expressed his dislike for the idea of local lockdowns, considering them to be unfair and hard to enforce (this would change significantly as Wales moved into autumn).

After England's announcement a Welsh Government spokesman said: "This is science-led, and if the advice changes, then we will re-consider. However, as things stand, it is unlikely that we will have localised lockdowns as we are planning to avoid them in the first place. We have adopted a cautious and public health-led approach to easing of any of the lockdown restrictions and you didn't see thousands of people on beaches in Wales over the bank holiday. Importantly these relaxations of restrictions can be quickly reversed if there are any unintended consequences."

In the background the Durham Dom saga was rumbling on. On *Newsnight* the outstanding journalist Emily Maitlis, best known for making Prince Andrew dig himself the world's deepest hole (though not sweating at any point), delivered an incredibly powerful opening monologue on the BBC's flagship news program. It is so strong it is worth sharing it in full:

Dominic Cummings broke the rules.

The country can see that and it is shocked the government cannot. The longer ministers and Prime Minister tell us he worked within the rules the more angry the response to this scandal is likely to be.

He was the man, remember, who always got the public mood. Who tagged the lazy label of elite on those who disagreed. He should understand that public mood now. One of fury, contempt and anguish. He made those who struggled to keep the rules feel like fools and has allowed many more to assume the can now flout them.

The Prime Minister knows all this but despite the resignation of one minister, growing unease from his back benchers, the dramatic early warning from the polls and a deep national disquiet, Boris Johnson has chosen to ignore it.

Tonight we consider what this blind loyalty tells us about the workings of Number 10. We do not expect to be joined by a Government Minister but that won't stop us asking the question.

The response was enormous. Maitlis was widely praised for her monologue which many felt summed up the mood of the nation on a story that had thoroughly transcended the Westminster bubble. However, some did not feel the same with the BBC receiving nearly 24,000 complaints that she had broken their strict impartiality rules. This prompted a statement from the broadcaster on Twitter which said: "The BBC must uphold the highest standards of due impartiality in its news output. We have reviewed the entirety of last night's *Newsnight*, including the opening section, and while we believe the programme contained fair, reasonable and rigorous journalism, we feel that we should have done more to make clear the introduction was a summary of the questions we would examine, with all the accompanying evidence, in the rest of the programme. As it was, we believe the introduction we broadcast did not meet our standards of due impartiality. Our staff have been reminded of the guidelines."

Maitlis would reveal months later that during this time she actually received a message from Dominic Cummings following the complaints in which he offered his support. Speaking to the *Tatler* she described it as "peak surreal getting a message of support from him in the middle of all the crazy stuff". Whether or not Maitlis did break the impartiality rules is open to debate but it is interesting to note she got more severely reprimanded by her employer than Dominic Cummings was by his.

Friday, May 29 was the latest point at which the Welsh Government was required by law to look again at the regulations. At the daily press conference First Minister Mark Drakeford said that the R rate "is no better today in Wales than it was three weeks ago and that continues to put a limit on our ability to make too many changes". The First Minister announced two key rules. The first being that people from two different households in the same local area would be able to meet up as long as they are outdoors and they maintain strict social distancing and hand hygiene. For some this was quite literally life-saving. With reports of mental health problems sky-rocketing, allowing people to meet their nearest and dearest (albeit at a distance) was a source of joy and relief that could not possibly be imagined before Covid. For many having their families so close but unable to see them was almost unbearable.

The second announcement by the First Minister was to introduce the 'five mile' rule, which allowed people to travel up to five miles for leisure activities. A similar rule was also introduced in Scotland, quite a contrast to England where Boris Johnson had declared weeks before that people could drive as far as they want.

The five mile rule was intended to prevent people from taking the virus into another community. The key point about it was that it was just that, a rule, not a law. The rule would be flexible for people based on where they live. Five miles travel in Cardiff allows you to reach a lot of people and places, whereas drive five miles in rural Powys and you may not meet anyone. Drakeford therefore said that if you have to drive more than five miles to buy groceries, you can drive that same distance to meet others.

At the press conference he said: "The scientists say to us that the further you travel the greater the risk of spreading the virus. The small headroom that we have does allow us to offer some additional freedom. That freedom has to be bounded. It has to be bounded by a sense of what is sensible and precautionary. A five mile distance… is a rule of thumb for people to apply to their own particular geography. By staying local you are helping to keep Wales safe."

This was Drakeford's MO for lifting lockdown restrictions: he believed by lifting just one restriction at a time you would be able to see the impact that action had. The logic being that if you were to lift five different restrictions at once and cases were to go up you would not know which of the lifted restrictions had prompted the spike in cases. It is worth noting the First Minister's desire to lift the lockdown restrictions every three weeks. In part this was to do with the legal necessity whereby the Welsh Government (and the UK Government) were obliged to review the restrictions every three weeks. However, there was also some science behind it. If, for example, the First Minister was to suddenly reopen schools, pubs and sport stadiums at the same time there would almost certainly be a rise in cases, especially given how widely the virus was circulating in the community at this point. However the key indicators for a spike in cases, such as more positive tests, more GP contacts, hospital admissions, deaths etc would take up to three weeks to be evident. If everyone in a sports stadium caught the virus it could be weeks before we saw any change in deaths and hospital admissions. At time of writing it is believed that the virus can incubate for a maximum of fourteen days (though the average is more like five) so policy makers cannot reasonably see the impact of lockdown changes until weeks after the event. This is why Drakeford was so hesitant to lift the lockdown quicker, despite the large amount of political flack he took, particularly from the Welsh Conservatives.

Easily forgotten in the euphoria of actually being able to see people we love from (from a 2 metre distance) was that not everyone in Wales actually got to enjoy this. The advice for the 130,000 people in Wales who have been advised to shield had not changed and they were still told to stay home. This created a really tough challenge of conscience for the people who lived with them. If you lived with a person who was so at risk they were not allowed to leave their house, could you really justify meeting your friends in the park when you could take the virus back to your shielding family? It was a judgement call and there was no easy decision – we should not forget that there were far more than 130,000 people who had to stay shielded at this time.

The week finished with a wave of Black Lives Matter protests across the UK and wider world. Hundreds of people gathered in Cardiff city centre the first large gathering in the city since the weekend where lots of angry Scots were told there was no rugby match and the Stereophonics hosted the first ever mass virus spread to the tune of 'The Bartender and the Thief'. While social distancing was maintained at the protest this was the beginning of a series of judgements people made to decide if immediate public safety trumped the desire to speak out against social injustice.

12. An Attack on the Fundamentals of Humanity

June 1 to June 21
Wales' confirmed Covid-19 cases – 14,054
Wales deaths – 1,347
UK confirmed cases – 250,347
UK deaths – 37,529

If anyone had suggested three months before that a granny seeing her grandchildren in a park would be the biggest news on June 1 you would either think they were crazy or that it was the slowest news day in history. With Mark Drakeford announcing that people could now arrange to meet up with friends and family at a social distance in a park, people were able to finally see loved ones after exactly seventy days in lockdown. The news was flooded with emotional reunions on park benches, by lakes or on beaches. The five mile rule was now in place, though it still meant people could not travel a long distance to see friends and family. However, it was now possible to sit down together and enjoy each other's company.

With many babies born during the lockdown period this was the first opportunity for some to see their grandchildren. Though the pictures and videos from the day warmed the heart they also showed the inherent cruelty of the virus and the measures necessary to control it. The sight of people standing metres from their nearest and dearest but unable to hold or touch them was a reminder that the virus had not just attacked respiratory systems and vital organs. It hadn't just preyed on the old or weak. It had not just wreaked havoc on our economy. It had attacked some of the fundamentals of humanity. Human beings are naturally sociable creatures who crave interaction with one another. Especially at times of crisis and fear, coming together instills a sense of safety and belonging. To meet your parent, child, grandparent, grandchild or best friend and not hug them feels fundamentally wrong. Not only had many people been starved of contact with those they love most, when this contact came back they were not allowed to get close enough to hold each other. Over this period I spoke to several people who remarked how strange it was to see people sitting close together or hugging when they watched a TV series or film. It is hard to express the damage this can do to the collective wellbeing of the population. It wasn't just not being able to hug those outside your household, it was the fact that the act of cwtching could be potentially deadly. The negative connotations to such a warm, natural and human behaviour acted to keep us apart even as we came back together. It took away that comfort at a time when we all most needed a cuddle.

June also marked the beginning of the Welsh Government's Test, Trace and Protect (TTP) strategy, which represented the only way of coming out of lockdown in any meaningful way while retaining control of the virus. It involved moving away from the previous testing regime, which focussed on people in hospitals, care homes and symptomatic critical workers. Under TTP, anyone in the community with symptoms was eligible for a test. Anyone who tested positive then gave a list of people with whom they have had contact and a team of contact tracers would get in touch with them to advise them to self-isolate for 14 days – even if they have had no symptoms and tested negative.

A contact is defined as someone who has been:
- Within one metre of the infected person, has been coughed on,

has had a face-to-face conversation, had skin-to-skin physical contact, or been in other form of contact within one metre for one minute or longer.

- Within two metres of the infected person for more than 15 minutes.
- Have travelled in a vehicle with – or in a plane near – the infected person.

This raised a few questions, the first being why wait for the person with symptoms to have a test before starting contact tracing? If they may have the virus it is surely vital to trace their contacts as soon as possible to prevent further spread? Though this is logical there are other elements to consider. First, at this point in time only 12% of tests were bringing back a positive result. This meant that the vast majority of people asked to isolate for half a month would not have the virus, an enormous imposition on people's lives. They may have kids or live alone and need to make arrangements for shopping. If they have a job they will probably only be able to claim statutory sick pay over this period.

The other question the announcement raised was why Wales hadn't been contact tracing much earlier? This is very important. Countries like South Korea and Singapore, widely accepted to have been among the best for managing the virus, all employed large scale testing and tracking of potential coronavirus sufferers. During the early stages of the pandemic the UK was also doing this, however Scientific Advisor Group on Emergencies (Sage) papers from February revealed modelling suggesting only a maximum of 50 cases could be traced each week[1]. Whereas countries in the Far East, which had previously suffered epidemics were prepared, the UK simply was not. It meant waiting months before a similar system (though with several teething problems) could be set up. These previous epidemics were not secret, policy makers knew they had happened and were likely to happen again. It was yet another example of how learning from the past was again hindered by combination of squeezed budgets, short term thinking and exceptionalism.

This TTP system was quickly put to the test as the epicentre of the virus in Wales was quickly shifting from the south to the north. By June 2 Betsi Cadwaladr Health Board, with 2,787 cases, had overtaken Cardiff and Vale with 2,730. The strange thing about this was that the virus in North Wales seemed to be taking off after lockdown restrictions had been brought in. There was part of a pattern which showed the virus moving south to north and east to west.

Though the spike in cases in the north was concerning, several factors hidden in the numbers were worth considering. First, was the health board itself. Betsi Cadwaladr University Health Board has more than its share of serious problems. It was placed into special measures in 2015 with 'areas for tangible improvement' including governance, leadership and oversight; mental health services; maternity services at Ysbyty Glan Clwyd; GP and primary care services, including out-of-hours services; and reconnecting with the public and regaining the public's confidence.

Despite clear issues the health board is also comfortably Wales' largest which means that judging it simply on the amount of cases (or deaths) is not the most useful metric. For example in cases compared to population there was more than met the eye.

As of August 10, Wrexham (one of the six local authorities covered by Betsi) had the highest number of cases per 100,000 of the population at 998. However, Merthyr Tydfil was second with 961. Though Denbighshire (also Betsi) was third with 844, Anglesey and Flintshire were about on par with Cardiff and Newport and had considerably less Covid cases than RCT in the Valleys. Cases were still going up during a lockdown period and people were understandably concerned. There was a perception that the north of Wales was an afterthought, especially when it emerged that it was taking up to 90 hours to return tests (the target was between 24-48 hours) with many tests still having to be sent to Cardiff for analysis. As anyone who has ever travelled from the north to the south of Wales will tell you, it is one of the most frustratingly slow drives a person can make (though stunningly beautiful if you take the right route #A470trumpsM5).

At this point I interviewed Public Health Wales consultant in communicable disease control, Graham Brown. He told me that the reason for the increase in cases was simply that they were conducting more tests in the area. He said: "When you go looking for Covid-19 you find Covid-19." Apart from the scary realisation that despite a stabilisation and drop in Wales-wide deaths there remained Covid-19 community transmission in every part of the country, I wondered why there had suddenly been a sudden focus on testing in the north? Well look no further than your fridge for that one.

June saw two separate outbreaks in meat processing plants in North Wales, one at the 2 Sisters factory in Llangefni, Anglesey, and the other at Rowan Foods on Wrexham Industrial Estate. By August there were more than 300 cases identified at Rowan Foods following extensive testing of staff and tracing of their close contacts. It is no coincidence that the two outbreaks occurred in similar facilities. Throughout the early months of the epidemic there had been several outbreaks in slaughterhouses and meat packing plants across Europe. In Germany's North Rhine-Westphalia more than 1,500 of 7,000 workers tested positive for Covid-19 resulting in 640 000 residents being put back into lockdown. These facilities were to the virus what St Mary Street is to hen and stag parties – a perfect breeding ground.

A combination of lower temperatures, very high or very low relative humidity and metallic surfaces on which the virus can survive a long time are all perfect for the coronavirus. Plus the noisy working environment means workers have to shout loudly, spreading virus-filled water droplets further. In addition the workers themselves are more likely to be young and therefore asymptomatic, allowing the virus to spread through the population without detection. Several researchers at the time suggested that a further factor was many of the staff in such plants are migrant workers, exposed to overcrowded accommodation and transported on overcrowded buses. In addition, people on low incomes or with insecure employment are less likely to isolate when they have symptoms for fear of penalties or being unable to live on statutory sick pay[2]. Back in April staff at Rowan Foods in Wrexham staged a walkout in protest at the working conditions in the light of the unfolding pandemic with North Wales Police attending multiple times to "assist in providing assurances and guidance to key workers around travel to work"[3].

Speaking of meat and feeling sick, the start of June also saw the reopening of McDonalds drive-thrus with long queues appearing all over Wales as people welcomed the return of the Big Mac. Less welcome was that within two days we started to see the return of McDonalds wrappers and rubbish to many Welsh roadsides – not 'lovin' it'.

Moving into June, plans were being put in place for limited reopening of part of the economy, and debate sprang up around the wearing of masks. Leading doctors called on Welsh Government to change its position on face coverings, arguing that they should be worn in places where people were not able to socially distance. British Medical Association (BMA) Cymru Wales council chair, Dr

David Bailey said: "There still remains a considerable risk of infection, and emerging evidence has shown that if mouths and noses are covered when people are in areas where they cannot socially distance, it may help in controlling the spread of infection of Covid-19 and therefore save lives." The UK Government had announced that from June 15 face coverings would be compulsory on public transport with the exception of people with certain health conditions, disabled people and children under the age of 11. The same measures were not introduced in Wales until almost six weeks later on July 27.

By this point many parents at their wits end with regard to home schooling were given a light at the end of the tunnel when Education Minister Kirsty Williams announced that all pupils would be able to return for limited periods during the week from 29 June. This came with the caveat that only a third of pupils would be allowed into school at any one time, in order to maintain social distancing. In some ways this was very welcome news, however though parents wanted their kids to return to school, their overwhelming desire was for them to do this safely.

Ms Williams announced the end of June reopening on Wednesday June 3, during the Welsh Government daily briefing. The next day Wales' Chief Medical Officer Dr Frank Atherton was up for the daily presser and said that the June reopening was actually the "second best option". He said: "When I was discussing this with the Education Minister my preferred option would have been to reopen the schools perhaps towards the end of the summer in August to give us a little bit more time. I understand that was not attractive to the unions and so we've got a second best option which is that we're going to re-open the schools towards the end of June for a short period of time with very different arrangements so that can be done safely. I think we can do that safely. We do need to monitor it and track it. It will be for a limited period of time. That will give us the summer to understand what has happened to levels of infection and it will basically give us more information which is what we need to manage this pandemic."

Understandably, when the man responsible for leading the medical profession in Wales says that the way schools were reopening was not his preferred option, people ask why the Government is opting for a different path – especially when it comes to children. The comments by Dr Atherton prompted outcry from across the political spectrum. Clwyd South Conservatives accused the Welsh Government of preferring "the advice of the unions – their biggest donors" to the advice of the nation's chief medical officer with Conservative shadow education minister Suzy Davies saying she was "a little concerned that the science from the experts we're all meant to be following doesn't seem to have reassured the unions"[4]. The unions themselves said the medical advice had not been shared with them during the talks on re-opening schools. David Evans, the lead official for the National Education Union Cymru said: "If he's [Atherton] trying to blame the unions for the return of all year groups in June then that decision was made by the minister, not by us. His suggestion is that there is a great inherent risk going back in June than later in the year. In that case why did the minister take that decision?"

Evans claimed that the Union had responded to the Welsh Government saying their members' preference was for a return in September "which would have put them in an even safer zone than Dr Atherton was referring to [August]. We said if September was not available then the preferred option was to open to limited year groups six, 10 and 12. We did this after sounding out members and from responses from hundreds of them. We had only from last Friday to 4pm on Monday to respond. A very limited time. We were never given a copy of Dr Atherton's advice to Kirsty Williams. There was a line in a document saying a chief science adviser said August would be a better date, but we did not get any further information, or the options considered. There was no line saying June was the second best option."

The Education Minister had to go on Twitter to defend herself following Dr Atherton's comments saying: "The decision to enable children to have some time in school ahead of the summer break puts the safety and wellbeing of learners first and foremost and is fully in line with the scientific advice. We also explored reopening schools later in the summer but this would have involved a complete structural change to the school year. Both approaches were fully endorsed by the Chief Medical Officer for Wales and the Wales Covid-19 Technical Advisory Group."

All in all, it wasn't exactly a confidence inducing reopening announcement for teachers, parents or staff.

Elsewhere the ripples set off by George Floyd's killing had become an unstoppable torrent as protests in support of the Black Lives Matter movement continued, leading to concerns that the gatherings would contribute to the spread of the virus. On April 7, protesters at a Black Lives Matter demonstration in Bristol had torn down the statue of a controversial slave trader Edward Colston and thrown it into Bristol harbour, a fitting end that his statue met the same fate as many of the African slaves transported to the Americas. The removal of the statue was both celebrated and condemned, with some seeing it as the well overdue removal of an appalling celebration to a disgusting and reprehensible past but others viewing it as the destruction of British history. This is a nuanced and worthy debate which is explored further in the chapter looking at how the virus affected non-whites.

There was one group within society which witnessed the toppling of this statue which also disapproved, however these were not people who valued nuance. On Saturday, June 13 large numbers of far right groups, many with connections to football hooligan firms, descended on London to, erm, 'protect statues'. Unfortunately for both the police and the statues this mainly involved getting absolutely bladdered and trying to fight anything that moved (at least that was good news for the statues). Videos emerged of a sea of increasingly red faces (whether from sunburn or booze, it was hard to tell) acting like a drug fuelled Arthur Shelby from Peaky Blinders as they launched bottles and fireworks at police. This was all back dropped to a...er... 'stirring' rendition of 'God Save the Queen' which gave everyone goosebumps (though this could have been a physical reaction to the amount of cocaine disappearing up noses).

Two images really stood out. The first was 28-year-old Andrew Banks from Essex who was photographed urinating next to the memorial to PC Keith Palmer who was stabbed during the March 22, Westminster attack in 2017. Tottenham fan Banks admitted he had travelled to London with other football fans to 'protect statues' and said that he had drunk 16 pints on Friday night into Saturday morning and had not been to sleep. He was sentenced to 14 days in custody, after pleading guilty to outraging public decency at Westminster Magistrates' Court[5]. I don't know Banks but I can't imagine he was kept awake at night by the hypocrisy of pissing on a memorial during a mission to protect statues – though who can keep awake after 16 pints?

The other picture that gained huge attention was the image of black man Patrick Hutchinson who carried one of the 'statue protectors' to safety. The striking image showed Mr Hutchinson carrying white Millwall fan Bryn Male from the middle of the protest after Mr Male was hurt. Speaking afterwards Hutchinson told Channel 4 News: "I was thinking to myself – if the other three police officers that were standing around when George Floyd was murdered, had thought about stopping their colleague from doing what he was doing like we did, George Floyd would be alive today still"[6].

The two biggest news stories in early June were coronavirus and the intense spotlight on the ingrained, systemic prejudices against people of colour within society. These were not separate issues, they were inextricably linked. Just like gender inequality, poverty, prisons, the care system, an underfunded health service, inequality for BAME people is yet another crack in society which we have failed to fill, and true to form coronavirus turned that fissure into a canyon. The virus was disproportionately killing more people of colour, due in part to genetics. The BAME community has a very specific gene called sickle cell trait. This makes blood more prone to clotting. In its later stages, the Covid-19 infection causes micro clots in the lungs, sickle cell perpetuates that clotting tendency. However, a huge factor in the high levels of BAME deaths is the result of social inequality which I will examine later.

The dual issues of Covid and BAME inequality are important in framing political stories that are relevant to readers. By early June a huge amount of data and stats around the subject existed and it would have taken a matter of minutes to write a story headlined: 'Almost 65% of all health care workers who have died across the UK have been BAME people'. Add the stats in a table, a stock image of a black nurse, a quote from a politician, a comment from the head of a charity and embed a tweet from some celebrity saying '#BLM' – boom, story written and you haven't even had your morning coffee yet. But there is one massive problem with this story: barely anyone will read it.

Speaking from experience, when stories are based on stats, or worse, a politician's quote, they are not read. The reason the '65% of all health care workers' story would bomb is because it doesn't mean anything to most people. This is not because people in Wales are racist bigots who do not care about the plight of BAME health-care workers, but because people do not respond to stats, they respond to people. As discussed in Chapter 2, the death stats, '100 people died of Covid-19 today' elicits far less of a response than a picture of a woman headlined 'Sarah, mum-of-three, dies of Covid three months after getting married'.

So telling the story of how coronavirus affects people of colour requires a different approach. The best way to present an issue that affects a minority and make it accessible and engaging to the majority of people is to present the human side of a story because... people respond to people.

To tell the story of how people of colour and those from less well off backgrounds were been impacted by the pandemic I spent a week speaking to people in Cardiff's Butetown area. The old Tiger Bay is a place really close to my heart, I had written features about the area before and found it to be one of the most welcoming and tight communities I have ever reported on. This is not to say there are not challenges, there are real issues with drugs and 46% of children there grow up in poverty. But growing up in poverty does not mean growing up without love and it is down to the compassionate and supportive spirit of the Butetown community that many children are able to thrive despite more limited opportunities.

During the week I spoke to dozens of people within Butetown, which is one of the most ethnically diverse places in the whole of Wales, and one thing became very clear, not all lockdowns are created equal. Being locked down in a house, with a garden, in a suburb, is not the same and being locked down in one of the fifteen storey tower blocks on Loudoun Square in the heart of Butetown. This is in no way to say that lockdown was easy for anyone, we all have our own problems, but the two situations are not the same.

Saabira (not her real name), a mum in her mid-thirties of Somali origin who lives there talked about the realities of living in a block, and therefore sharing community space, with people who may have the virus. "People in my block have had the virus," she said. "I knocked a neighbour's door for some salt and the woman was shouting to stand back because they had coronavirus. It is terrifying. My mind was working overtime thinking 'had I seen them last week'? Could I have got it? Have they already spread it? It is a very real threat. You do feel that if you get it you are likely going to die."

If you want an example of how the coronavirus lockdown disproportionately affects people who live in flats look no further than the lifts. The tower blocks on Loudon Square have two lifts each – and sometimes only one of them is working. During lockdown you, quite understandably, could only have two people in the lift at any time in order to maintain social distancing. However, with 15 floors people could be waiting a long time for an empty lift to arrive, and because of this many people would simply opt to take the stairs. This is however not an option for disabled people, frail people, elderly people or parents with prams. The perverse situation arises that only people who have no choice to enter the moving, infectious, metal covid boxes are those with underlying health conditions. For an insight on how the virus changed even the most basic fundamentals in life look no further than the mum who told me about how she now has to tell her young kids not to hold the handrail as they descended multiple stories because of the danger from all the other hands that had touched it that day. Add to this the challenge of homeschooling families of six children, in a flat, when you have one laptop between you, and the education is not in a parents' first language. Even in the kids' downtime there is not the option of playing in the garden, which is just a small grassy communal area shared by hundreds.

This is to say nothing for the overwhelming anxiety that comes from knowing that, as a person of colour, you are more likely to die from the virus. "I have had one cousin who caught it," Saabira said in the article[7]. "She is a care worker and works with the elderly. She is a mother with three children. Her kids didn't get it because she quarantined herself in her bedroom. I know people who have died. One was a man who was the first person my dad met when he arrived in Cardiff. No one was able to visit and comfort his wife since his death."

My investigation into Covid in Butetown wasn't just doom and gloom, it was also a tale of hope. I spoke to four different community groups who were delivering food packages and support to those shielding or with little money. It gives you hope for humanity, many were dead on their feet but were giving up their time (and frankly at the height of the virus risking their lives) to help others.

This piece on Butetown gave real insight into what it is like to be a person of colour and/or poor during the lockdown. It put faces to figure and stories to stats. Ultimately it is journalism about people that informs readers not "politician X says this is bad". But the biggest reason that this kind of journalism makes a difference is because people read it! One of the biggest challenges of political journalism is making politics relevant and interesting. The story about Butetown was a political story. It showed the impact political decisions from way before the coronavirus crisis have on normal (whatever that really means) people. I spend a huge amount of time explaining to politicians, special advisors and political PR officers why their press release from them "calling for a change to X" is not a story. There are a significant number of politicians who really believe that just because they have said something, it is newsworthy – no.

Take Senedd committee meetings. There is a belief among many in political circles that they should all be reported' as a matter of public record. But why? If no one is going to read a dry story about a Senedd committee (and believe me, they don't) what is the point in writing it? It would be more productive to use that time to write something else. The only people who are going to read it are the politico types who would follow it anyway. It is all available on the Senedd website if people want to look it up. There is of course an argument for the BBC to cover this as they are not a business who have to drive revenue in order to exist.

Yet this is not to say that Senedd committees are unimportant. A colleague or myself watched or read the transcript of every Senedd committee and took some great stories out of them which were really important public interest journalism. However, we would rarely report these stories as 'committee chairwoman says...'.

Take domestic abuse, for example. If a committee publishes a report that refuges are overwhelmed and are turning women away that is a hugely important story to tell. But the story is the women themselves who are being turned away, not the committee who produced a report on them. To tell that story in a way that will be read by people who don't have an existing interest in the issue you need to speak to the women affected, the charities desperate to help but which don't have the resources. That is when to introduce the 'politics', when it has been demonstrated to readers why it matters, that real human beings are suffering as a result of political decisions.

Many, many politicians and political party press officers do actually understand. They realise that just their comment does not a story make. Though there are some who are either so wrapped up in their own importance or so monumentally boring (or both) that you can't believe the stuff they send out. One Welsh MP sent out a press release saying that they had been to a local shop to tell them to 'keep up the good work' during the pandemic – that was it! I can't imagine even the people in the shop would find it interesting and want to read that.

Before rowing back from this wild tangent I seem to have found myself on I just want to talk about 'click bait' because it is a criticism thrown at around a great deal, but more than ever during the crisis. True click bait is an article which is headlined in a way that is misleading. This usually takes two forms. First, the headline exaggerates the content of the article. For example the headline states: 'Watch the hilarious moment House of Commons Speaker brutally put down Jacob Rees-Mogg' but the content is just Sir Lindsay Hoyle saying 'will the right honourable member please calm down and take his seat'. Or, the headline has nothing to do with the content of the article. The headline might say: 'Watch the hilarious moment House of Commons Speaker brutally put down Jacob Rees-Mogg', and the content is a list of the best viagra brands on the market.

But it would not be a click bait headline if the Speaker of the House had actually said: 'I understand why the Member North East Somerset is upset, I too would be devastated if my 500 page book on the Victorians had only sold 734 copies in its first week but can you please take your seat'. This is simultaneously brutal, hilarious, directed at Jacob Rees-Mogg and said by the speaker – therefore is not clickbait.

People have a tendency to simply label any headline that is written in a way that will make you want to click on it as 'click bait'. This ignores the fact that literally every online news headline ever written is designed to make you click on it. Of course they are, because the story is a news organisation's product. You don't see an advert for a Mars Bar or a Ford Mondeo on the TV and suddenly start shouting 'buy bait, buy bait'!

On June 10 the 1,500 Dragon's Heart Hospital in the Principality Stadium was downgraded to standby status which meant that it would not be run as an active hospital but will remain available for now in case of future demand. Despite its enormous capacity and cost the Dragon's Heart Hospital treated only 46 patients before it was put on stand-by. It could be argued this was a total waste of money, though that would be the same as complaining about unused lifejackets on a cruise. Not having to use them should be seen as a success not a failure.

The nineteen field hospitals across Wales cost £166m of Welsh Government funding for their set up, construction, and equipment. In just six weeks they nearly doubled hospital bed capacity in Wales along with 138,000 pieces of equipment including beds, imaging equipment, syringe drivers, and medicines. It was a remarkable achievement that was replicated across the border with the UK Government and its Nightingale Hospitals. Back in February when China was throwing up huge hospitals seemingly overnight there was a real perception that we couldn't possibly do that. But in the construction of the field hospitals we got a glimpse of what is possible for the government when it put appropriate resources, time and political capital into it.

As we moved into mid-June the UK Government were engaged in a fight they couldn't possibly win. A golden rule of politics is that if you are forced to make a concession, don't fight it. If something is inevitable do it as quickly as possible and take the credit for it. A change of course preceded by delay means a loss of credit and looks like indecision. The fight the government was embroiled in was with a 22-year-old Mancunian – should be easy right? Except that the 22-year-old was also an England international footballer with 3.2 million Twitter followers', which brought a different dynamic to the fight. Even more unfortunate for the UK Government was that the fight was around feeding poor children over the summer, and they were on the side of not feeding them. The result was inevitable.

With growing financial pressure on families throughout the country there was pressure on the Government to extend the £15/week free school meals throughout the summer for children from low income families. It decided not to. Mr Rashford took up this campaign revealing that he had used foodbanks and depended on free school meals as a child. On Twitter he wrote: "When you wake up this morning and run your shower, take a second to think about parents who have had their water turned off during lockdown." Secretary of State for Work and Pensions Therese Coffey made a play for the title of 'Tone Deaf Tweet of the Week' by replying to a link to the tweet saying simply, "Water cannot be disconnected though."

The optics of the whole affair were pretty terrible for the UK Government. Johnson, facing a rebellion of some back benchers, performed a U-turn, leading Rashford to comment: "I don't even know what to say. Just look at what we can do when we come together, THIS is England in 2020."[8] As we begin publication the whole debate has a risen again over the autumn half term break.

In Wales the continuation of free school meals had been announced on April 22 with free school meals, money, or vouchers for food valued at equivalent of £19.50 a week, in a £33m scheme. It is hard to argue with this as a policy but one should also hesitate to celebrate the fact that such a scheme is required in the first place.

The period ended on a crap note with research by a consortium led by Bangor University which monitored the amount of Covid-19 in the sewage system. In May[9] it was discovered that traces of the virus could be found in faeces up to 33 days after a person had the disease. Further investigation discovered that regular monitoring of the sewer system could act as an early warning system for outbreaks in a particular area, up to a week before people started presenting at testing stations. From the start of August the pilots being led by Bangor University would be able to monitor 75-80% of people in Wales' waste to see if there is any coronavirus genetic material. Not only that but they are also able to spot new mutations of the virus as well. It was this evidence that led the First Minister to conclude in the autumn that travel from the north west of England had contributed to a series of North Wales outbreaks in September.

13. The First Wave Ends

June 22 to July 6
Wales' confirmed Covid-19 cases – 15,602
Wales deaths – 1,502
UK confirmed cases – 276,581
UK deaths – 39,892

At the start of the crisis much was made about a 'four nation approach' to tackling coronavirus. The UK went into lockdown as a whole and, in the early days, both Drakeford and Johnson repeatedly signalled their support for a collaborative strategy in the fight against the virus. Even though health is a devolved issue and each UK nation was able to dictate its own lockdown rules this made sense. After all, Covid-19 infects the cells lining your throat, airways and lungs just as effectively whichever side of a border you live. For Wales having a coherent, aligned strategy with England was more important than it was for Scotland, because of geography. The Scottish/English border is just 96 miles long whereas the Welsh/English border is 160[1] (Offa put Hadrian's effort to shame). Not only is the border significantly longer but it is also more densely populated and more porous, with thousands of people working or being educated in a different country to the one they live in. The merits of such a strategy were accepted across the political spectrum. Conservative MS and then Shadow Health Minister Angela Burns described a four nation strategy as "the only sensible approach to take" to getting on top of the virus[2]. First Minister Mark Drakeford said that it was his preference that "all four nations retain a common approach to lifting the restrictions" though said he would also "take the right decisions in the interests of the people of Wales"[3].

There had been signs of this united front becoming strained towards the end of the first lockdown period in April with different administrations announcing the continuation of the restrictions at different times. The illusion of a united front, at least at the highest levels of Government was stretched further when in May the Prime Minister had told people in England they could drive as far as they wanted for "unlimited outdoor exercise"[4].

When the next lockdown cycle began on June 22, the differences in approach by the four UK nations was so stark it was impossible to argue that there was still a unified strategy.

The difference in the rules around meeting people were:

Wales – Meet an unspecified number of people outside but only from two households.

England – Groups of up to six can meet with two households allowed to meet indoors and stay overnight.

Scotland – People from one household can meet outdoors with people from up to two other households – no more than eight in any group.

Northern Ireland – Up to six people able to meet indoors.

Though each nation had slightly different rules they were not widely different. Clearly it is not ideal to have slightly different rules because it leads to confusion in the messaging, however it showed that each administration was working from the same set of evidence.

However, in other parts of the lockdown rules, such as masks or home working, the discrepancies were wider. Take face coverings on public transport. In Wales and Northern Ireland face coverings were not mandatory though people were advised to wear masks if crowded. The Welsh Government suggested they should be worn on busy public transport but this was only guidance, not compulsory. Health minister Vaughan Gething went on the record saying "further scientific evidence is needed on the benefits to the wider public of wearing face coverings"[5]. By contrast, in England and Scotland face coverings were compulsory on public transport, which was in line with the then World Health Organization (WHO) advice.

It was a similar story for people working from home, with the advice remaining in Wales that people work from home where possible, with only essential retail remaining open. In England those who could not work from home were being actively encouraged to go to work.

The differences in policy led to some bizarre situations. For example, the Bridge Inn in Kentchurch and the Angel Inn in Grosmont, Monmouthshire are about a mile apart and separated by the river Monnow that marks the Welsh/English border. The Bridge Inn was allowed to open by the UK Government on July 4 with customers able to go inside and have a pint. But the Angel would not be able to serve customers indoors until almost a month later on August 3 (they could serve outdoors from July 13).

Why the difference? All the UK nations are drawing from basically the same evidence base yet were drawing significantly different conclusions. Whichever side of the border you happened to sit, this is a cause for concern. If England were lifting lockdown restrictions too quickly then the UK Government was putting lives at risk. If the Welsh Government were lifting the restrictions too slowly it was unnecessarily crippling the Welsh economy. If Wales and England were two wildly different countries in metrics like healthcare provision and demographics it is understandable how both Governments can read the same advice and draw such different conclusions – but this is not the case. Both the Welsh and UK Governments were criticized for their respective decisions. The Cardiff Bay administration was slammed by their political opponents as over cautious and doddery. By contrast Westminster was labelled as gung-ho, putting the economy before lives.

The consequences of the different approaches were seen on both sides of the border. In England the city of Leicester was ordered into the UK's first ever full local lockdown with non-essential shops and schools closed again after a spike in positive cases. In Wales, there were calls from the tourism industry for clarity as people cancelled holidays in Wales to rebook in England and Scotland due to the uncertainty over the lifting of restrictions. The CEO of North Wales Tourism, Jim Jones, called on Drakeford for clarity around dates for re-opening, saying he understood "how careful Mark Drakeford is being" but "the most frustrating thing for our businesses is the not knowing and being left in limbo". He added: "We have thousands of people who depend on their livelihoods in this sector who have poured their heart and soul into it." The First Minister was not to be moved and when questioned in press conferences would always say: "This is an economic crisis as well as a health crisis but the view I have taken, and it is the view many, many economists take, is that by doing the right thing by people's health you are doing the right thing by the economy.[6]"

At the beginning of July it became clear how little Boris Johnson valued communication with his opposite number when it was revealed by the First Minister that he'd had no personal contact with the PM, whether by video, telephone or in person since May 28. It should be said that Drakeford could have picked up the phone to the Prime Minister. However, the First Minister did repeatedly call publically for increased dialogue with Number 10. When you reflect, for the Prime Minister of the UK not to have a conversation with the most senior politician in Wales for over a month, during a global pandemic is remarkable. For context, one of the EU's institutions is the Council of Ministers. It is divided up into nine separate councils for different areas of policy such as economics, agriculture and education. At these sessions the minister responsible for that area meets with their 26 counterparts. Three of these councils meet every single month, and these countries are not even close to the levels of interconnectivity that exists between Wales and England.

As anyone who has ever opted for the biodegradable bags at Aldi instead of the bags for life will tell you, as soon as there is a small tear, the whole thing is going to fall apart. The inevitable risk of lifting the lockdown wherever you happen to be in the UK was that once you give an inch people may take a mile (or the piss). A message of 'stay home' is not just easier to enforce, it is also easier to understand and is less open to interpretation. As lines are blurred, compliance is inevitably going to fall.

The lines were not so much blurred as violently vomited on when hundreds of young people turned up at Ogmore-by-Sea on June 25 , seemingly for a party which descended into a brawl and several arrests. Normally a gathering of people like this would have been fairly minor news, but after months of lockdown it created something of a scandal. Dr David Bailey, chairman of the British Medical Association's (BMA) Welsh Council, said it was 'extremely concerning' while one NHS worker told WalesOnline it was "a kick in the teeth to everyone who obeyed the rules. It's pathetic selfishness." The First Minister warned that he would be forced to stop lifting restrictions if such behaviour continued. The scenes in Ogmore were not isolated incidents. Cardiff Bay would see large gatherings of young people every time there was a sunny weekend throughout July.

Despite these incidents, the vast majority of people, of all ages, were obeying the rules. Even when restrictions were lifted there were huge parts of the population who simply avoided pubs and shops like the plague (literally). The incidents in Ogmore and the Bay were predominantly young people, who, due to their age were at a fairly low personal risk of suffering serious health issues from the virus. When such pictures emerge there is always a sudden plenitude of social media posts chastising 'young people' for their reckless ways or selfishness.

Clearly the people breaking the rules here are selfish prats. But it would be lazy and unfair to characterise all young people in this way. The vast majority of young people did obey the rules and I really felt for them. Those in school had been unable to see their friends for months and had seen their education all but stopped. Those at university had what should have been the best time of their life ruined (and will be paying extortionate fees for decades for the privilege) and those trying to get work or placements had hardly any opportunities. On top of this they were as a generation labeled selfish because of the actions of a few dickheads.

You see it all the time, if we observe someone who is different to us doing something wrong you will define them by that difference. Whether that be their gender, race, religion or age. If you were in your seventies and you saw a bunch of other pensioners getting pissed up at the beach instead of saying 'all these selfish old people' you would say 'all these selfish dickheads'. We all know that one male prat who, while describing someone cutting them up on a motorway, would say if it was a female 'I was cut up by this woman driver' whereas if it was a bloke doing it would say 'I was cut up by this dickhead'.

I think this is one of the reasons we have such a toxic way of talking to each other, especially about politics, especially online and especially when everyone is scared and looking for a scapegoat during a pandemic. Every single place, country, age group, race, religion (or none) and gender has a fairly even amount of dickheads.

Anyway, I digress

With the economy opening up it was important for the Welsh Government to continuously monitor the virus to check if was gaining a foothold again (probably due to those bloody millennials). Conducting this monitoring was more nuanced and complicated than you would expect. In the first few months of the crisis the figure that every politician and journalist would focus on was the 'R-rate', the amount of additional people each person with the virus would infect. If it was 1 there was no change in the overall level, if it was below one the amount of cases would fall, if it was above one (even by a little bit) cases would rise rapidly due to exponential growth. It was a really useful figure in those early parts of the lockdown because there was so much Covid in the community. However, after three months it ceased to be so useful. Imagine if only three people in the whole of Wales had coronavirus. If they all infected three people each there would be an R rate of three, which would be a massive number and, if allowed to continue would of course be a serious worry. However just nine people having the virus is not a reason to pull the whole country into lockdown even with the R rate technically at three, especially if they were all concentrated in one place like a factory. As infectious disease epidemiologist at Imperial College London Dr Anne Cori described it: "I see a lot of discussions about incidence vs Rt as a measure of how well (or how badly) we are controlling this pandemic. I think both matter. Incidence is how far you are from the wall and Rt is how fast you are headed into it or away from it." As Wales left lockdown the Welsh Government's Technical Advisory

Group developed a more sophisticated way of assessing the risks of Covid which were divided into 'circuit breakers' and 'early warning indicators'.

There are five circuit breakers which, if any of them reached a certain level, would cause an immediate lockdown. They were, doubling/halving times of hospital admissions for coronavirus (this is how quickly the amount of people with the virus in hospital is doubling – but does not include people who caught the virus in hospital); Covid-related hospital occupancy; Covid-related ICU occupancy; overall ICU occupancy (if, for example, there are not many coronavirus cases but ICU was full because of seasonal flu, there would still be a justification for going into lockdown as any spike in Covid-19 cases could overwhelm the NHS); and the reproduction number or 'R-number' (if it were to stay above 1.1 for an extended period a lockdown would be ordered).

Below these circuit breakers were the early warning indicators. These are much broader and, as the name suggests, gives decision-makers advanced warning if a spike is on the way. If multiple indicators start flagging up it could trigger local lockdowns if they occurred in particular places, or perhaps a stopping of any further lifting of restrictions. The early warning indicators are:

Transmission/Incidence
- Number of confirmed Covid-19 cases
- ZOE prevalence data (% of population with Covid-19)
- NHS Direct / 111 calls related to coronavirus
- NHS online activity related to coronavirus
- NHS primary care consultations related to coronavirus (phone and face to face)
- NHS Community nursing visits related to coronavirus

Mortality
- Total number of Covid-19 deaths

PPE
- Level of PPE supplies: total
- PPE stocks for individual items including: disposable gloves, disposable plastic aprons, disposable fluid-repellent coverall/gowns, surgical masks, fluid-resistant (Type IIR) surgical masks and filtering face piece (FFP3) respirators.

PPE levels as an indicator are more nuanced than 'above X items good' and 'below X items bad'. It also involved how quickly Wales was going through the stocks. For example, seven million gloves would be seem like a large number. However if Wales is using 1 million pairs a week it is a very low number compared to what is needed. The health experts consider the speed of use, not just stock levels.

When we look back on the crisis, one of the most iconic scenes will be the Downing Street press conferences. In a time of streaming services, recording live TV and thousands of channels, with the exception of live sport there are very few occasions when the nation collectively stands still to watch something. Downing Street press conferences were different. On March 23, around 26 million people tuned in to hear the lockdown announced. From then on it became a regular feature of life with many watching every day without fail. Certain broadcasts were more popular, the ones at the end of each lockdown cycle sparked particular interest, Boris Johnson's confusing pre-recorded announcement on May 10 got a staggering 24.35 million viewers (three times more than the most popular FA Cup final). As time passed the numbers began to drop but they were still pulling in viewing figures that most TV executives would die for. Even when there wasn't a big announcement there was still immense value in these sessions, it allowed the UK Government to be held to account, challenged and made to commit to the record. If democracy dies in the dark then the press conferences were a big spotlight. However, on June 23 the UK Government announced it was extinguishing this light. The Downing Street spokesman told the daily lobby briefing: "We'll continue to hold press conferences to coincide with significant announcements, including with the PM. We will be publishing all of the data which has previously been included in the press conference slides on Gov.uk every weekday."

Though this was the switching off, the UK Government had long been slowly turning down the dimmer switch. At the start of June it had cancelled press conferences on Saturday and Sunday citing low viewing figures. Following Dominic Cummings' totally lawful ride on the Vision Express there was a significant drop in the number of scientific or medical experts on the Downing Street briefing. In the immediate aftermath of the Cummings affair Chief Nursing Officer Ruth May was seemingly dropped[8] from the broadcasts after she declined to endorse Boris Johnson's advisor at the practice session beforehand.

England's deputy chief medical officer Jonathan Van-Tam also refused to toe the party (AKA Dominic's) line, saying he was happy to answer questions. "In my opinion the rules are clear and they have always been clear," he said. "In my opinion they are for the benefit of all. In my opinion they apply to all." Not all advisors stuck their head above the parapet with chief scientific officer, Patrick Vallance responding to questioning that he did "not want to get involved in politics"

Cummings and Johnson did not seem to like that scientists were much less pliable than Cabinet Ministers. Research by the i Newspaper[9] found that for the first 11 weeks of the Downing Street briefing from mid–March until the end of May, there was a weekly total of between eight and twelve scientific or medical experts alongside ministers. In the first two weeks of June this dropped to four and three respectively. On Friday, June 5, Mr Hancock became the first minister to appear without an official (though perhaps that number would have been higher if he had counted himself both entering and leaving the room like his unusual counting of tests). The falling numbers of medical and scientific experts cannot solely be blamed on the Cummings saga. There were also suggestions about underlying disagreements about the lockdown lifting strategy, however this was mainly England specific.

Despite the PM no longer appearing regularly at a press conference no one could deny the Johnson family were taking the fight against the virus seriously. The Prime Minister's father, Stanley Johnson, travelled to his villa in Greece ostensibly to make the property 'Covid-proof', though there are no rules in Greece forcing landlords to 'Covid-proof' holiday lets . The trip was widely condemned with Johnson Senior (a towel over his shoulder) saying he was going to be there for a week 'to organise the house'. Speaking on LBC Boris Johnson refused to criticise his Dad, saying the media should raise the issues with him.

On July 6 I was able to type one of the most wonderful sentences I had written since the start of the pandemic: "No new deaths from coronavirus have been recorded in Wales". For the first time since we had gone into lockdown 105 days earlier, no deaths had been reported to Public Health Wales. The last day with no deaths reported was on March 19 and at that point only two people in Wales had been killed by the disease. Now into the start of July, 1,531 people had died of the virus according to official figures from PHW, though this only counts those who died after a positive test. It does not include the ONS figures which include where Covid was named on the death certificate, or the numbers of excess deaths which is a more accurate reflection of the amount of people killed indirectly by the virus and the measures to contain it.

It is almost impossible to decide a spot to end the chronology of coronavirus in Wales. How do you draw a line under a virus we may never fully eradicate? There are so many arbitrary lines which could be drawn and say this is where the first (but alas seemingly not last) wave ended. For the people who lost loved ones, jobs or livelihoods on the other side of that line these distinctions mean nothing. Yet lines must be drawn else every history book would just be the beginning of the world from big bang to present.

Part II

14. PPE – Left Undefended

"Not in the slightest. For a long time we have not had enough people, or enough equipment. It is just more of the same."

That was the answer one nurse gave me when asked if she was surprised there wasn't enough adequate personal protective equipment (PPE) available for healthcare workers at the start of the pandemic. The lack of the most fundamental and basic protection for the people caring for our sick and vulnerable was dubbed a 'national scandal' by health experts during March and April[1]. Hindsight is not any kinder. The failure to provide PPE where it is needed is tantamount to corporate manslaughter. It is the equivalent of sending soldiers into battle without body armour or a helmet.

If this had been a sudden and surprise invasion then perhaps the shortages would have been justifiable – it is hard to prepare for something that is unpredictable. Except we did know it was coming. Even if we ignore that Exercise Cygnus demonstrated how utterly unprepared we were for a pandemic (and we should never allow our politicians off the hook for this), there was still time to prepare for the arrival of coronavirus in the UK. Our politicians watched and waited for eleven weeks while the virus tore through other countries, they could have prepared our troops for the battle we knew was coming but they didn't.

To stretch the military analogy further, instead of equipping them correctly they just got every other person in the country to clap them as they slowly marched towards the enemy as they were mown down.

The term 'corporate manslaughter' is really serious, it should not be thrown around. Having reported on the entirety of the pandemic in Wales I am strongly of the opinion that the lack of preparedness for the pandemic in terms of PPE directly led to the unnecessary deaths of hundreds of people – many of whom were on the frontline of the fight to save others from the disease. Clearly all the many issues in preparation and response to the virus added to both the amount of unnecessary cases and deaths. Lack of testing, poor communication, bad governance, systemic shortcomings in our care sector, and deep rooted inequality all killed people in Wales during the pandemic; however these reasons were more complex, multifaceted and nebulous More than anything else the lack of PPE was the factor you can point to and say 'that is why these people died'. Though a nurse may have been more statistically likely to die because he/she was black, or overweight, or poor, the fact that she was forced to inhale a deadly virus because the right mask was not available is why that virus was able to infect the lining of their throat, airways and lungs.

The story of PPE during the crisis is divided into two parts. The first is a roughly six week period in March and April when Wales was hit by an unprecedented spike in demand for PPE. After a few months, as the situation stabilized, global production increased and the Welsh Government was able to secure some large deliveries from abroad. The second part came later in the crisis and at time of writing is still continuing, centred upon the guidance on when, where and how to wear a mask or face covering.

With the initial shortage it is important not to underplay the seriousness of the situation in Wales. In March and April WalesOnline was inundated with contacts from people all over Wales who were lacking some of the most basic equipment, and it wasn't just in hospitals or care settings. While shops were locking down, pharmacies had remained open to provide their essential service. Raj Aggarwal is a pharmacist and owner of Central Pharmacy in the Roath area of Cardiff. Speaking to WalesOnline[2], he described how they "were given no personal protective equipment by the health service but managed to purchase some at extortionate prices to protect the staff". The staff in that pharmacy, who by the very fact they had remained open were key workers, had to rely on what could at best be described as an 'unconventional supplier' for this vital equipment. Mr Raj Aggarwal said: "Luckily a local sixth form college, St David's in Cardiff, realised our plight and managed to make us some visors with their 3D printer, which was really welcome." In Newport, the very centre of the epidemic in those early days, the council issued a plea to businesses and organisations to give them any spare PPE they had to "help protect the city's front line workers".[3] It was not low risk office-based staff that needed the PPE to do their jobs – these were carers, social workers and refuse collectors. They were absolutely essential.

The shortages were also affecting the very frontline of the virus. Within the first three days of going into lockdown Dr David Bailey, chairman of the British Medical Association's Welsh Council, said that some GPs were having to wear goggles from DIY shops in a desperate bid to protect themselves. Dr Bailey said: "We've heard from members on the frontline who are anxious over the adequacy of PPE currently being provided to healthcare professionals in Wales as well as those experiencing shortages. We welcome the commitment from Welsh Government to follow WHO guidance regarding eye protection, however we've heard from GPs who feel they are putting themselves at risk because the eye masks which have been delivered to surgeries are completely inadequate and do not cover their eyes appropriately – some are opting to wear goggles bought from DIY stores they already had at home. This is unacceptable.

The Welsh Government must find a reliable way to substantially increase the production and distribution of PPE as well as ensuring what is being provided is appropriate. No healthcare worker should be putting themselves at risk."

It wasn't just goggles that were scarce. Bangor GP, Dr Catrin Elis Williams, said that general practitioners were expected to 'ration' their PPE and to use it only on patients who were strongly suspected of having Covid-19[4]. "However we are finding as time goes on that elderly people in particular are presenting with confusion and cannot tell us that they have a fever," she said. "We are being expected to provide care and put our own health at risk by rationing our use of PPE." So in a developed, wealthy country with plenty of warning, key workers were begging for basic equipment. Pharmacists described themselves as 'lucky' that a local sixth form college could make them visors. GPs were rationing their PPE, having to decide how much of a risk was posed by the sick person in front of them and whether they needed to use their scarce resources. These are decisions that should not have been required, both for the safety of the GP and for every subsequent patient they would see.

The stories about the lack of PPE were inevitably followed by stories of deaths. Gareth Roberts was a 65-year-old grandfather and nurse. He had come out of retirement in 2015 and had been working extra shifts in Llandough Hospital. A family friend said he had told her he was going to work with just a 'paper mask, plastic gloves and a pinny'[5]. As we would also see with the policy to only test care home residents with symptoms, the obvious shortages led to a belief that the Welsh Government was tailoring its guidance on PPE usage to manage dwindling supplies, rather than to maximise the safety of workers.

This was a key finding by the Senedd's Health, Social Care and

Sport Committee in their 'Inquiry into the impact of the Covid-19 outbreak, and its management, on health and social care in Wales' report published in July 2020. It found "there was a perception amongst some staff that advice on appropriate use of PPE, agreed on a UK-wide basis, changed according to what was available rather than what was needed" adding that "a failure to communicate effectively in the early part of the outbreak led to confusion about what PPE was appropriate to use in different circumstances"[6].

Speaking on BBC *Question Time* on March 26, Richard Horton of *The Lancet* medical journal lamented the response of elected representatives in his characteristically direct way. He said: "I am sorry to say this but it is a national scandal. We knew in the last week of January that this was coming. The message from China was absolutely clear. There was a virus with pandemic potential that was hitting cities. People were being admitted to hospital and ICU units and were dying. I am not just hearing that not only is PPE not available but it is the wrong kind of PPE. What we have isn't even to WHO standards. How could we allow this to happen? The hypocrisy of clapping NHS people but not supporting them to go into that front line is tragic, and I am sorry to say it is preventable."

The following day I spoke to Cardiff surgeon Chris Wilson who echoed these sentiments: "Poor preparation is one thing...but the lack of PPE is quite another, and represents a failure at a local level and at the Welsh Government level. Furthermore there has been a lack of honesty and transparency over these shortages, with rationing disguised as policy. The health policy makers have a lot of serious questions to answer when we're through the worst of this."

All of these clear and obvious issues were happening just days after Deputy Chief Medical Officer for England Jenny Harries told the UK on March 20 that "the country has a perfectly adequate supply of PPE" and that supply pressures had now been "completely resolved". This is not to suggest that Ms Harries was being deliberately misleading, but something that is perhaps even worse, that neither the UK or Welsh Government had any clear grasp of the scale of the problem they were dealing with or a clear idea of their own stockpiles.

While both governments should rightly be strongly condemned for their inability to adequately prepare for the storm they knew was coming, once the storm was here, it was inevitable they were going to struggle as every country in the world battled to secure supplies of PPE. Like every other facet of the Covid-19 crisis, the PPE debacle was not a new problem, but rather the bursting of a series of long festering wounds, one of which is reliance on overseas suppliers.

On April 21, health minister Vaughan Gething admitted that Wales had only enough of all items of PPE to last for 'a few days'. Up until that point 48.3 million items of PPE had been issued across Wales since the start of the crisis with fluid-resistant gowns and masks the two most in demand pieces of PPE. Mr Gething told the press conference that "some of our regular international suppliers have cancelled contracts, saying they are no longer able to sell outside their country. And in other cases supplies are taking longer to arrive." To put into context how much Wales relies on PPE supplies from abroad, even after a large mobilisation of home-ground manufacturing to supply protective equipment, as of July 2020 90% of Wales PPE supplies still came from abroad. This leaves the country immensely vulnerable.

This is not to say that manufacturers in Wales did not step up – they absolutely did. In chapter five we saw how web designer, Richard Blackwell supplied healthcare workers with visors using 3D printers. However, he had to put his supplies on hold while tests were carried out to make sure they were up to standard. This was a challenge that the Welsh Government and Public Health Wales came up against time and again. I received over a dozen messages from people who had contacted the Welsh Government and offered to produce PPE and were furious that they had not been taken up on their offer immediately. But decision makers were in a tricky position because they had to certify all this PPE to make sure it was both safe to use and able to properly protect people. With so many businesses offering to help this was a challenge and the government had to prioritise the factories that could supply the most PPE in the shortest time. So suppliers which could supply 200,000 gowns a week would necessarily take precedence in receiving accreditation compared to one that could supply 1,000.

Another festering wound that the PPE issue exposed was highlighted by members of the Royal College of Physicians (RCP) when they gave evidence to the Senedd's Health, Social Care and Sport Committee, namely that the majority of PPE masks are designed for men. The Committee's inquiry found that "despite the high proportion of female clinicians working in the NHS, PPE masks are largely designed for male frames. One RCP member told us that they only passed fit testing when the mask was tied very tightly – something that they worried might not be replicable in an emergency situation."

Gender inequality exposed by coronavirus was highlighted by the greater number of working age women contracting the virus than men. The design of PPE is a further example. For context, the majority of GPs in Wales are women[7], as are nurses, and the idea that most of our PPE is not designed in a way that will be effective for those people is outrageous. Again this is not just a Covid/healthcare issue. In her book *Invisible Women*, campaigner Caroline Criado Perez drew attention to how equipment in other public services made it more likely that women would die or suffer injury. Take police stab vests, which are designed around a male frame and take little account of the fact that the person wearing the vest will have breasts. This means the vests can lift up thereby exposing the abdomen, or be so restrictive or uncomfortable that they are removed. Whilst researching for this book I spoke to one woman who is an officer in the British Army. While not wanting to be named she explained how the helmets issued don't accommodate hair buns (which rules dictate the hair should be in), causing the helmet to sit unnaturally high above the neck, thereby obscuring vision.

Another issue highlighted by the PPE crisis was the difficulty of competing in a global market. The decision to leave the EU and the resultant isolation, leaves the UK as a much smaller fish in a pond that remains the same size. In a global marketplace size really does matter. Being the biggest kid on the block (or fish in a pond), rightly or wrongly puts you at the front of a lot of queues. Even when the UK was still able to join such schemes a *Guardian* investigation revealed that[8] Britain missed three opportunities to be part of an EU scheme to bulk-buy masks, gowns and gloves and did not attend key talks about future purchases.

The merits of being (or not) part of a larger bloc are replicated in the UK. All the devolved nations had individual responsibility for the procurement and distribution of PPE and approached it in slightly different ways, especially in distribution. Chapter 5 relates how a wholesaler was accused of reserving PPE just for English care homes. In Wales, the distribution of PPE is coordinated by NHS Wales Shared Services Partnership, working with the Joint Equipment Stores that service local authorities[9]. This was supported by a website established by the Welsh Government where health and social care organisations could request PPE. Despite Wales,

England, Scotland and Northern Ireland all taking individual responsibility for PPE there was also a joint four nations group headed by Public Health England to secure international supplies where all four nations would receive a share of the PPE bought. In the first week of April, 20 million items of PPE were distributed to the devolved nations from the UK procurement process and there were weekly meetings of a four-nations oversight board[10]. This close working and mutual aid saved parts of both Wales and England from running out of PPE at different points in the crisis. Vaughan Gething indicated that it was only because of PPE being transferred from other UK nations that Wales was able to get by at the time it was 'two days' from running out. Similarly, Wales received two enormous PPE shipments from the Far East into Cardiff Airport (one flight from Hanghzhou, China, contained 600,000 fluid resistant gowns and 1.2 million fluid resistant surgical masks) some of which were able to shore up other struggling parts of the UK.

It was not only the lack of PPE that pointed to shortcomings in UK society, it was also the suppliers paid by the tax-payer. An investigation by *The Times*[11] found that contracts for personal protective equipment (PPE) worth more than £180m have been awarded to companies owned or run by prominent supporters of the Conservative Party. The investigation identified twelve contracts handed out by the government to three firms with links to Tory donors or members, with one company (co-owned by a Conservative donor) a supplier of high street beauty products being awarded a £65m deal to provide facemasks to the NHS. The donor had previously given several thousand pounds to Michael Gove's 2016 leadership campaign. When the contracts were awarded Mr Gove was the Minister for the Cabinet Office, which was the part of the UK Government responsible for NHS procurement. It should be noted that at the time the UK Government said that ministers were not involved in the selection of the companies in question, "proper due diligence is carried out for all government contracts" and that it was awarded based on 'clinical need'.

How unethical all this appears. It is clear and obvious and will be covered in more detail in other chapters. At time of writing details of less than half of the £5.5 billion of contracts to produce PPE had been made public, so there may be more revelations to come.

Once the lockdown started to take effect and international supply lines became more secure the focus of the PPE debate shifted from 'why isn't there enough?' to 'when should the public be wearing it?'. This debate primarily centred around the wearing of masks. This is still very much a live issue. By the time you are sitting on your sofa or toilet immersing yourself in this great book, the debate is likely to have moved on significantly, but it is still possible to do some analysis of the topic.

Throughout the first four months of the pandemic the UK went its own way on advice on masks. By the end of June Italy had made masks compulsory on public transport and places where it wasn't possible' to social distance inside or outside, and masks were compulsory in all German public spaces. For many Asian countries that had performed most effectively in containing the virus, masks were a key part of their strategy.

This was not so in Wales. On May 12, after people in England had been advised (not compelled) to wear face coverings in public, Chief Medical Officer for Wales, Dr Frank Atherton, released a detailed statement as to why Wales was taking a different approach. In it he said that "The evidence from SAGE shows a small, but marginally positive effect on reducing the risk of a coronavirus infection in others" when wearing a mask. He listed three reasons why Wales had not taken the same steps. First, the Welsh Government feared that issuing advice to wear face masks would reduce the amount of PPE available for front line care workers (which gives credence to the accusation that guidance was issued based on amounts of PPE supplies rather than safety). Secondly, it was felt that people with symptoms might be more likely to leave their homes because a mask gave a false sense of security. Finally came concerns over discrimination. Some people are not able to wear masks due to certain health conditions and there were concerns that they might become the focus for abuse. When masks were eventually made mandatory many people who were unable to wear them took to wearing sunflower lanyards to indicate their hidden disability.

Wales would remain behind the curve on face coverings throughout the summer. It wasn't until July 13 that Mark Drakeford announced that they would be compulsory on public transport, and even that rule would not come into effect until July 27. By contrast Scotland introduced mandatory face coverings on public transport on June 22 with exceptions only for children under five and people with certain medical conditions. The First Minister said: "For the sake of simplicity and consistency, as well as being part of our plan to help reduce the risk of transmission while on public transport where it is not always possible to maintain a 2m physical distance, it will become mandatory for people to wear a three-layer face covering while travelling – this includes taxis."

Though the words 'mask' and 'face coverings' are used fairly interchangeably, the Welsh Government was also very specific to talk about a three-layer face covering as opposed to a mask. This is because the WHO recommends a minimum of three layers in a face covering, which should include: an inner layer of absorbent material, such as cotton; a middle layer of non-woven material, such as polypropylene and an outer layer of non-absorbent material, such as polyester or polyester-blend.

The lack of PPE for our health care workers was truly scandalous – a total failure of governmental planning that resulted in people dying. The true tragedy is that the situation was made worse because our NHS are so dedicated, making do with few resources. These shortcomings have been going on for over a decade of which the lack of PPE during the Covid crisis was just (hopefully) the pinnacle.

To understand what happened and why read again the quote from the nurse at the start of the chapter. When asked if she was surprised at the lack of PPE she simply said: "Not in the slightest. For a long time we have not had enough people, or enough equipment. It is just more of the same." This sums it up. Her reaction to her country and her employer failing to equip her wasn't fury, it wasn't surprise, it was just a shrug of the shoulders. Every winter our hospitals are stressed to breaking point, even without the virus, with wards often significantly understaffed. Managers are regularly ringing round agencies trying to get numbers to recommended levels. Our NHS staff just have to carry on. An example the nurse gave me was that if a seriously ill patient who weighs 22 stone falls on their way to the toilet you do what you can to help them up. It may be that you don't have enough colleagues around to do it in a way that is safe for staff but what can you do? Leave them on the ground? Even if you have the equipment to lift them will it be available? Even then will it be the right size? For a decade we have expected our healthcare workers to go without, they have been conditioned to expect not to have everything they need, to just make do. They are told to report it when wards haven't got enough nurses, but what is the point? There is not enough staff and there is not enough money. The NHS has been carried on the back of these people and it functions because they care. But caring cannot stop you catching a virus, if anything it will make you more vulnerable. Some of the people we counted on most to protect us when the virus came died because our elected politicians failed to learn the lessons of Exercise Cygnus, the virus in China/Italy and a decade worth of NHS winter crises.

15. Care Homes: Wales' Predictable Disaster

Two overlapping themes arise frequently in looking at the pandemic: that coronavirus was a predictable disaster and that the virus worked its way into cracks in our society, widening them into chasms.

These themes reach their zenith in the area of care homes. Unlike many of the issues we have looked at so far, social care in Wales was already a canyon long in the making. In a political climate where being adversarial is king, it is testament to how convoluted, complex, stretched and struggling the social care system is in Wales and the wider UK, that there is near universal cross-party agreement for the need for reform. Decade after decade reports are churned out, recommendations are made and policy makers make the odd small nip and tuck at the system like a Hollywood plastic surgeon but eventually the botox always wears off.

Though it has become very in vogue in recent years for politicians to call for reform, in reality no Government, whether in Westminster or Cardiff Bay has got to grips with how to structure and ultimately fund our care sector. There are many reasons why but first and foremost no change has been made because the task is immensely complicated, hard and expensive. It will likely take more than one election cycle for the impact of any reforms to take effect. In an age when political machinery is primarily geared towards having favourable headlines after tomorrow's 6 a.m. pips on Radio 4 than planting trees under whose shade they will never sit, there is little appetite for wasting political capital on such mundane issues as supporting our most vulnerable.

By June 19, a total of 717 of the most vulnerable people in society had died from the virus after it had entered care homes. A combination of poor and slow decision-making in a system already gasping for air, cost hundreds of Wales' care home population their lives. Not only did these people die before their time, but often, because they had Covid, they died alone, unable to see their families because of the need to contain the virus. There were stories of people with severe dementia, unable to understand why their families were not there, asking if they had done something wrong, trying to take in why the only humans they saw were behind a visor, goggles and mask. Attempts to understand the terror and anxiety that both them and their families must have gone through makes the heart hurt.

WalesOnline and the *Western Mail* were very alert to this and led the way in how we covered this issue during the crisis. Not just here in Wales but we were ahead of the curve of many of the UK nationals. I really believe that most people get into journalism to cover big, important stories and to give a voice to those with none. There is no bigger story in the first half of 2020 than coronavirus and care homes and I am proud of how we covered it.

To truly understand how the disaster unfolded a brief overview of how social care works in Wales is necessary. Even those with an active interest in this policy area can be somewhat overwhelmed by its complexity so this will be an overview of the sector. If you want more information I strongly recommend the paper 'The future of care in Wales' by Cian Siôn and Michael Trickey from Wales Fiscal Analysis, which is a research body within Cardiff University's Wales Governance Centre I will draw heavily on this for the first half of the chapter[1].

As we have seen, the NHS in Wales is probably more complicated than is needed for a country only a little larger than Greater Manchester. It is like a trifle with layers including seven health boards, three NHS trusts, Public Health Wales, the Welsh Government, the Community Health Councils, the National Delivery Group and NHS Wales Shared Services Partnership: pretty complicated, right? This is nothing compared to the patchwork system that is the social care sector. If the Welsh NHS is a trifle at least it is still one organisation. However complex, however multi layered, it is still one organisation at the end of the day. In comparison social care in Wales is a massive bowl of alphabetti spaghetti, it should all come together to spell out something but instead it is a confused jumble that doesn't make any sense. This is the lived everyday reality that patients, relatives, staff, managers, care home owners and local authorities have to try to navigate to the detriment of all.

Formal service provision is fragmented, with over 1,000 separate providers. This is especially so in residential care. In the whole of Wales only 9% of care homes are run by local authorities, with Cardiff, Powys and Torfaen having no council run homes. Adding together homes for adults of all ages but not children's residential homes, there are 1,056 adult residential homes in Wales, of which 263 provide nursing care.

The funding of care provision for older adults is a mixture of taxpayers' money from the Department for Work and Pensions benefits, Welsh Government funding, local authorities and the NHS, alongside payments by individuals and families, plus voluntary donations. Yet all of these payments are dwarfed by the amount of unpaid care which is administered by families and friends within peoples own households. An exact figure is hard to pin down but two separate reports[2] estimate that paying the market rate for the care provided by relatives and friends would add up to £8 billion (for context, the Welsh NHS budget for 2020/21 is £8.74 billion).[3]

Focusing just on care homes, residents are divided into those whose care is fully funded from the public purse and those who self-fund. Generally if you have savings or assets worth £50,000 or more, you're expected to self-fund the full amount of your residential care home costs (though some people qualify for NHS funding in some circumstances under NHS Continuing Care).

The amount of money being spent on care in Wales by both self-funders and the taxpayer does not mean that care providers are necessarily raking in the cash. Local authorities offer care homes different weekly fees, with large discrepancies between councils. Care Forum Wales, an independent representative body for care providers, routinely publishes what it dubs the 'Cheapskate Awards' which it claims illustrates the 'postcode lottery' of care home funding. The numbers are stark, with the average fee per person in the lowest paying council (Powys) coming in at £555 per week compared to £762 at the highest paying (Cardiff)[4]. Some local authorities pay as little as £80 a day for people in residential homes. As one home owner told me: "You would struggle to get a hotel for that let alone care." There are also discrepancies in funding by the seven health boards which, according to Care Forum Wales chair Mario Kreft MBE, amounts to 29 different ways of doing things. There is also significant evidence that self-funding residents are subsidising the low fees paid by local authorities with people paying out of their own pockets pay 25% more for a similar service[5].

Issues in the sector do not end there, with pay for people working in social care notoriously low. Fewer than half of professional personal care workers are paid above the real living wage and for the past 10 years there has been no improvement in pay relative to inflation. When compared to similar developed countries the UK is a stingy payer[6], it remains to be seen if such low pay for such essential workers will be tolerated by the public post-Covid but it seems unlikely there will be fast action to remedy the discrepancy. Taking into account that approximately 80% of all care workers are female, this means that the low pay disproportionately hits women.

Behind all this there remains the spectre of our aging population looming in our futures. As we live longer the question of social care will not go away. Studies estimate that in twenty years time there will be 53,700 older adults living with severe dementia in Wales, twice as many as now[7]. Though some of this extra demand could be met by providing care within people's own houses, it seems likely that some expansion in care home places will be needed. However, the amount of beds available in Wales has hardly changed since 2010.

So Wales has a stretched and underfunded system, with poorly paid staff and a Byzantine system of communication and organisation. Enter Covid-19 stage left.

Before lambasting the Welsh Government for a series of woeful shortcomings in their handling of care homes during the crisis the question must be asked if it could have done better. It could be that because the virus was so destructive, so aggressive and so easily transferred that the 717 care homes deaths were inevitable. To assess the Welsh Government in challenging circumstances it is worthwhile comparing their performance to other countries. Where unfortunately, Wales does not come out well in international comparisons. There are over 23,000 registered beds in Welsh care homes with occupancy of about 92 % going into the crisis. With 717 dead out of a care home population of 21,160, Wales lost 3.4% of all residents (all figures taken from mid-June 2020). Compare this to New Zealand (0.04%), Germany (0.4%), Canada (1.5%), Denmark (0.5%). Even Italy, a country with less notice of the virus than Wales and whose health service was overwhelmed, performed better

(3.1%). Though Wales did perform better than the UK as a whole which lost 5.3% of its care home population, this is no cause for self-congratulation. Not performing quite as badly as someone else is no defence, especially when one considers that the virus took root in London weeks before it established itself strongly in Wales.

If more people were dying in Welsh care homes than in other countries the question needs to be asked: why? Ultimately the virus has to get into a care home, once there it is in what could be considered the perfect environment for it to thrive: dozens if not hundreds of people, many with weakened immune systems and underlying health conditions. Not only will the virus be more likely to affect these people, it is also in perfect environment for spreading the virus with more lines of transmission than an ill-advised Stereophonics concert. Providing direct care cannot be done at a distance, it is hands on; care-workers literally get their' hands dirty – a perfect setting for Covid-19. It was vital therefore, that coronavirus' did not cross the threshold.

For the virus to infiltrate it has to come through the front door, and in multiple press conferences both Mark Drakeford and Vaughan Gething identified three avenues of entry: visitors, staff and residents. Visitors were stopped from entering homes very early in the crisis, meaning that only two ways that the virus could have got inside was through staff coming into work or through new residents, usually from a hospital discharge. The latter were particularly risky because Welsh hospitals in March and April were full of the virus as it peaked. With a virus that could be both symptomless and take several days to incubate the risk of someone with an unnoticed infection entering the home was high. The only way to prevent this was, to use the now famous advice from the WHO, to 'test, test, test'.

But the Welsh Government did not. It was not until April 29

that Vaughan Gething changed the policy to allow the testing of all new residents. Until that point, only those with symptoms were allowed to have a test. On June 21 a WalesOnline investigation exclusively revealed that 1,097 patients were discharged from hospital to care homes without a test during March and April 2020. As of June 5, ONS figures suggested that nearly a third of Wales Covid deaths had been within care homes[8].

It is essential when analysing the quickly unfolding events of the pandemic to not simply be wise in hindsight. As it suddenly dawned on policy makers that a tsunami was about to smash into us in March, there had been a rush to clear hospital capacity with elective procedures cancelled and patients urgently discharged. These were understandable actions, after all we had seen the impact of the virus on the Italian health service. However, just like the last twenty years of policy making, care homes were forgotten in the equation.

So why were these people not tested? This was a question that my colleagues and I spent a long time seeking to answer. The first and most obvious answer seemed to be that there was limited testing capacity. After England gazumped Wales and took the 5,000 tests a day that had been agreed with Roche (see Chapter 16 on Testing), the allocation of Wales' scarce testing capacity was closely monitored. Could it be that the decision to test asymptomatic residents was a question of resources management, with tests being prioritised for front line healthcare workers in hospitals? Well according to the Health Minister this was not the case.

In a press conference, showing the same flash of anger at questioning as when he exploded at Jenny Rathbone in the Senedd, Vaughan Gething replied furiously 'you are wrong' and steadfastly denied testing capacity had anything to do with the decision. He went as far as saying that even with 'treble the amount of testing capacity', he still would not have allowed testing of people without symptoms in care homes adding the reasons for the delay was basing 'decisions on advice and evidence. The advice and the evidence changes.'

Mr Gething's point would have been stronger if his version of events had not been totally contradicted by the First Minister a week later when Mark Drakeford said in Plenary: "The reason why we changed the guidance was not because the clinical advice had changed, but because we recognised the need to give confidence to people in the sector."

Mr Gething's stance was further weakened when considering the scientific evidence base he was drawing on at the time. My colleague David James and I reviewed several of the papers published with the minutes of the UK's core scientific advisory body Sage, on which all the devolved administrations of the UK are represented. It is this research that informs the advice which Wales' technical advisory cell and Scotland's own Covid-19 advisory group tailor to the situations in their respective countries and give to their ministers.

The Sage minutes of March 31 include an NHS England paper[9] written by Professor Stephen Powis dated the same day which addressed specifically the risk of 'nosocomial transmission', looking at the extent to which transmission within hospitals from patients to healthcare workers and vice versa had become one of the key sources of the outbreak across the UK. Professor Powis was unequivocal about the risk that people in hospital with no symptoms posed, saying: "A key additional risk is transmission of coronavirus from non-diagnosed Covid-19 positive patients or staff, i.e. those who are asymptomatic or pauci-symptomatic (presenting few symptoms)." He was also absolutely clear about why these patients were not being tested. "We must consider public perception and workforce expectations of testing," wrote Prof Powis. "In most Trusts there remains insufficient testing capacity to test NHS and other critical staff away on sickness absence with suspect COVID-19 or self-isolating, and all sectors are under significant pressure. With the current pressure on the NHS and social care it could be perceived as inappropriate to prioritise those apparently well."

It is important to note that the document related to NHS England, however there are a couple of points to draw from this. First, it was seen by the advisors of all the devolved administrations on the Sage committee. And secondly, at the time of release significant divergences in policies between England, Wales, Scotland and Northern Ireland had not yet emerged. The document clearly shows that people with no symptoms in hospital were not being tested because there was not enough capacity to test all the doctors and nurses and care workers at home self-isolating – and health bosses thought it would be inappropriate. Lack of testing capacity was clearly at the heart of this issue.

It wasn't just that authorities in Wales were advising homes to take in residents discharged from hospitals without a test, they were actively pressuring them to do so. I spoke to one Port Talbot care home owner called Nigel Clark who told me he was under intense pressure to take discharges from hospital into his homes during this period and that the pressure came after he refused to take anyone without a test. He told me: "We decided on the official day the lockdown started. We had been told to stop visitors coming in that week. We decided that if family members cannot come in the home we can't take others without a test. The residents are so vulnerable. They [Welsh Government] would only give a test on people showing symptoms. We took the decision because of the risk of them being asymptomatic. There was pressure. We were under tremendous pressure to take people from the hospitals. One of our resident's children lives opposite the home. To tell them they can't see their family but take people without a test would have been unacceptable."

At time of writing the dust is just settling on the care home disaster in Wales, but already investigations, reports and enquiries are starting to unpack the events. A report commissioned by the Extraordinary Regional Partnership Board (ERPB), an emergency governing body set up to allow quick decision-making across Swansea and Neath Port Talbot during the coronavirus pandemic, found some serious shortcomings in how the situation was managed. Listed under 'challenges' the report listed ten particularly damning conclusions:

1. There was a "presumption that the efficacy of testing was such that there was only value in testing symptomatic residents and staff between day 1 and day 5 of those symptoms".
2. There were examples which "appeared to indicate a possible breakdown of communication between Health Board, Public Health Wales, local authorities, and individual care homes".
3. Shockingly that information that an individual resident was infected was not passed to the responsible care home in a timely manner.
4. National guidance led to an over-reliance on the presumption that infection could be safely managed within a care home setting, meaning that infection is likely to have been transferred into some care homes "as part of the national strategy to ensure capacity within the acute hospital setting".
5. It took "longer than ideal" to agree a principle to not knowingly transfer infected people – surely this is obvious?
6. Even after that principle was agreed the implementation "was

not as effective as it should have been", and therefore, some clinicians continued to operate on the basis that once an individual was medically fit for discharge, they could be transferred to a care home setting, even if still Covid positive.

7. In a small number of cases, there were examples of miscommunications between between Health Boards, Public Health Wales, local authorities and individual care homes meaning that individuals were discharged on the presumption that they were not Covid positive when in fact, they should have been known to be so.

8. There was a "over-reliance on symptomology" and then testing within the first 5 days of those symptoms (as per PHW advice) meant that asymptomatic staff and residents are likely to have been introducing infection into care home settings.

9. National guidance on mass testing of care home staff and residents took too long to develop. They added that "the knowledge that asymptomatic transmission was known to be a factor in high rates of care home deaths in other countries" prior to the surge in this country, makes it particularly difficult to square the national and public health guidance.

10. Subsequent mass testing has identified that asymptomatic staff have continued to work and, therefore, have been a possible source of infection transmission for longer than necessary.

Checkmate, gin and Yahtzee right?

Lack of testing could also have contributed to the virus entering care homes through staff. The determination by the Welsh Government to only test symptomatic staff meant that asymptomatic workers were able to move around homes unknowingly spreading the virus. This was a cause of real concern among workers, especially because they were more likely to be asymptomatic as they were younger and healthier than residents.

Though it was covered in depth in Chapter 7 it is worth reflecting on how the Welsh Government attempted to appease care workers not only for the lack of testing but also for the shortfalls in PPE – the £500 gift. Though a good thing in principle this policy was so rushed and poorly thought through it ended up sending money ring fenced for Wales back to the Treasury through tax.

Throughout this crisis, it is my observation that the care homes themselves were often a step or two ahead of the Welsh Government in their policies. The refusal to take in hospital discharges without a test despite significant pressure to do so is one example of this. One letter I saw from Public Health Wales to a South Wales care home owner summed this up. When asking about whether they should be testing all people coming into their homes the PHW expert told them there was no point testing someone who was asymptomatic. The PHW expert said: "There is no test to see if the patient is 'incubating' Covid after exposure, until they develop symptoms, which may be up to 14 days post exposure". Despite the fact that many care homes took it upon themselves to try to isolate all patients coming in, the PHW official said in the letter: "I wouldn't advocate this as routine practice for any patient coming out of hospital."

I spoke to Glyn Williams, who owns the Gwyddfor care home in Bodedern, near Holyhead on Anglesey. He had read an article in *The Lancet* medical journal back in February that suggested there was a possibility of asymptomatic transmission. Mr Williams told me: "The evidence that was cited was an example of a pre-op patient who within hours managed to infect 14 healthcare professionals before the onset of symptoms" adding "I thought 'Jesus this is a biological threat'. We have to treat this like biological warfare."

Later in the crisis several Welsh care homes would again be ahead of the curve compared to the Welsh Government. In June Mr Williams said: "If you look at the European Centre for Disease Control recommendations for recovering Covid patients it clearly states that at least two negative tests are required within 48 hours of discharge. So we have implemented that policy ourselves. We are implementing a higher standard. We have said to Betsi Cadwaladr Health Board that they must provide us with two negative tests within 48 hours of discharge and they must have been isolated during that period or we simply won't take them."

When reflecting how the virus unfolded in care homes we shouldn't forget that this had all been predicted. Exercise Cygnus found that local responders had raised concerns about the expectation that the social care system would be able to provide the level of support needed if the NHS implemented proposals entailing the movement of patients from hospitals into social care facilities.[11]

The reason the care home disaster matters is the devastating effect it had on human beings. It was entirely predictable in a system that was already on its knees. Even those residents who did not get the virus were subject to lower standards of care as staff were forced to self-isolate for a lack of testing.

Like the quality of a person, the quality of a society should be judged on how it treats their most vulnerable. In the social care sector ours has utterly failed, not just during the pandemic but for a generation. It didn't have to be this way during the crisis – as international comparisons show. There were political decisions that led to these deaths. It is easy to say 'the advice was this' but science, especially on new and developing diseases is not exact. There are judgement calls to be made and these are political decisions to be taken by elected politicians: it is why we voted for them. They were under immense pressure and people make mistakes, but to doggedly spout 'we were following the science' when care home owners with a subscription to *The Lancet* are making better informed decisions a month ahead of policy-makers, simply doesn't wash. This is compounded by the fact the health secretary then reacted with indignation at reasonable questioning of what has been shown to be poor decision making is not what you would hope from people who stood for election on the promise they can make our lives better. The buck stops with them.

Note

This is a very fluid and developing situation and everyday we know more about the virus. At time of writing some very early research has suggested that the size of the care home may have been a contributing factor in virus taking root in a care setting. Having read the paper and interviewed the author there is nothing to suggest that the virus did not enter through staff or hospital discharges. At time of writing the research has not yet been peer reviewed but I bring it to your attention to point out that it is likely that our understanding around what happened will increase week on week as more data becomes available.

16. Testing Times

The story of coronavirus testing in Wales is focussed around two occasions where Wales was undercut by the UK Government. Well perhaps one and a half occasions, how much Wales was helped or hindered is a matter for interpretation (and perhaps your political outlook).

Covid-19 is a disease where testing really matters. Many cases of infection are asymptomatic and a significant proportion of people are totally unaware that they have, or have had, the virus. Unfortunately, these people are still able to spread the disease. The reason it is hard to put an exact figure on how many people have been asymptomatic is because people are only likely to be tested when they are displaying symptoms. So when people around Wales and the UK sat down to watch the Downing Street/Welsh Government press conferences, they got only the tip of the iceberg when the number of new cases was announced.

Covid tests are not just important in identifying who has the disease and should self-isolate or be treated. As one public health official said to me: "the thing that matters with a test is what you do with the result". A positive test is about far more than the individual, though of course that is important. Beyond that person, these results(should) lead to all of their recent contacts being made aware that they too are at risk and need to self-isolate and potentially be tested. Furthermore, the test is vital for helping epidemiologists and policy makers understand what the virus is doing (are cases increasing in a particular location), who it is infecting (including age, gender, race, occupation, location), where is it infecting them (is a particular workplace, holiday destination, church a risk?), thereby informing an overall plan. Without good quality tests, planning and policy are made in the dark, and as every overconfident man who goes to the loo in the night without turning the light on can attest, it is surprising how far off the mark you can be.

The countries that responded most successfully to the pandemic almost always offer the best illustration of the crucial role of testing. All had quality, large scale testing, with quick turn around times at the heart of their strategy. In February South Korea saw a surge in cases from 31 to more than 4,200 in two weeks. They responded by setting up 500 testing sites which had tested more that 100,000 people by March 3[1]. The first drive through test centre opened there on February 26, before Prime Minister Boris Johnson boasting about 'shaking hands with everybody'" when he visited Covid patients in hospital.

The leading experts all agreed that testing should not just be a part of a country's strategy, it should be the bedrock. On March 16, WHO Director General Tedros Adhanom Ghebreyesus told a news conference in Geneva: "We have not seen an urgent enough escalation in testing, isolation and contact tracing – which is the backbone of the response. Social distancing measures can help to reduce transmission and enable health systems to cope. Handwashing and coughing into your elbow can reduce the risk for yourself and others. But on their own, they are not enough to extinguish this pandemic. It's the combination that makes the difference. As I keep saying, all countries must take a comprehensive approach. But the most effective way to prevent infections and save lives is breaking the chains of transmission. And to do that, you must test and isolate." He then issued his now famous line: "You cannot fight a fire blindfolded. And we cannot stop this pandemic if we don't know who is infected. We have a simple message for all countries: test, test, test!"[2]

Much like PPE the bulk of the story of testing played out in a frenetic three weeks around the beginning of lockdown. Trying to pin down exactly what happened and when can be a quagmire. There are teams of people within the Welsh Government and the Welsh NHS who are spending time focussed on tracking, documenting and monitoring audit trails and correspondence for the inevitable inquiries and finger pointing to come. Conversations and interviews with both political and management figures within the Welsh Government, Public Health Wales and the health boards as well as answers given to Senedd committees have revealed a cocktail of chaos and mistakes, but also exceptional resourcefulness and a clear demonstration that Wales has the ability to do things its own way successfully.

There were two flash points between Wales and the UK Government that define testing in Wales during the early weeks of lockdown. The first was the UK Government's commandeering a deal the Welsh Government thought it had made with pharmaceutical company Roche to supply 5,000 Covid tests a day. The second was the setting up of a mobile mass testing centre at the Cardiff City Stadium by Deloitte under UK Government instruction without telling the Welsh Government it was happening.

First to the collapse of the Roche deal. At the very start of the crisis Wales was quicker than England when it came to setting up community testing units. These were small scale units that could test roughly 100 people a day. In England, testing was very much hospital-based with little community testing where the general public with symptoms could be tested. The health boards in Wales had been tasked with setting up community testing and had responded. The main issue wasn't actually about the ability to test people, it was a lack of lab capacity and the global scarcity of the reagents.

With the WHO championing testing and countries like Germany and their large pharmaceutical industry testing on a far greater scale both the UK and Welsh Governments were under pressure from the public, media and opposition parties to up their capacity. This led to a series of promises and targets which neither government would hit. On March 21, Wales set a target of 6,000 tests a day by April 1, 8,000 by April 7 and a target of 9,000 by the end of the month. Matt Hancock said that England would hit 100,000 day by the end of April. The Welsh Government had reasons to be optimistic about scaling up its testing capacity as they believed it had secured a written agreement with Roche to provide 5,000 tests a day – quite a coup for a country the size of Wales.

However this deal was never fulfilled because the company agreed to supply those 5,000 tests to the UK Government instead. Although these tests would be split between all the nations in the UK, including Wales, only 19% of the Roche tests ended up being used in Wales[3]. This led to almost a week of confusion when health secretary Vaughan Gething refused to name the company involved even when it was put to him directly. This bizarre refusal ended in Plenary on April 1 when Mark Drakeford said: "So, we did have a deal; it was a deal that we had; it was with Roche. We believe that it was a deal that ought to have been honoured."

The situation appeared all the more strange when I approached the company and they issued a statement saying: "We maintain that Roche never had a contract or agreement directly with Wales to supply testing for COVID-19. Our absolute priority and focus at this time is to support the UK Government and NHS to scale up testing across the whole of the UK, including in Wales. As part of

the centralised roll-out of testing, we will continue to speak to colleagues at Public Health Wales to move this forward as quickly as
possible."

Either way, the Roche deal falling through completely obliter-
ated any chance Wales had of hitting its 9,000 target. Public Health
Wales, responsible for scaling up testing, now had to tear up its plans
for thousands of tests a day in the near future. There is no getting
around the fact that the UK taking over the deal screwed Wales over.
The benefits of being part of a larger union are significant, especially
when it comes to purchasing power, but on this occasion Wales was
treated by the UK not as a partner and family member, but as just
another country in the cut-throat international marketplace.

That begs the question of why Mark Drakeford and the Welsh
Government were so hesitant to call out the UK Government and
Roche for selling Wales down the river? It would certainly have
been politically expedient for Drakeford to do so as he was taking
severe criticism for failing to speak up for Wales. After Tracey
Cooper, the chief executive of Public Health Wales (PHW), told
the Senedd's health committee on May 7 that the UK Government
had stepped in and commandeered the deal between the Welsh
Government and Roche, Plaid Cymru Shadow Health Minister
Rhun ap Iorwerth, MS, said: "Public Health Wales' confirmation
today that the UK Government did step in to take 5,000 tests a
day off Wales and to subsume them into the general testing pool
raises serious and fundamental questions about how UK Government views Wales. What we've seen is the gazumping of a deal
negotiated for the benefit of the Welsh public, and Labour Ministers
were too weak to stand up to UK Government." Surely any politician would have been throwing Boris and Roche under the bus,
not taking the criticism themselves?

There are a number of factors at play here. Consider politicians like Nicola Sturgeon who make great political capital out of attacking the 'Tories', 'the UK Government' and 'Downing Street'. This serves her really well, as shown in polls[4] that gave her a far higher approval rating for her handling of the crisis than Boris Johnson despite the fact that, particularly in the early stages, they made broadly the same decisions. It is easy for her to project a 'them against us mentality' that speaks well to her base and shifts any blame for her own failings.

Mark Drakeford does not have the same luxury. As a Labour politician and a man who is pro the union, he does not want to feed into the narrative often used by Plaid Cymru that Wales is constantly being shafted by England. It is a tricky line for him to tread and means he can't lean back on the classic Sturgeon defence for shortcomings: 'it's Boris' fault'.

Another factor to consider is that, especially in those early weeks of the lockdown, everyone was really just winging it. The global shortage of PPE and testing reagents (as well as other basics like bags and swabs) meant that Wales was likely to be very reliant on the scale of the UK Government's resources and purchasing power through the crisis, so the Welsh administration was hesitant to publicly rebuke its neighbour.

However it is my opinion that these are just secondary reasons for Drakeford's hesitation to go on the attack against the UK, even when they had clearly dumped Wales up the testing creek without 5,000 paddles. It is a matter of temperament. Mark Drakeford has shown time and again that his preference is always for communication and collaboration. This is a pain for the humble journalist that just wants him to say outright that "Wales has been shafted" but instead he just straight bats it back down the wicket like Geoffrey Boycott. To continue the sporting analogy, he is far more a Roy Hodgson than a Jose Mourinho. I really don't believe that it is an orchestrated strategy or ploy to cultivate this public image, it is merely a reflection of the man himself. This is a double edged sword for him politically as it leaves him open to accusations of being dull, doddery and lacking dynamism. In an age when politicians seem to either be manicured, media trained into oblivion, robotic politicians (think Raab, Hancock et al) or, for want of a better word, 'characters' (Farage, Johnson and the gang), Drakeford doesn't really fit into either mould. Throughout the crisis his popularity rose (helped by the fact people in Wales now knew who he actually was) and a key part of this was his forensic, detail orientated and unflashy oratorical style which was a real juxtaposition to the Prime Minister.

To return to testing. Wales was now floundering, trying to increase its testing capacity from other sources as well as the scraps it was given from the new Roche deal. Things were not going well and on April 14 it was announced that only 770 tests had been conducted the previous day – well short of the 5,000 promised. What made this even worse was that there was still spare capacity in the system. Speaking at the press conference health secretary Vaughan Gething blamed the shortfall on a lack of referrals for frontline workers to have tests, but admitted the daily capacity was 1,300 a day, adding that he was frustrated the 'maximum capacity' for testing was not being used.

He blamed the local authorities for not making the referrals: "We need to do much more to maximise the capacity that exists. It is really frustrating for me that we haven't maximised that capacity. Every part of the system needs to refer their staff to make sure the capacity is used. I know, for example, that 12 local authorities have referred in their social care workers to have tests. But actually every local authority can make use of that and we have the capacity to test over 100 social care workers each day. That means those referrals need to be made. My frustration is, I am sure, borne out and multiplied by frontline staff who are waiting and self-isolating at home who think if they had a test they would understand they are Covid-free and return to work."

It is worth mentioning the daily capacity for testing because it can be somewhat misleading. If you heard "Wales has capacity for X amount of tests in a day", you will naturally assume this is every day – but it isn't. The maximum capacity is based on how many tests could be done on one day if everything was thrown at it. The following day the numbers would be well down because all the reagents etc would need to be replaced. This figure also works on the assumption that all staff employed in the process will be available that day. But of course people get sick and take annual leave. We saw the impact of the throwing everything at it approach when Matt Hancock bragged about hitting the 100,000 tests a day target – the subsequent days there was a fall in testing numbers.

On April 20 the 9,000 tests by the end of the month target was abandoned by the First Minister. He told the press conference: "We're not going to get to the 5,000 figure that we had hoped to get to by the middle of this month." Abandoning the target was highly embarrassing for the Welsh Government and was big news. Though, it seems that some people were not even aware there was a target in place. In what was one of the weaker performances from a senior official I have seen, PHW chief exec Tracey Cooper told the Senedd's health committee on May 7 she was 'not familiar' with Welsh ministers' original aim to carry out 9,000 daily coronavirus tests.[5]

Wait, what?! The head of PHW, the organisation tasked with delivering the Welsh Government's testing target, did not seem to even recognise it existed? The scrutinising MSs were 'shocked'. Angela Burns commented: "I'm sure that you don't need me telling you that one of the real drivers of this is about trust, and to say that there has been evasion over the questions or a lack of straight answers to the questions that [have been put] forward would be an understatement. I am genuinely shocked that Public Health Wales is saying publicly and on the record that they were not aware of the Government's commitment, that the Government said very loudly, very clearly and in multiple media, that there was an ambition for 9,000 testing capacity by the end of April." Ms Burns added: "You are the chief executive of Public Health Wales and that is a major, major Government commitment." It seemed that even without England's help, the Welsh Government was perfectly capable of undercutting itself.

The second flashpoint between the UK and Welsh Governments came over the setting up of mobile test centres. As the country went into lockdown there was an acknowledgement that mass testing was going to be the way to get on top of the virus and manage any lifting of lockdown restrictions. Though the details had not been ironed out, officials and decision makers knew that mass testing would be key. This meant that many of the smaller community centres were not going to cut it. The need was for testing centres that could handle thousands of tests a day, not hundreds. Public Health Wales was tasked with devising this strategy.

They were looking at locations around Wales including the Cardiff City Stadium and the Liberty Stadium. These sites would cater for densely populated urban populations with home testing planned for rural areas. Meanwhile, the UK government had five centres that they wanted to set up around the UK and they had earmarked Cardiff as one of them. Health planners in Wales were then were shocked to see on Twitter that white tents were being set up in the car park of the Cardiff City Stadium. The UK Government had taken it upon themselves to enlist the company Deloitte to begin the construction of a testing centre.

Neither Public Health Wales nor the Welsh Government seemed to know anything about the new centre. Health is a devolved issue, the UK Government has no jurisdiction to implement policy related to health within Wales. It is the same as Mark Drakeford organising a test centre in Bath or Nicola Sturgeon setting one up in Carlisle. It could be argued that there was no real issue here – Wales now had a drive in test centre in the middle of a pandemic, was that really something to moan about? The problem was that Wales had had no input into the system it was now expected to use. The data gathered would not be automatically integrated into the Welsh systems and the UK Government's testing systems were not anywhere near as robust as those planned by PHW. The UK Government was using spreadsheets and manual input for people's details whereas Wales had an integrated clinical system which meant that if you are registered with a Welsh GP it would feed into the Welsh infrastructure. It was on a secure NHS network whereas the UK one was with Deloitte. In the coming month Deloitte would look to improve their system, introducing QR codes and a booking portal.

Throughout the crisis this would be a clear difference in the Welsh and English approaches to testing. In England the focus was totally on the quantity of tests – the more the better. In Wales the focus was the opposite, with everything aimed at delivering good quality tests with thorough and robust data collection to allow for detailed analysis. In reality both sides went too far in their respective directions. England ended up with lots of tests which were not able to give them as much information as they could have because they were too busy trying to stop Matt Hancock looking like a fool by missing his target. In Wales they could have tested far more people if they had been willing to compromise slightly on conducting the perfect test with perfect data.

A good example of the incompatibility of the Welsh and English models for testing is the tests themselves. As this chapter is literally about tests it will be useful to understand how these tests are conducted. As someone who sat through hours of technical briefings with scientists to explain how it works I can confirm that the process is complicated, but put simply it is this:

When samples have been taken they are put in the dry tube and sent to the lab. There, the sample is then put in a solution that breaks down the cells in which the virus lives. It breaks down the fat and protein around the outside of the virus, leaving a mixture of proteins and fats which is then washed away with a range of different salts, chemicals and detergents. This leaves a purified form of the virus's genetic material, called RNA. An enzyme is then used to turn the RNA into DNA (what we have in our body). Next, more of the material is then created by using another enzyme, heating it to 98C and then letting it cool. This process is repeated forty-eight times to see how much of the virus' genetic material is present and if they have a positive sample.

At the start of the crisis, for self-tests analysed in Welsh labs, the person was required to use a cotton bud and swab right at the back of the throat. This is placed in a dry tube and sent off for analysis. English tests require people to swab twice[6]. One goes deep in a person's nose and the other in their throat. They are then placed in about half a tablespoon of fluid. The Welsh version is less invasive, more pleasant for patients and doesn't require the fluid for transport. Wales has been using dry swabs for about fifteen years, a technique developed for transporting samples of flu from areas of rural Wales where it took more time to get samples back to labs. According to experts I spoke to, samples are actually more secure on the dry swab and other countries have been contacting Public Health Wales to copy the method.

PHW took over the Cardiff City Stadium testing centre which it ran until it was handed on to Cardiff and Vale Health Board. It was then, along with all other Welsh drive-in centres taken over again by Deloitte and is part of the Lighthouse Labs network which answers to the UK Government. The Lighthouse Labs had serious issues and failings later in the year, which unfortunately fall outside the scope of this book.

The end result of the whole debacle is that the testing system in Wales is now extremely complicated because both English and Welsh models are being run simultaneously. Because some tests are going to Welsh labs and some to Lighthouse labs mix-ups are regularly made. Samples with a single dry swab often end up at the Lighthouse labs and double swab wet samples at Welsh labs – neither is equipped to test the samples supplied in error. The situation is confusing for members of the public, who don't know if they should be contacting the health board, PHW or ringing 119 This in turn leads to delays that make it all the harder to contain the virus. Often people trying to find out where their test went would be best placed to simply ask if they had a swab up their nose or not in order to work out if it was a Welsh or English lab it will have gone to.

At time of writing Wales' is attempting to move out of its first' lockdown. A key part of moving out of lockdown or other restrictions will be how well Wales' Test, Trace, Protect program works. It is still too early to give a verdict but the current signs are promising with 90% of people reached. However there remain issues with the turnaround times for tests. The figures on delivery of test results for 21 June in Wales reported only 64 % of hospital tests were delivered within 24 hours, with a lower percentage for community testing and drive through facilities.

There have been other hiccups along the way with examples of people in Scotland receiving test results meant for people in Wales[7], plus one day when nearly 10,000 tests were added to the daily figures in just 24 hours due to a backlog in non-NHS labs. It is clear that rolling out mass testing is no easy task. But the whole process was made so much harder by 5,000 tests being taken away from Wales at the start of the process. This does not absolve the Welsh Government from blame, the fact the head of PHW says she didn't even know there was a target is nothing short of astonishing. For the first months of the pandemic, the virus tested Wales far more than Wales tested for the virus.

17. The Impact of Coronavirus on People of Colour

Before we start I first want to address the use of the acronym BAME (Black, Asian and minority ethnic). Personally I don't like using such a broad catch-all acronym. Just the 'Asian' part of the acronym covers an entire continent with a huge range of ethnicities, races and cultures. It is clumsy.

Unfortunately, it is used so widely in reports, studies and analysis that it is hard to interpret and present some information without using it. I have opted not to swim against the tide and will use it within this chapter for simplicities sake, but it is worth bearing in mind that the acronym has limitations.

During the first wave, Coronavirus killed a far higher proportion of BAME people in Wales than white people. Analysis for the period March 2 to May 15 2020 shows that, after taking into account size and age structure of the population, the number of deaths involving Covid-19 was highest among males of black ethnic background at 256 deaths per 100,000 population and lowest among males of white ethnic background at 87[1]. Data for admission to critical care in Wales found 12.8% were from BAME backgrounds. When compared to the population of Wales there was a higher proportion of people from Asian and other ethnic backgrounds admitted to critical care with Covid[2].

It was an issue that quickly began to emerge during the crisis and when combined with the killing of George Floyd and the

Black Lives Matter protest, it became one of the defining themes of the entire first wave of the Covid pandemic. But as with other problems that emerged during the crisis, such as care home deaths, it is impossible to effectively analyse the impact of the virus on BAME people without first understanding the context.

To get to the heart of this story we need to look at the statistics surrounding BAME people in Wales. As I have demonstrated several times during the book, the problem with telling stories about human beings using stats is that numbers are inherently dehumanising. This is not really about X number of people of colour living in poverty it is about the first generation migrant, who can't speak English or Welsh, is unable to access services he/she is entitled to, therefore lives in an overcrowded house, has poor quality food, and whose poverty means that he or she is more likely to die before their time because of this disease. That is the story. But in order to see the bigger picture these statistics must be investigated, always keeping in the forefront of our mind that big numbers should multiply revulsion, sadness and desire to change – not diminish it.

As we review and analyse the data, all of the usual disclaimers and caveats about the pandemic being an unfolding and developing situation still apply. Every week understanding of Covid in Wales grows. It makes the job of journalists, authors and commentators more difficult; the story of coronavirus and its effects will likely still be developing a decade from now, and history and events rarely have an end point.

The phenomenon of BAME people being more likely to die from coronavirus played out across the entire United Kingdom. UK Government figures[3] showed that the highest age-standardised diagnosis rates for Covid-19 per 100,000 population were in people of Black ethnic groups (486 in females and 649 in males) and the lowest were in people of White ethnic groups (220 in females and

224 in males). After accounting for the effects of gender, age, deprivation and region, their analysis of survival among confirmed cases shows that people of Bangladeshi ethnicity had around twice the risk of death when compared to people of White British ethnicity. People of Chinese, Indian, Pakistani, Other Asian, Black Caribbean and Other Black ethnicity had between 10 and 50% higher risk of death when compared to White British.

What was also interesting about this data was that Covid didn't just set a new trend, it reversed an existing one. Death rates may have been higher for black and Asian ethnic groups when compared to white ethnic groups but this is the opposite of what was seen in previous years, when the all cause mortality rates were lower in Asian and black ethnic groups. In the pandemic, all cause mortality was almost four times higher than expected among black males since the start of the crisis, almost three times higher in Asian males and almost twice as high in White males. Among females, deaths were almost three times higher in black, mixed and other females, and 2.4 times higher in Asian females compared with 1.6 times in white females. The issue with this data is that it was not possible to include the effects of occupation, comorbidities (multiple conditions at once) or obesity in the calculations. These are also important factors because they are associated with the risk of death and are more commonly seen in some BAME groups.

Looking at the data specifically for Wales in relation to BAME employment, housing and poverty (all of which are known factors to increase a person's risk level from Covid) the stats are telling. A paper from Statistics for Wales from June 22, 2020[4] suggested that people from some BAME backgrounds are more likely to be a key worker than their white counterparts. More than half of employees of Bangladeshi ethnicity are critical workers, and half of black, African, Caribbean and black British employees work in critical roles. People of colour are also overrepresented in several high risk professions in Wales. Despite BAME people making up on 5.2% of the Welsh workforce they make up 11.2% of health care workers, 22.8% of chefs (who are at risk because of their often cramped working conditions) and 40.2% of Welsh taxi drivers and chauffeurs.

The risks are also increased when it comes to housing. A total of 77% of ethnically black people in Wales live in a rented property, and of those renting nearly twice as many live in a socially rented property compared to a privately rented property. Asians are the BAME background most likely to live in a property they own though this is still 13 percentage points lower than the equivalent figure for whites.

It isn't just that BAME people are more likely to rent, along with the inherent instability that comes with that form of living, but the quality of the housing is relevant. Several BAME ethnic groups are more likely to live in overcrowded housing than whites. In 2011, 28.7% of Gypsy or Irish Travellers and 27% of Bangladeshis lived in overcrowded housing which is defined as having fewer bedrooms than they need to avoid undesirable sharing, whilst 19.4% of black people and 18.5% of Arabs did so compared to 4.9% of white British people.

Location is also of significance. Analysis of data from the Welsh Index of Multiple Deprivation (summarised excellently in a paper by Scott Clifford[5]) found that almost 11% of the people living in the most deprived 10% of small areas in Wales were from a BAME background which double the proportion of BAME people in the total population. At the other end of the scale, a mere 3.3% of people living in the least deprived 50% of small areas were BAME. An appalling 34.9% of people from a black ethnic background were living in the most deprived 10% of small areas. These people are more likely to die from the disease with the ONS evaluation of

Covid-19 deaths by local area and socio-economic deprivation (from the start of March to end of May) showing that the most deprived areas mortality rate for coronavirus deaths were 109.5 deaths per 100,000 population, almost twice as high as the mortality rate for the least deprived areas of Wales (57.5 deaths per 100,000 population). As we discussed in Chapter 12 there were also genetic factors that likely contributed to the higher mortality rates among BAME people as well as higher incidence of obesity, with black adults the most likely of all ethnic groups to be overweight or obese[6].

To their credit, authorities in Wales were quick to recognise the increased risk the virus posed to people of colour. On April 21 Vaughan Gething[7] said in a written statement that "there is growing evidence Covid-19 infection is having a disproportionate impact on people with BAME backgrounds" and that "many of the health or social care workers who have sadly died ... were from BAME backgrounds". He added that as "we do not fully understand the reasons for such impact ... an urgent investigation is required to understand the factors involved". Subsequently the First Minister Mark Drakeford launched an investigation which, showing the Welsh Government's trademark flair for creativity and branding, came up with the "all-Wales Covid-19 Workforce Risk Assessment Tool"[8]. Developed by orthopaedic surgeon Professor Keshav Singhal this would help BAME people working in the Welsh health system to calculate their particular risk by giving themselves a score. Anyone who scored seven or more were considered 'very at risk' and had to work from home or at least not interact with patients. A score between 4-6 suggested considering modifying duties and carrying out a PPE review.

The criteria included:

- If you are aged between 50-59 = one point
- If you are aged between 60-69 = two points

- Male = one point
- If you identify as one of the BAME or mixed race groups = one point
- Cardiovascular disease. Are you on any treatment for hypertension (high blood pressure), atrial fibrillation (irregular heart rate), heart failure (had a heart attack), or have you had a stroke or mini stroke = one point
- Diabetes (type one or two) = one point
- Chronic lung disease (including asthma, COPD, interstitial lung disease) = one point
- Chronic kidney disease (any stage 1-5) = one point
- Sickle cell trait, thalassaemia trait or other haemoglobinopathy = one point
- If your BMI is more than 30 = one point
- If a member of your immediate family (parent under 70, sibling, child) has been in ITU or died with Covid-19 = one point

One place the Welsh Government did not get credit was for its data collection around the issue. A report by Professor Emmanuel Ogbonna of Cardiff University[9], commissioned by the Welsh Government, heavily criticised the lack of record keeping in Wales. Prof Ogbonna found that ethnicity of people dying with coronavirus did not start to be recorded as a matter of course through the Welsh Clinical Portal surveillance e-Form until May 6. Even after that date the form was only completed about two thirds of the time. With ethnicity not being included on death certificates it is far harder to properly understand the impact on minorities[10].

At the same time as the risk assessment was being released, Black Lives Matter (BLM) protests were taking place all around Wales. The first was in Cardiff on May 31 when hundreds of people gathered in front of Cardiff Castle for what was the first mass gathering in the capital since lockdown was imposed. The next weekend on June 6 the Cardiff protest had grown to 2,000 people with a smaller protest involving several hundred taking place in Swansea. Over the next seven days there would be similar protests in Barry, Bridgend, Newport, Carmarthen, Llanelli, Cardiff Bay, Brecon, Aberavon Beach and in Chippenham Fields in Monmouth.

I hesitate to call these demonstrations 'political' protests because there is nothing political about saying that black lives matter. It is simply a statement that any right thinking person will agree with. It would be the same as calling a banner saying 'murder is wrong' or 'love your children' political. I have covered a lot of protests on a whole range of issues. It involves speaking to protesters (and counter protesters) as well as liaising with organisers and the police. I have never experienced a more respectful or peaceful demonstration than those I observed in Wales over those three weeks. Social distancing and mask wearing were carried out by the vast majority. The protest in Barry saw the crowd addressed by members of the Stephen Lawrence Campaign. The event organiser was the lawyer Hilary Brown, who summed up the mood saying: "We are not going to play into the stereotypical images that people have of activists when they come together for a cause. So our behaviour today is going to be impeccable. Why? Because black lives matter."

For the rest of Wales, seeing large groups of people gather (however well distanced) was a cause for concern. For months people had been staying inside and not seeing loved ones, often to their own great detriment. This was for their personal survival but also for the wider protection of the NHS and society. To see people gather in this way caused uproar in come circles. UK health secretary Matt Hancock called on people not to join the protests saying: "Like so many, I am appalled at the death of George Floyd. I understand why people are deeply appalled and upset. But we are still facing a health crisis and coronavirus remains a real threat. For the safety of your loved ones, do not attend large gatherings, including demonstrations, of more than six people this weekend." These concerns were perfectly reasonable and legitimate. Arranging to meet in large groups was obviously dangerous, and if they weren't why the hell had the public spent the previous two months indoors? Expressing concern about them was a perfectly natural and understandable response. Because someone publicly expressed concern about spreading a virus that has been killing people doesn't mean that their concern is coming from a place of bigotry or prejudice (though of course many people who are that way inclined did jump on the criticism of the protests).

It is my personal view that it would be clearly incorrect to say that the BLM protests did not negatively impact upon the fighting of the virus. Not only did the protests themselves likely contribute to at least some contagion but the precedent they set likely reduced future compliance. However I remain convinced that they were a net positive for Wales and Welsh society.

The most eloquent point that I have seen made on this topic came from Jeremy Konyndyk on Twitter. He is a senior policy fellow at the Center for Global Development focussing on humanitarian response and global outbreak preparedness and he previously served in the Obama Administration from 2013-2017 as the director of USAID's Office of US Foreign Disaster Assistance (OFDA), where he led the US government's response to international disasters. His comments are quite extensive and are USA focussed but they apply to the situation in Wales as well. He said:

> I've been reflecting on the tumult last week over how to support
> the BLM protests while still supporting social distancing. A lot of

critics argued that I and others were 'conflating medical and professional expertise with other political beliefs, damaging [our] credibility.'

With the benefit of some distance and reflection, I want to address that again. I'll start with a quick story. Just over a year ago I traveled to Eastern Congo to assess WHO's work on the Ebola outbreak there. I went to Butembo, then the epicenter of the outbreak.

Much of E. Congo has been at war for years. In Butembo I met with leaders of local NGOs and civil society. Amazingly, 200 people showed up for a small meeting. Packed the room. And they didn't want to talk about Ebola. They wanted to talk about SAFETY.

Speaker, after speaker, after speaker talked about safety and security. "Why didn't the government and UN care about insecurity here before Ebola arrived?" "Why did you send peacekeepers to protect Ebola teams, but not to protect us from conflict?" (Applause across the room)

In their minds – understandably – Ebola was not the biggest threat to their safety. Conflict and insecurity were – and had been endangering them much longer than Ebola. We spent a lot of time talking about that. My rusty French got a workout.

But they needed me to hear them on that before they were ready to dialog on Ebola. We ended up talking for two hours before I finally had to head off. There's a lesson in that. People who feel fundamentally unsafe and unheard will probably care about that more than a virus.

Black Americans have been fundamentally unsafe in this country since before its founding. And public health officials have no grounds to tell them that legacy should come second to the virus. Both are valid public health crises. Both threaten lives. Both need to be solved.

And finally the country is hearing them. It would be great if the movement sparked by George Floyd's killing had happened when we weren't mid-pandemic. But if you know a way to conveniently reschedule a country-wide spontaneous mobilization for racial justice, I'm all ears.

So I see the protests as a net public health good, given the sea change they have sparked in views on racial violence. And I see it as valid, given their importance, to treat them as an 'essential' public activity, just as we would something like voting.

It is disingenuous to think that this does not apply to Wales too. Black people are not being killed by the police at the same rate as across the Atlantic but the figures are still stark and representation within police forces is still far too low.

As an example, every summer I write the same story about BAME representation in Welsh police forces when the figures for the previous financial year are released in June. For the year 2019/20 the representation of BAME people in Welsh forces remains seriously low and is even worse for the numbers for women of colour in Wales' four police forces and how many non-white occupy the highest positions.

It must be remembered that Wales is overwhelmingly white in terms of demographics and it would be silly to demand that Dyfed Powys police, whose force area is just 2% BAME, to have 25% BAME officers. However, comparisons to population numbers are not good.[11]

- In Dyfed Powys Police, 1.3% of its officers are BAME compared to 2% of the population. Of the 12 BAME officers only two are women (both at constable level). There are 10 BAME male officers of whom only one is above the rank of sergeant.
- In Gwent Police, 2.2% of its workforce as BAME people compared to 3.9% of its population. Between March last year and March this year the force had a net loss of one BAME officer. The force has only one BAME female officer and 27 male. Only one is above the rank of constable.

- North Wales Police has 0.9% BAME officers compared to 2.5% of the population. It has only two female officers who are BAME.
- South Wales Police has 2.6% BAME officers compared to 6.6% of the population. There are 22 female officers, only one of which is above the rank of sergeant.

This means that in the whole of Wales there are just seven BAME officers above the level of inspector and just one of those is a woman. Anyone who ever suggests that there is a simple solution to a complicated problem is usually lying and lack of representation in police forces is a very complicated problem – one that police forces are working hard to rectify. Of course there is likely an element of prejudice to this, but there are other factors such as how BAME people perceive the police. In many countries of origin for first generation immigrants the police are figures of fear and exploitation, not a respectable career to be pursued like medicine or law. This makes recruitment from small BAME communities difficult. The same can absolutely be said for journalism. In the main, newsrooms are overwhelmingly white places and, again, it is a complicated problem. Part of the issue is that, to get into many areas of journalism you need work experience and expensive professional qualifications. If you don't have the money or contacts it is very hard to get a foot in the door, especially as pressure on local newspaper budgets has reduced the amount of trainee and internships available. To head off the people on social media who like to chirp off over this issue, I am not advocating for people unqualified for a job to be appointed over stronger candidates, I am suggesting that the current system in no way provides equality of opportunity across a huge range of important and influential professions.

Nowhere is a better reflection of how much the BLM movement applies to Wales and how a lack of representation in police forces is detrimental to people of colour than in the data around restraint. The 2017 Report of the Independent Review of Deaths and Serious Incidents in Police Custody[12] found that use of restraint was more prevalent in cases of BAME individuals who have died in police custody than in deaths of white people. The report also found evidence to suggest that dangerous restraint techniques and excessive force are disproportionately used on BAME people as well as the fact that in 2014/15 people who identified themselves as black or black British were three times more likely to be arrested for notifiable offences than those who identified as white.

Stop and search stats are not better. In England and Wales between April 2018 and March 2019, there were four stop and searches for every 1,000 White people, compared with 38 for every 1,000 Black people. The divide is clear when you look specifically at Welsh police forces. Dyfed Powys has a rate of 5 per 1,000 white people compared to 40 for black people. South Wales is 7 white compared to 42 black. Gwent is 3 white compared to 25 black. North Wales is 3 white compared to 9 black[13].

This is not to say that progress has not been made, not just in the police, but also in society generally. In his independent review into the treatment of and outcomes for BAME individuals in the Criminal Justice System, MP David Lammy said:

> It is true that, in wider society, overt racial prejudice is declining. For example, the proportion of people who say that they would mind if a relative married someone from a West Indian or Asian background has fallen significantly over the last two decades.
>
> It is also the case that younger generations, who have grown up in a more diverse country, report lower levels of prejudice than their parents and grandparents' generation. Social norms are changing."

However he adds: "Nevertheless, some prejudice that was overt is now covert. A recent study in the US found one particular racial slur against African Americans is searched for on Google seven million times a year.

Sometimes, prejudice can be subtler. Consider, for example, when the word 'gang' is used, rather than 'group', in public discourse about crime. It can be used to signal ethnicity rather than to describe the links between a group of suspects."

Without doubt we still have such a long way to go and that is why the BLM protests absolutely applied to Wales. Prof Ogbonna quoted in his report a 2017 survey by The National Centre for Social Research that found that 26% of a representative sample of British public described themselves as 'very' or 'a little' prejudiced against people of other races. A 2014 European Social Survey found that 18% of UK respondents believed that 'some races or ethnic groups are born less intelligent' and 44% believed that 'some races or ethnic groups are born harder working'.

As of March 2020 there were estimated to be 186,600 BAME people living in Wales, this equates to about 6% of a population of 3.1 million. When something doesn't affect the vast majority of people, it is far more likely to not to receive the attention it deserves. After all, 6% is a very small number right?

But as a thought experiment let's look at a group of a similar size and imagine how things would have played out differently if the stats had been reversed. According to the 2011 census, children aged 0-4 years old numbered 178,301 in Wales – 5.8% of the then population. Picture the reaction if the headline had been 'Coronavirus killed a far higher proportion of children under four than adults'. Clearly in some ways this is not a direct comparison, nothing creates the same reaction in humanity as threats to children. However, it demonstrates the ability of human beings to distance themselves from inequalities that they perceive as not their business. The racial inequalities on which coronavirus has thrown a light are all our problems. The demographics of Butetown are likely to be far more reflective of Wales in 2050 than they are now. This is a wound we cannot allow to fester – mainly for reasons of simple humanity but also because of economic and social imperatives. It is utterly unsustainable to have a society where a person's skin colour is such a big determinant of their life prospects, lifespan and stake in a society that is as much theirs as anyone else's.

18. Cardiff Bay and Westminster Relations – Walking in Lockstep?

On April 19 Matt Hancock wrote an article in which he laid out the virtues of a united, four nation approach to tackling the virus[1]. At a time when UK Government ministers were still trying to channel their inner wartime Churchill, his piece oozed togetherness as he talked about the 'crucial contribution' Wales was to make. As well as defending their poor record on PPE, Mr Hancock's main theme was one of togetherness. "Right from the start the battle against coronavirus has been a shared UK fight. The virus doesn't care about borders and neither can we." He added: "Our four Chief Medical Officers work closely together to coordinate data and scientific insight. And whether in Wrexham or Reading, Cardiff or Coventry, our core goal is to protect the NHS and prevent it from being overwhelmed. In the end it's not a Welsh Health Service or an English Health Service but a National Health Service. We are all on the same team and we will all get through this together, as one United Kingdom."

The same noises were coming out of Cardiff Bay where First Minister Mark Drakeford was a vocal proponent of a united and collaborative approach from the very beginning. Despite the fact that at the end of April he said that Wales' approach may be different 'at the margins' to other parts of the UK he added that "a UK way of doing things remains a strength"[2]. As we went into May, five weeks after Wales, England, Scotland and Northern Ireland went into lockdown together, Mr Drakeford was still keen, saying "a four nations approach works best for Wales" and that the four governments should "begin to lift lockdown through a set of common measures implemented to a common timetable"[3].

Clearly, at least publicly, both sides wanted to work together to overcome the virus in the United Kingdom. Yet despite this, the next three months would see sniping, public disagreements, a UK Government minister actively lobbying against his Welsh counterparts, a significant divergence in lockdown policy and the highest office holders in the respective administrations not speaking for two months. Yet the line still coming out of Downing Street in particular was that the UK had never been more united.

What happened and went wrong? Was the period of March to July a period of unparalleled (the word 'unprecedented' has been used enough for one year) co-operation between the UK nations or was it more like a dysfunctional marriage, only staying together for appearances and passive aggressively commenting on the fact that the other came home late/forgot to tell them their policy on facemasks? Actually, it was both. Relations between Westminster and Cardiff Bay were, like so much of the Covid crisis, entirely predictable – it was never going to go smoothly. To begin with there is the UK's entirely haphazard constitutional and devolution settlement. This will be covered in far greater detail in the next chapter 'The State of the UK' but suffice to say that the current arrangements were so disjointed that even if both administrations had been ideologically aligned it would have been hard to maintain constantly good relations. And there was no ideological alignment beyond a vague desire to do what is best for the country, and that is surely the aim of every politician (you would hope...).

It is impossible to list every single exchange, disagreement and flashpoint between all parts of the UK and Welsh administrators throughout the crisis. Not until the dust has settled and inevitable public inquiries are under way will all the details really be known. However, there was still plenty played out in the public domain and even more that can be gleaned from daily conversations with politicians and their advisors.

Even when the First Minister was saying on May 4 that the "four nations approach works best for Wales" cracks had already begun to show. Back in April, with the first lockdown review approaching, it was clear to everyone that the restrictions would have to be extended. Drakeford had been using his daily press conference to voice his desire for the UK Government to convene a meeting to confirm the continuation of the restrictions in order to give the public clarity. With the PM still in hospital fighting the virus and the UK Government not making any announcement publically on the extension of lockdown, Mr Drakeford declared unilaterally on April 8, that Wales was keeping the lockdown rules for another three weeks to "allow people to plan for the week ahead". Earlier the same day on the Downing Street lobby call the Prime Minister's spokesman had refused to say whether the lockdown would be extended.

Sniping came on May 3 after England 'hit' its testing target of 100,000 tests a day by the end of April. Speaking on BBC Radio Wales, Vaughan Gething suggested that the Department for Health and Social Care were simply doing so many tests because they felt obliged after setting a target: "England have gone out and created lots of capacity very quickly and they have then gone out and used that capacity. The challenge from a policy point of view is that there is clearly a difference but that is partly because England decided that having set a big target they needed to go out and use all the tests."

Mr Gething didn't stop there adding that he felt the English strategy was not underpinned by evidence, and implied that the way the UK Government had counted the tests was not entirely accurate. "Now other people will tell you about how many of those tests are actual tests or tests that have been sent out," he said. "But part of the difficulty we've had is that the scientific underpinning of how and why you extend that policy isn't something where there has been a fully informed debate and we don't see that the science supports all of the differences in policy and the testing reach in England." In addition to these criticisms the health secretary also lambasted the UK Government's online test booking system which at the time was telling people tests 'are unavailable in Wales'. He said: "It is really unhelpful because that does give a misleading impression about the availability for tests in Wales for people who need to have tests done. When actually we have different methods of getting tests to the people that need them."[4]

It wasn't just between Wales and Downing Street that disagreements were starting to be made public. For several days ahead of Boris Johnson's announcement on Sunday, May 10, there was a series of leaks about the PM's road map out of lockdown. It seems that none of this had been discussed with the devolved administrations despite the fact they were supposed to be moving in lockstep. This led to Scottish First Minister Nicola Sturgeon saying at her daily briefing that she would 'not be pressurised' into lifting measures prematurely and that Scotland could take a separate path on easing lockdown restrictions. She added that no decisions had yet been made at Cobra meetings despite the appearance that the UK Government had already decided on the course of action to take[5].

Sturgeon's comments were followed the next day by some from Drakeford (almost like they were co-ordinated). At his press conference the First Minister followed his usual modus operandi, by keeping his criticism measured and wedged between compliments and encouragement like a true shit sandwich. "My summary would be that it has been a bit of a fits and starts experience," he said when he was questioned. "But when we have discussions with UK ministers – and we have had discussions on Wednesday, Thursday and Friday this week – when we have these discussions they work well, they are open and they are engaged. What I have tried to argue for is a more reliable pattern of that engagement. We tend to get it and then it doesn't happen for a while then it resumes again. When we have it, it is good."

This assessment also saw what would become one of the First Minister's buzz phrases throughout the crisis when he would talk about what he wanted from Cardiff Bay/Westminster relations – a "regular, reliable, rhythm". He added: "It would be better from my point of view if it had a regular and reliable pattern so we can maximise the desire of all four governments from across the United Kingdom to work closely together. The more we talk the more we understand each other and the more we are able to deliver on that ambition."[6]

Come Sunday, May 10 there was the announcement itself by Mr Johnson which we discussed extensively in Chapter 8. This led to the first significant divergence in the messages coming from the different administrations. This in and of itself does not point to a disagreement or lack of cordiality between Cardiff and London. One of the key points of devolution is that decisions can be made closer to the people they affect. It may have been perfectly correct for England to have less stringent lockdown restrictions. England is not Wales and UK Government ministers and Welsh Government ministers, presented with the same scientific data, can quite reasonably come to different conclusions given the specific circumstances facing their particular country. However, the way that these measures were announced and, for want of a better word, marketed, by the respective administrations pointed at best to a fundamental lack of communication and at worse to a wilful lack of clarity. We have discussed how the Prime Minister (who we should not forget is the Prime Minister of Wales as much as he is the Prime Minister of England) failed to make clear distinctions that now existed between the lockdowns in Wales and England which made it more difficult to enforce the vital lockdown within Wales and we have previously discussed the frustration this caused for Welsh police chiefs.

It is hard to fathom why the Prime Minister did not make it clear that the new rules only applied to England. The lack of clarity left many inside the Welsh Government furious. One source told me that they understood it to be a deliberate and calculated decision. An effort to cultivate an image of a PM speaking for Britain, not just for England – an attempt to portray to his base that there was no alternative way forward other than that been taken by his administration. Whether this is the case it is hard to be sure, certainly the frequency of this vague messaging through the crisis suggests this interpretation is accurate. However, everything was so poorly delivered and managed around the May 10 announcement that one cannot simply rule out the omission of any England/Wales/Scotland/NI distinction as simply being an oversight. Whether deliberate or by accident, the continued failure to distinguish the fact that, on the subject of lockdown, Boris Johnson did not speak for Wales suggested a disdain and contempt for devolution.

It didn't take long for the First Minister to speak out publicly again. On Friday, May 15 he told his press conference that the relationship between the respective administrations was working in 'fits and starts' adding that there had been no conversations about lockdown since the week before.[7] Mr Drakeford said: "This week has been one of the stops in the stop-start process. Last week in the run-up to the announcements [on lockdown changes] we had good meetings on four out of five days. But now a whole week has gone by without any meeting of that sort. One out of three weeks has now gone by without any contact of that sort. We don't want to see a sudden splurge of contact in the days before a decision has got to be made."

Considering we were facing perhaps the UK's biggest ever peacetime threat, Drakeford revealed that many of the meetings on very serious topics were bizarrely "called together at very short notice, often to discuss things of very great importance". The First Minister seemed all the more annoyed that the UK Government had seemingly reneged on a pledge to make these dialogues more regular and reliable. He also said in his press conference:

When we had the last COBRA meeting I felt there was a commitment there to have these discussions on a more regular and predictable basis. I immediately followed that up by communicating with the UK Government, hoping to see that in place this week. It is a disappointment to me that that rhythm has not been established.

The reason I am disappointed is simply because I am committed to a four-nation approach.

Getting a four-nation approach becomes more complicated and challenging as we move out of lockdown. Therefore you need more conversations, more opportunities to share information, share perspectives, share ideas and hammer out a common way ahead. Without the opportunities to have those conversations, I think that becomes more difficult.

It also seemed from the First Minister's comments that though the communication from Westminster was 'ad hoc', the communication between the other devolved administrations (all of which were also run by different political parties) was flourishing, as Drakeford also said in that press conference that his conversations between the other devolved administrations were "almost always more continuous than they are with the UK Government because we have a whole series of responsibilities that we discharge and that we learn from one another".Yet at the same time the Conservative Secretary of State for Wales Simon Hart was announcing that all was rosy and that the UK and Welsh Governments had worked closely together 'every step of the way'.

The issue of communication only got worse from that point. When England made the wearing of face masks mandatory on public transport on June 4, the First Minister of Wales, whose country shares a highly connected rail and bus transport network, found out at the same time as everyone else did, during the Downing Street press conference. "We hadn't any explanation why they had come to that conclusion, or a point to the evidence of why they'd done it," Drakeford would comment on the decision, adding "We can't have a system where a guard has to walk up and down a carriage shouting for people to put their face masks on [when they cross the border] for example."[8]

As June continued the disagreements between Simon Hart and Mark Drakeford would become more pronounced. In an interview with the i newspaper published on June 7 the First Minister said that Wales would remain largely shut this summer with the possible exception of some self-catering accommodation.[9] This prompted Simon Hart to send Drakeford a letter on June 9 in which he lambasted him for failing to follow the lead of other parts of the UK and begin to reopen tourism. The Secretary of State for Wales said that there had been 'only 41 new cases across Wales' on the day the article had been published and that 'none of those' were in the tourist dependent areas of Carmarthenshire, Pembrokeshire, Powys or Monmouthshire. He added that "bold leadership is needed to get the country back on its feet" and that the Welsh Government had a responsibility to "restart the engines of the economy".

The war of words escalated with Wales deputy transport minister Lee Waters telling BBC Radio Wales Breakfast: "It is clear… the UK government is departing from the advice of SAGE, it has given up [on] a science-led approach." This culminated on June 17 when Simon Hart wrote another letter, this time to MSs and local council leaders in Wales urging them to pressure the First Minister to set out a roadmap for reopening tourism.[10] The Welsh Government response was dismissive with a statement being issued saying: "We thank Mr Hart for his advice, but the First Minister makes decisions based on safety and science rather than lobbying efforts by UK Government Ministers."

The Llywydd (speaker of the Senedd) Elin Jones tweeted: "I really don't take kindly to this political tactic. I will decide on my own representations on behalf of my constituents and do not need to be told what to do by a UK SoS." The matter continued on into the daily press briefing where Vaughan Gething commented that Mr Hart had "the luxury of not being a decision-maker" and that it was "a clumsy and ill-judged intervention".

There was no doubt that, despite the criticism, the Welsh Government's cautious approach was well received by the public. The Welsh Barometer opinion poll for ITV Cymru Wales showed that, in answer to the question 'Is the Welsh Government handling the crisis well?' only 29% had said yes on March 20. This increased to 41% on April 7, 56% on April 27 and 62% on June 1. By contrast when the same question was asked about the UK Government, by June 1, those answering yes had fallen to 34% from a high of 59% in April.[11]

Simon Hart may have just been trying to make political capital.

To show that while the doddery Welsh Government was being, well, doddery, the UK Government were getting things done. But if we work under the assumption that the aim of the letter was a genuine attempt to salvage the summer for beleaguered Welsh tourism we need to ask why this particular method was used. The decision to send the letter to MSs and council leaders asking them to lobby the Welsh Government is clearly not an ideal way to conduct intergovernmental communication. Even the UK Government would have to agree that in an ideal world this would not be how to go about their business. This suggests that it was a method of last resort, that all other avenues had been pursued and there was just no other option left. Yet this suggestion falls down when we look at the communication, (or lack thereof) between Boris Johnson and Mark Drakeford throughout the early summer period of the crisis.

Between May 28 and July 31, the Prime Minister and the First Minister had no contact via phone, video call or face to face. Pausing to think about it, it is utterly ridiculous that, in the middle of a pandemic, the leaders of two of the most interconnected countries in the world didn't once have a conversation for two months.

It is important to remember that Boris Johnson is not just the Prime Minister, he is also the 'Minister for the Union'. This was a new title that he took upon himself when he entered Number 10, ostensibly to signal ongoing commitment to strengthening the union between the UK nations. The UK government also made Chloe Smith the Minister for the Constitution who was responsible for maintaining 'integrity of the Union'. Cynics would suggest that the fact that this title was never added to any of his governmental or parliamentary biographies, and that Ms Smith was never replaced in her role when she was moved to the Cabinet Office in February 2020, points to merely paying lip service to Union and devolution settlement, not actively nurturing it.

This was certainly the view of the First Minister who, when I questioned him on July 6, said:

> If you are Minister for the Union, then speaking to the component parts of the union would seem to me a sensible way of discharging those responsibilities. If we had had more of those opportunities, there are many issues which we have come across, we could have shared our experience of reopening schools for example, we could have heard directly from the Prime Minister about the experience over this weekend reopening hospitality. I wanted more conversations not because I want to have arguments with anybody. I just want us to share, learn and do better and I think we would have done better if we had had more opportunities.

There are plenty of examples where the communication and relations between the Welsh and UK Government's has been poor. From the moment a Deloitte testing centre turned up in a Cardiff City Stadium car park and the UK Government took 5,000 tests away from Wales, there have been issues, challenges and disagreements. Even Simon Hart reported to the Senedd's Finance Committee on July 13 that it had been a 'tense and occasionally strained relationship.' However, despite the Prime Minister's inexplicable lack of contact with Drakeford, it is still fair to say that there had been unprecedented levels of co-operation at lower levels of government. In the middle of May I was given a leaked list containing all of the meetings, letters and video conferences between the UK and Welsh Governments. From the day we went into lockdown until May 14 there were over one hundred such communications (excluding contact between special advisers) including ministerial implementation group meetings often attended by both the Office for the Secretary of State for Wales and

Welsh Government ministers. Beyond this, several committee hearings have been told the chief medical officers for all four nations talk on a regular basis with clinical discussions and public health strategy discussions taking place frequently. The scientific advice from the UK's Sage committee and its subcommittees are also a resource used by all of the devolved governments through their scientific advisors.

There absolutely were frustrations at ministerial level with the Welsh Government frequently expressing public fury that the UK Government made announcements on new policies without also outlining the budgetary and Barnett consequential impacts on Wales. We would often hear from the First Minister in press conferences that England 'announce first and plan second'. But below the surface of ministers and party politics, there was clearly substantial levels of cooperation between England and Wales in the early parts of the crisis. What the challenges highlight is that our current system is not remotely equipped to deal with serious problems that require speed, efficiency, communication and co-operation from the bottom to the top of our governments.

19. The State of the UK

To truly understand why the UK performed so poorly in how it handled the Covid-19 pandemic it is important to look at serious structural failings that stretch back through the twenty-first century and beyond. To put it in the 2020 lexicon, you need to understand the UK's myriad of underlying health conditions. In terms of what you would look for in a healthy, functioning, democratic polity, the United Kingdom is sick. If it were a person, it would have been shielding since the beginning of March and New Zealand would have been dropping off its Tesco deliveries at the end of the drive.

For a democratic system to work it must be, among other things, robust, flexible and accountable. All the component parts of that system need to buy into and nurture it. Long term planning is essential. While seeking necessary reforms is important, they should all be driven towards fostering the long term health of that system – not undermining it in pursuit of short term political expediency.

Repeatedly we have seen how rather than nurturing democracy, elements of the UK Government in particular, has appeared to actively try to undermine it – and 'undermine' is absolutely the correct word; to 'erode the base or foundation'. This is not to suggest that coronavirus is in any way the cause of this seemingly relentless attack on our democratic foundations. It is the running theme throughout this book that Covid simply accelerated the process and has brought the underlying sickness into starker relief.

It is possible to write at length on how the virus demonstrated the true extent of the sickness of UK democracy, for the fundamentals of good governance were lacking, how political addiction to spin allowed misinformation to thrive and become accepted and normalised, how social media fuelled misinformation and attacked expertise, how the government's response to the virus made a compelling case for devolution and how, five months into the pandemic, support for an independent Wales is at an all time high. These are not individual issues in separate vacuums, they are all different symptoms of the same diseases which all in turn feed and interact with one another.

Looking at democracy and political culture the issues are clear. However old and well established, all democratic systems are fragile. They require the collective agreement of those in power to maintain the rules of engagement and buy into the idea that safeguarding that democracy is an intrinsic good, and their responsibility. The strongest institutional framework in the world, with constitutionally assured checks and balances will fall apart if enough people within the system don't work within the mutually agreed rules – see Trump in the USA. Institutions are made strong not simply by the written rules that govern them, but by the ingrained adherence to norms of behaviour and customs. All the major safeguards within our democracy came under pressure in the last four years and this has been accelerated by the Covid crisis.

For several years the Conservative Government has attacked the judiciary and wider legal system and sought to cast it as an opponent to be overcome, not a fundamental pillar of any democratic country. The Home Secretary Priti Patel has talked about how the removal of asylum seekers crossing the English Channel continued 'to be frustrated by activist lawyers'. At the same time Government insiders say that Dominic Cummings wants 'to get the judges sorted'. In 2020 the Government has been the subject of several high profile judicial reviews[1] that have found the its actions to be unlawful, including the detention and attempted deportation of 25 Jamaican nationals without access to legal advice, and in not allowing Shamima Begum to return to the UK for a fair hearing[2]. On July 31 the UK Government response was to create an independent panel to "examine if there is a need to reform the judicial review process"[3]. Judicial reviews are simply doing their job, they rule on whether the Government has acted unlawfully. They are the sign of a healthy democracy, an acknowledgement that governments (like citizens) will sometimes step over the line of legality and establish if this has occurred. Despite the UK Government's portrayal, this is not an attack on the lawful Government, it is an attempt to make sure the law applies to all, even the law makers.

It is on the subject of equality before the law that we see fundamentals of democracy yet again under attack. The idea that every person in this country is dealt with equally before the law is a pillar of any democratic state but one which has been chipped away at for a long time. Aided by sensationalist headlines, legal aid for those who cannot afford representation has been portrayed as an affront to society rather than a vital cog within it. This has allowed a succession of governments to slash the criminal legal aid budget in England and Wales from over £1.2 billion in 2007/08 to £879 million in 2018/19. Civil legal aid has not been spared falling from £1bn in 2010/11 to £600 million by 2015/16[4]. But a far starker representation of how the law does not apply to everyone equally was Dominic Cummings' high speed optical exam which has already been discussed extensively.

It is not just in law where there is the appearance of double standards. Questions of ethics and morality have also arisen. It is common to have heard in recent years after some political scandal, 'there was a time a politician would have resigned for that'. This phrase was widely used in July when Housing Secretary Robert

Jenrick refused to resign (and Johnson refused to sack him) after it was suggested he rushed through approval for a housing development plan for Conservative donor Richard Desmond[5]. It stands alongside the huge number of government contracts for the production of PPE given to companies with strong links to the Conservative Party which add up to at least £180m, though the Department for Health insist that 'proper due diligence' was carried out and it has 'robust processes in place'.

Allegations of cronyism within the UK Government were common throughout the crisis, with the continued appointment of Dido Harding to senior positions a clear example. Married to Conservative MP John Penrose she was the CEO of TalkTalk during their 2015 cyber attack, for which her handling received strong criticism. A Conservative peer, Baroness Harding was put in charge of the UK Government's contact tracing program, which was widely criticised for lack of efficiency and poor value for money as well as an app riddled with delays[6]. She was then rewarded for this in a way that even the relentlessly failing upwards Boris Johnson would have been proud when she was appointed the inaugural chair of the National Institute for Health Protection which combined Public Health England, NHS Test and Trace and the analytical capability of the Joint Biosecurity Centre under a single body[7].

Close links between our elected representatives and the businesses awarded government contracts are not just a London phenomenon. In August 2020 I wrote a piece about how former Wales Secretary Alun Cairns was being paid £15,000 a year to advise the Crumlin based BBI Group which had a role in producing coronavirus tests for the UK Government. To earn his £15,000 a year salary, which is in addition to his salary as an MP, the representative for the Vale of Glamorgan Mr Cairns is required to advise the company for 70 hours a year (less than six hours a month) equating to just over £214 an hour – nice work if you can get it. If it sounds odd that a former Government minister can take up this role, that is understandable. Former ministers are not allowed to lobby the UK government for two years after leaving office, and during this twenty-four month period they must seek permission from the Advisory Committee on Business Appointments to accept such roles. The committee, which was headed by former Tory cabinet minister Lord Eric Pickles, ruled that though "there was an inherent risk it could be perceived your contacts might assist BBI Group unfairly" Mr Cairns would be allowed to take up employment with the company but said he could not lobby the UK Government on behalf of the company or advise them directly on the work of the UK Government. If he is not going to be advising them on the work of the UK Government or lobbying the UK Government for the company it begs the question what will he be doing? Perhaps he has great expertise on immunoassay development.

But again this is not a new thing that Covid has allowed, it has merely allowed it to flourish like never before. Further examples of how entrenched these potential conflicts of interest can be are to be found with the two most recent Welsh Secretaries – Alun Cairns and Simon Hart.

In my role at WalesOnline I have trawled through Mr Cairns' declarations of interest for the last decade. Donations to his election campaigns extend well beyond the Vale of Glamorgan. He received significant donations from Alexander Temerko, a Ukrainian-born oil and gas businessman who was previously an arms tycoon, whose companies are involved in infrastructure sectors including offshore oil and gas, offshore renewables, interconnectors and onshore gas. Temerko has given Conservative politicians more than £1m since the Kremlin-connected entrepreneur was given British citizenship in 2011.

Before the 2019 election a donation of £5,000 was given to Mr Cairns from one of the companies Mr Temerko is involved in, AQUIND Ltd. In April 2014 he gave another £5,000 in a personal donation followed the same year with £5,000 but this time from another one of his companies, Offshore Group Newcastle Ltd. Mr Cairns also received two tickets for the Chelsea Flower Show in both 2011 and 2012 worth over £2,200. These came from a Japanese tobacco company at the same time he voted against a bill banning smoking in cars carrying children and vocally opposed plain packaging on cigarettes[8].

Mr Temerko has also given significant funds to the campaigns of Simon Hart who received £10,000 in 2014 from Offshore Group Newcastle. The same year he accepted two tickets to the Chelsea Flower show worth £1,404.00 from Japan Tobacco International, when just three months before he was one of only 24 MPs who voted against tabled amendments to the Children and Families Bill which would enable the UK government to introduce regulations requiring plain packaging for tobacco products and making it an offence to sell e-cigarettes to children under 18. Another amendment would have made it an offence for an adult to buy cigarettes for anyone under the age of 18. Hart had previously also been one of 50 MPs who wrote to then health secretary Andrew Lansley expressing serious concerns over plans for plain packaging on cigarettes saying: "There is no reliable evidence that plain packaging will have any public health benefit; no country in the world has yet to introduce it. However, such a measure could have extremely negative consequences elsewhere."[9]

There are also questions to be asked about the quality of Government ministers more generally. Ideally the Cabinet would be the cream of the crop, where the most able and talented politicians of their day will come together to run the country to the betterment of all. However, the criteria for entry into the Cabinet that faced the coronavirus crisis was not ability or acumen, but seemingly snivelling loyalty. As the *FT* wrote in its leader on May 26: "The foundation of this UK government is a bunker of close allies surrounded by a lightweight, supine and largely ineffectual cabinet chosen mainly for their commitment to Brexit or their loyalty to Mr Johnson in last year's Conservative party leadership contest. With the possible exception of Rishi Sunak, the chancellor, and Michael Gove, the cabinet office minister, few show the gravity demanded of a secretary of state. More heavyweight conservatives are meanwhile banished to the backbenches"[10].

This brings us to misinformation, disinformation and more spinning than Stripping the Willow at a New Year ceilidh. Politicians have always used situations and events to fit their own political agenda. However the hypocrisy, half-truths and sleight of hand we have seen in the UK since the EU referendum has been quite incredible. Only last year Boris Johnson opted to prorogue the very Parliament whose sovereignty was so sacrosanct that he had argued for leaving the EU in order to safeguard it. He prorogued it in order to stifle opposition to his proposals around Brexit. If the judiciary is a key pillar of our democracy then Parliament is the keystone which locks everything together. Much like the international Covid comparisons in daily briefing, parliamentary primacy and sovereignty was vital until it was no longer politically expedient.

In the general election that followed contempt for another pillar of democracy was shown by how the Dominic Cummings election campaign was orchestrated. The gaffe happy Prime Minister was kept out of public view as much as possible. Whereas other party leaders faced questions from then BBC journalist Andrew Neil,

Johnson avoided them. At one point he even seemed to take refuge in a fridge when confronted by a reporter from Good Morning Britain (it turns out democracy dies in the cold as well as the dark). But beyond this there was seemingly a systematic drive to employ subterfuge on a co-ordinated scale.

At one point the Conservative Party press office rebranded its' Twitter account @CCHQ as 'factcheck UK' for a televised election debate which made their account look like one of the independent fact checking charities such as FullFact. By any definition this is disinformation. The Tories were unapologetic, with Dominic Raab saying on the BBC the next day "no one gives a toss about the social media cut and thrust"[11]. At the same time the party created a website called labourmanifesto.co.uk which attacked the Labour party and then paid for it to be an advert on Google any time someone searched 'Labour'. There were also examples of Conservative councillors creating Facebook pages and websites which claimed to be politically neutral and then simply spammed pro Tory content. The whole rebranding of a Twitter account was a pretty weak attempt to mislead, but it is impossible to argue that it wasn't disinformation funded by the ruling political party (this is not to underplay the disastrous campaign by Jeremy Corbyn which was as weak as your nan's PG tips). But if you want to understand the hypocrisy of all this deception it comes from a tweet by the Cabinet Office just the week before. In it, the UK Government account tweeted a public information campaign saying: "Disinformation isn't always easy to spot. Make sure you know what to look for. Use the SHARE checklist. Don't feed the Beast." In an accompanying video a little green goblin warns people about information online which is 'purposefully misleading'.

The issue of misinformation and disinformation coming from social media in particular is enormous and the impacts were really stark during the coronavirus crisis. In April a mobile phone mast serving the emergency NHS Nightingale hospital in Birmingham was targeted by arsonist crackpots under the impression that the introduction of 5G caused Covid-19. Fears and opposition to mask use have been widely spread on Facebook and, especially early on in the pandemic, all sorts of false cures were circulating. Ultimately the only way out of the grim, lockdown limbo is a vaccine and yet these will also meet with opposition.

Idiots online are spreading lies and false science about vaccines and these so called 'antiVaxxers' have the potential to risk the herd immunity we will need if we are going to get back to any sense of normality. This is not even to begin to talk about misinformation around climate change.

Overcoming disinformation is incredibly difficult and ultimately takes a concerted and consistent effort from government. There is a reason why everybody now knows that smoking is bad for you, because of a sustained message from our lawmakers. But they will never cure the ailment of disinformation because they are part of the disease. How is it possible to reverse a growing society wide contempt for academics and science when senior members of Government have fought referendums on the back of us 'having enough of experts'? As Dominic Cummings and Barnard Castle showed, when the Government, who we should be holding to a higher standard than any, say 'do as I say not as I do' the entire spell is broken. The problem is that at the moment it's politically expedient for the Government to spread misleading information and half truths, for example Matt Hancock and the 100,000 tests a day target – cloaks, daggers, smoke and mirrors.

There are plenty of examples of an aversion to scrutiny, the UK Government's early refusal to name the members of SAGE, for instance. When politicians are determined to mislead it is the role of journalists to hold them to account. A free press is essential to a functioning democracy but again, during the virus there was evidence of the fourth estate weakening. There was much fuss made about how open Number 10 was with its daily briefings but as soon as the questions got tough over Cummings, and the unfolding shambles of tackling the virus, journalists were no longer allowed to ask follow up questions, with attempts being quickly muted. This is not an anomaly. Back in February political journalists boycotted a Downing Street briefing after the PM's most senior communications adviser, attempted to exclude reporters from news providers such as the *Mirror*, the i, HuffPost, PoliticsHome and the *Independent*[12]. This in itself was not a new tactic as during the 2019 general election the Tories banned the *Mirror* from joining all other major news providers on Boris Johnson's battle bus following negative coverage[13].

The challenge for journalists comes from the rise of social media and the decline in newspaper revenue. With social media and a smartphone everyone now has a voice. In some ways this is fantastic, people who are victims of power or in need are able to share their plight and shine a light on their situation. It is also a prime breeding ground for misinformation. In 2018 a picture circulated on Twitter of an aerial view of a large crowd of hundreds. The caption said it was a mass protest in London for far right activist (and at time of writing ironically a refugee in Spain) Tommy Robinson to be released from prison. This was widely shared when in fact it was neither a protest, in London or recent. It was a group of Liverpool fans, in Liverpool, celebrating the 2005 Champions League final. A real journalist, at a real publication is trained to assess and scrutinise that image[14]. A random person on Facebook is not. A random bloke with one Twitter account has the potential to reach as many on social media as a highly trained epidemiologist. Not all opinions are created equal and good journalism is about being balanced by giving prominence to the informed voices.

Not that everyone trusts journalists. A 2019 Ipsos MORI poll found that only 26% of people trusted journalists to tell the truth (though this was almost double the figure for politicians)[15]. Trust in some journalists did see a small increase during the early parts of the pandemic. A YouGov poll in March 2020 found that trust in broadsheet newspaper journalists has hit a six-year high since the 2019 general election (40%), though trust in tabloids such as the *Daily Mail* and *Sun* continued to fall[16].

Social media has allowed politicians to speak directly to voters, and at first glance that can be considered a good thing. Politicians are always being accused of being disconnected so what could be better than the ability to have conversations with voters? This would be true if it was in fact a conversation, but it isn't. There is nothing two-way about it. It is just the government line being pumped into the eyes and brain of their electorate with the respective supporters and opponents calling each other 'cockwombles' in the comment threads. There is a reason that when he announced his 'stay alert' message on May 10, Boris Johnson pre-recorded it with no journalistic scrutiny. It is the same reason the government always put questions from the public ahead of the journalists at the daily briefing. It is the same reason that Donald Trump will take any opportunity to undermine the credibility of the journalists who scrutinise him. It is because journalists are essential in holding power to account, and governments that run on a populist ticket, hate being held to account. This is why trained and credible journalists are so vital to a functioning democracy, and why attempts to limit them should be seen as an attack on our society itself.

On reflection you can't really be surprised by the state of the UK political system. Angry – yes. Disappointed – yes. Disillusioned

— yes. Surprised? No. The UK's electoral system has done more than almost anything to ingrain the woeful shortcoming of governance today. First, is the adversarial political culture, a system designed for two parties but which contains over half a dozen. The very set up of the House of Commons is adversarial. Why the hell, in the twenty-first century, are our elected representatives 'two sword lengths apart'? No wonder we have a culture where it is better for politicians to have been seen to lie and mislead than be wrong. Yet the real cancer in the heart of politics in the UK is the voting system. The idea that the first-past-the-post method can still be defended is bananas.

Imagine if a group of thirteen friends went out into town and were trying to choose where they should go for a drink. Three want to go to 'Spoons for a beer, three want to go to a club, and three want to go to a wine bar. They all want to go to slightly different places but all nine agree they want alcohol. However, the other four want to go to Costa for a latte and pain au chocolat. Under first past the post all the boozers (and let's face it, probably the more fun people) have to go to sit pretentiously in a coffee shop. Moving on from yet another analogy in this book, the figures around elections tells the whole story.

In 2017 Theresa May was seen to have failed because she received 42.4% of the vote, which won her 317 seats and produced a hung parliament. The next election in December 2019, Boris Johnson was only able to increase his vote share by 1.2 percentage points to 43.6% but he achieved an enormous majority with 364 seats. Not because the Tories did much better, but because Labour did so much worse. And it isn't just about the two largest parties either. The Scottish National Party had one seat for every 26,000 votes they received. By contrast The Greens had 857,513 votes and only won one seat. Labour needed to win more than 50,000 votes to win a seat while the Conservatives only needed to win 38,000 votes to send a Tory to Parliament.

The reason this system is bad for both democracy and governance is that it means that parties are able to win large majorities by appealing to fewer people. If you can get your base to support you, and that base is geographically concentrated, you win elections. This means there is never any political advantage to compromise or convincing people with a different point of view. Year after year, election after election, this takes its toll on political discord and allows the extremes of the political spectrum to dictate the agenda.

On the subject of devolution, it is hard to look at the current set up and argue that it works well for Wales, especially in terms of investment and funding. As the previous chapter described, the pandemic has been both a challenge to devolution but also an awakening of Wales' devolved consciousness. Mark Drakeford saw a significant growth in popularity, his detail focussed style juxtaposed to the politicians in Westminster. There was vocal support throughout the crisis for Wales ploughing its own furrow with regard to the lockdown restrictions. It was the first time many had really considered that Wales could do things differently. Though most people knew there was a Welsh Government there has for a long time not been the clearest understanding within the wider population what is and isn't a devolved competency. The Covid-19 crisis was for many the first time there was a truly visible way in which the decisions in Cardiff Bay actively affected their day to day lives. This does not mean they all liked what they saw. An ITV-Cymru Wales and Cardiff University poll of Welsh adults carried out by YouGov from 29 May to 1 June 2020 found that support for no devolved government in Wales actually rose in the first months of the crisis by five points to 22% though it should be pointed out that support for more Senedd powers and an independent Wales also rose during that period[17].

The subject of independence was also stoked in Wales by the Covid-19 crisis. On July 15, after polls indicating support for independence was at an all-time high, the Senedd debated independence for Wales for the first time. There is no doubt the issue of an independent Wales has been brought more into mainstream debate by Covid as well as the Brexit vote. It is a fascinating subject and a debate that needs a separate book. However, I think it is important for the debate to not be about 'could Wales be an independent country' – of course Wales could be independent. The real question is should Wales be independent?

There are many arguments to be made by both sides but in the current state of the UK it is understandable why arguments in favour of independence are gaining traction. This needs to be put in context however, though support for Welsh independence hit an all-time high over the crisis this is still not an enormous number. That same ITV Cymru Wales and Cardiff University poll found that only 25% answered yes to the question 'Should Wales be an independent country?' This is significantly less than support in England for England being an independent country. Also, even though people support something it doesn't mean it is their burning passion. Most people want reform of the House of Lords but they don't vote en masse for the Lib Dems.

People of all and no political persuasion, are unable to look at the current system and think there is a robust democracy, ready for any challenge. Our democracy is currently very unwell. Until all the Home Nations are given as much thought and investment as the Home Counties, as we have seen in Scotland, support for independence will only grow.

Notes

Around the World in 60 Days

1. '对话"传谣"被训诫医生：我是在提醒大家注意防范- 综合- 新京报网.' "(http://www.bjnews.com.cn/feature/2020/01/31/682076.html)" 31 Jan. 2020, http://www.bjnews.com.cn/feature/2020/01/31/682076.html. Accessed 22 Jul. 2020.

2. 'China coronavirus outbreak: All the latest updates - Al Jazeera', 7 Feb. 2020, https://www.aljazeera.com/news/2020/2/7/china-coronavirus-outbreak-all-the-latest-updates-5. Accessed 20 Oct. 2020.

3. 'Listings of WHO's response to COVID-19.' 29 Jun. 2020, https://www.who.int/news/item/29-06-2020-covidtimeline. Accessed 20 Oct. 2020.

4. 'Plenary 29/01/2020' - Welsh Parliament - National Assembly... https://record.assembly.wales/Plenary/6078. Accessed 29 Oct. 2020.

5. 'CMO for England announces 12 new cases of novel... - Gov.uk.' https://www.gov.uk/government/news/cmo-for-england-announces-12-new-cases-of-novel-coronavirus-01-march-2020. Accessed 23 Jul. 2020.

6. 'No 10 and Department of Health clash over access to EU ....' 1 Mar. 2020, https://www.telegraph.co.uk/politics/2020/03/01/downing-street-department-health-locked-row-access-eu-pandemic/. Accessed 29 Oct. 2020.

7. 'What was Exercise Cygnus and what did it find? | World news....' 7 May 2020, https://www.theguardian.com/world/2020/may/07/what-was-exercise-cygnus-and-what-did-it-find. Accessed 29 Oct. 2020.

8. 'Boris Johnsons aides "told to keep memos short"'... - Daily Mirror, 23 Feb. 2020, https://www.mirror.co.uk/news/politics/boris-johnsons-aides-told-keep-21558629. Accessed 20 Oct. 2020.

9. '"I shook hands with everybody" says Boris Johnson weeks...' 27 Mar. 2020, https://www.theguardian.com/world/video/2020/mar/27/i-shook-hands-with-everybody-says-boris-johnson-weeks-before-coronavirus-diagnosis-video. Accessed 23 Jul. 2020.

10. 'Coronavirus: 60% of UK population need to become infected...' 13 Mar. 2020, https://www.independent.co.uk/news/health/coronavirus-herd-immunity-uk-nhs-outbreak-pandemic-government-a9399101.html. Accessed 29 Oct. 2020.

11. 'Coronavirus: Did "herd immunity" change the course of...' BBC, 20 Jul. 2020, https://www.bbc.co.uk/news/uk-53433824. Accessed 29 Oct. 2020.

12. 'Coronavirus UK: Boris Johnson won't shut schools to halt' 12 Mar. 2020, https://www.dailymail.co.uk/news/article-8103651/Pressure-mounts-Boris-

Johnson-ramp-Britains-coronavirus-action.html. Accessed 29 Oct. 2020.
13. '20000 deaths in UK from coronavirus would be "good outcome".' 17 Mar. 2020, https://www.walesonline.co.uk/news/uk-news/20000-deaths-uk-coronavirus-would-17939352. Accessed 29 Oct. 2020.
14. '"A National Scandal" A Timeline of the UK Government's ....' 11 Apr. 2020, https://bylinetimes.com/2020/04/11/a-national-scandal-a-timeline-of-the-uk-governments-woeful-response-to-the-coronavirus-crisis/. Accessed 29 Oct. 2020.

Stay Home, Protect the NHS, Save Lives

1. 'Tesco, Asda and other supermarket websites crash after Boris ....' 23 Mar. 2020, https://www.walesonline.co.uk/news/wales-news/tesco-asda-supermarket-websites-crash-17968779. Accessed 29 Oct. 2020.
2. 'Coronavirus: 18-year-old "youngest" to die in UK as fatalities ....' 23 Mar. 2020, https://news.sky.com/story/coronavirus-number-of-deaths-in-uk-rises-by-48-to-281-11962009. Accessed 29 Oct. 2020.
3. 'Coronavirus and devolution | The Institute for Government.' https://www.instituteforgovernment.org.uk/explainers/coronavirus-and-devolution. Accessed 22 Oct. 2020
4. 'Coronavirus: Four more people die in Wales as 71 new cases ....' 23 Mar. 2020, https://www.walesonline.co.uk/news/wales-news/coronavirus-news-cases-wales-symptoms-17964945. Accessed 22 Oct. 2020.
5. 'The NHS is launching a massive recruitment drive for drivers ....' 24 Mar. 2020, https://www.walesonline.co.uk/news/wales-news/coronavirus-jobs-nhs-staff-employment-17969744. Accessed 22 Oct. 2020.
6. 'Coronavirus: 20,000 UK deaths would be "good outcome", Sir ....' 25 Apr. 2020, https://news.sky.com/video/coronavirus-20-000-uk-deaths-would-be-good-outcome-11959254. Accessed 22 Oct. 2020.
7. 'Reasons why Gwent is a coronavirus hotspot | South Wales ....' 26 Mar. 2020, https://www.southwalesargus.co.uk/news/18336561.reasons-gwent-coronavirus-hotspot/. Accessed 29 Oct. 2020.
8. 'Coronavirus: Essex GP with "textbook symptoms" dies - BBC ....' 27 Mar. 2020, https://www.bbc.co.uk/news/uk-england-essex-52040991. Accessed 22 Oct. 2020.
9. 'Boris Johnson boasted of shaking hands on day Sage warned ....' 5 May. 2020, https://www.theguardian.com/politics/2020/may/05/boris-johnson-boasted-of-shaking-hands-on-day-sage-warned-not-to. Accessed 17 Jun. 2020.

A Death Warrant from the Grim Reaper

1. 'First Minister names company involved in collapsed ... - ITV Hub.' 1 Apr. 2020, https://www.itv.com/news/wales/2020-04-01/first-minister-names-company-involved-in-collapsed-coronavirus-testing-kit-deal. Accessed 5 Nov. 2020.
2. 'Coronavirus: Target reached as UK tests pass 100000 ... - BBC.' 1 May. 2020, https://www.bbc.co.uk/news/uk-52508836. Accessed 5 Nov. 2020.

3. 'Coronavirus: Planned surgery cancelled in Wales - BBC News.' 14 Mar. 2020, https://www.bbc.co.uk/news/uk-wales-51877667. Accessed 5 Nov. 2020.
4. 'Coronavirus: Hundreds of cancer patients "could die due to ....' 31 Mar. 2020, https://www.lbc.co.uk/news/uk/coronavirus-hundreds-of-cancer-patients-could-die/. Accessed 5 Nov. 2020.
5. 'The huge number of operations cancelled in Wales over the ....' 31 Jul. 2018, https://www.walesonline.co.uk/news/health/huge-number-operations-cancelled-wales-14969458. Accessed 5 Nov. 2020.
6. 'Almost a fifth of people with Covid-19 in Wales are healthcare ....' 3 Apr. 2020, https://www.walesonline.co.uk/news/health/coronavirus-testing-drakeford-staff-covid-18037427. Accessed 5 Nov. 2020.
7. 'Leak reveals shortage of coronavirus PPE in Northern Ireland ....' 30 Mar. 2020, https://www.theguardian.com/world/2020/mar/30/leak-reveals-shortage-of-coronavirus-ppe-in-northern-ireland. Accessed 5 Nov. 2020.
8. 'Surgery asks sickest patients to sign "do not attempt CPR" form ....' 31 Mar. 2020, https://www.walesonline.co.uk/news/wales-news/coronavirus-covid-19-surgery-patients-18012444. Accessed 5 Nov. 2020.
9. 'Thousands of prisoners are set to be released across Wales ....' 4 Apr. 2020, https://www.walesonline.co.uk/news/wales-news/thousands-uk-prisoners-released-coronavirus-18042718. Accessed 5 Nov. 2020.
10. 'Five-year-old child becomes youngest known coronavirus ....' 4 Apr. 2020, https://www.itv.com/news/2020-04-04/coronavirus-deaths-total-up-to-4-313-after-further-708-die. Accessed 5 Nov. 2020.

Please Take My Liberty
1. 'Coronavirus: 13,000 shielding letters in Wales go to wrong ....' 15 Apr. 2020, https://www.bbc.co.uk/news/uk-wales-politics-52283236. Accessed 29 Oct. 2020.
2. 'Supermarkets reject First Minister's claim that delay in ....' 22 Apr. 2020, https://www.walesonline.co.uk/news/politics/drakeford-supermarkets-vulnerable-shielding-delivery-18134507. Accessed 29 Oct. 2020.
3. 'Plenary 22/04/2020 - Welsh Parliament - National Assembly ....' 22 Apr. 2020, https://record.assembly.wales/Plenary/6291. Accessed 29 Oct. 2020.
4. 'Powerful letter from nursing leaders lays out concern at the ....' 9 Apr. 2020, https://www.walesonline.co.uk/news/wales-news/care-homes-ppe-testing-coronavirus-18066822. Accessed 29 Oct. 2020.

Thank You Key Workers
1. 'More than 1,200 face shields sat in boxes unable to be ....' 13 Apr. 2020, https://www.walesonline.co.uk/news/health/nhs-face-shields-coronavirus-ppe-18084027. Accessed 29 Oct. 2020.
2. 'UK economy could shrink by 35% with 2m job losses, warns ....' 14 Apr. 2020, https://www.theguardian.com/business/2020/apr/14/uk-economy-could-shrink-by-35-with-2m-job-losses-warns-obr. Accessed 29 Oct. 2020. See

also 'Chancellor Sunak warns of "tough times"'for UK economy ....' 14 Apr. 2020, https://www.bbc.co.uk/news/business-52279871. Accessed 29 Oct. 2020.

3. 'Far more women than men are being diagnosed with ....' 14 Apr. 2020, https://www.walesonline.co.uk/news/wales-news/women-covid10-coronavirus-cases-nurses-18091570. Accessed 29 Oct. 2020

4. 'The Welsh Government said they'd be doing 5,000 tests a day ....' 14 Apr. 2020, https://www.walesonline.co.uk/news/politics/testing-coronaviris-capacity-covid19-gething-18090009. Accessed 29 Oct. 2020.

5. 'Hundreds of Welsh fire service staff are self-isolating amid ....' 14 Apr. 2020, https://www.walesonline.co.uk/news/wales-news/fire-firefighters-testing-covid19-cronavirus-18087761. Accessed 29 Oct. 2020.

6. 'People are saying that PPE is being prioritised for care homes ....' 16 Apr. 2020, https://www.walesonline.co.uk/news/wales-news/ppe-carehomes-coronavirus-supplies-covid19-18096491. Accessed 29 Oct. 2020.

'What the F___ Is the Matter with Her?'

1. 'How many people in Wales have been furloughed ....' 15 Jul. 2020, https://www.business-live.co.uk/economic-development/how-many-people-wales-been-18599417. Accessed 29 Oct. 2020.

2. 'Coronavirus vaccine to be tested in UK from Thursday ....' 21 Apr. 2020, https://www.independent.co.uk/news/uk/politics/coronavirus-vaccine-uk-nhs-matt-hancock-latest-a9476901.html. Accessed 22 Oct. 2020.

3. 'Health Secretary walks away from questions over calls for ....' 24 Aug. 2017, https://www.itv.com/news/wales/2017-08-24/health-secretary-walks-away-from-questions-over-calls-for-inquiry-into-health-boards-actions. Accessed 29 Oct. 2020.

4. 'COVID-19 causes a SHiFT in the sands for proximal femoral ....' 14 Apr. 2020, https://www.boa.ac.uk/policy-engagement/journal-of-trauma-orthopaedics/journal-of-trauma-orthopaedics-and-coronavirus/covid-19-causes-a-shift-in-the-sands-for-proximal.html. Accessed 29 Oct. 2020.

5. '"t lay her to rest" - Wales Online.' 24 Nov. 2019, https://www.walesonline.co.uk/news/wales-news/murder-crime-haverfordwest-police-bradbury-17301586. Accessed 29 Oct. 2020.

6. 'Drug addict admits killing solicitor Alison Farr-Davies - BBC ....' 14 Mar. 2017, https://www.bbc.co.uk/news/uk-wales-south-west-wales-39272621. Accessed 29 Oct. 2020.

7. 'Cardiff Queen Street murders: Andrew Saunders gets ....' 28 Feb. 2017, https://www.walesonline.co.uk/news/wales-news/live-updates-man-sentenced-cardiff-12661338. Accessed 29 Oct. 2020.

8. 'Full letter to Welsh Government Deputy Minister and Chief ....' 22 Apr. 2020, https://www.welshwomensaid.org.uk/wp-content/uploads/2020/04/COVID-19-VAWDASV-Funding-Public-Letter-to-Deputy-Minister-22.04.2020.pdf. Accessed 22 Oct. 2020.

The Virus Can't Get You As Long As You Stay Aert

1. 'Campers get car stuck in sand after driving from Hereford to ....' 1 May. 2020, https://www.walesonline.co.uk/news/wales-news/campers-car-stuck-sand-after-18183198. Accessed 30 Oct. 2020.
2. 'Coronavirus risk "10 to 30 times higher" at one metre away ....' 5 May. 2020, https://www.walesonline.co.uk/news/politics/coronavirus-politics-masks-social-distancing-18201236. Accessed 30 Oct. 2020.
3. 'Coronavirus Scotland: Nicola Sturgeon warns she will "not be ....' 7 May. 2020, https://www.dailyrecord.co.uk/news/scottish-news/coronavirus-scotland-nicola-sturgeon-warns-21992625. Accessed 30 Oct. 2020.
4. 'Relationship between UK and Welsh Governments over ....' 8 May. 2020, https://www.walesonline.co.uk/news/politics/coronavirus-drakeford-westminster-covid19-virus-18221681. Accessed 30 Oct. 2020.

'Too Fast, Too Confusing and Too Risky

1. 'Coronavirus UK: Boris Johnson's exit strategy is in chaos ....' 11 May. 2020, https://www.dailymail.co.uk/news/article-8306539/Commuters-crowd-Tubes-Boris-Johnson-urges-Britons-work.html. Accessed 31 Oct. 2020.
2. 'Government's "road map out of lockdown" is too fast, too ... - BMA.' 10 May. 2020, https://www.bma.org.uk/bma-media-centre/government-s-road-map-out-of-lockdown-is-too-fast-too-confusing-and-too-risky-says-bma. Accessed 31 Oct. 2020.
3. 'Wales' First Minister has made a massive mistake - WalesOnline.' 11 May. 2020, https://www.walesonline.co.uk/news/news-opinion/wales-first-minister-made-massive-18235813. Accessed 31 Oct. 2020.
4. 'Labour health minister tucks into chips at picnic ... - The Sun.' 12 May. 2020, https://www.thesun.co.uk/news/11608940/labour-mp-breaks-lockdown-rules-chips-picnic/. Accessed 31 Oct. 2020.
5. 'Plenary 13/05/2020 - Welsh Parliament - National Assembly ....' 13 May. 2020, https://record.assembly.wales/Plenary/6325. Accessed 31 Oct. 2020.
6. 'Coronavirus: Change to guidance "nothing to do" with Gething ....' 13 May. 2020, https://www.bbc.co.uk/news/uk-wales-politics-52646400. Accessed 31 Oct. 2020.
7. 'No gowns included in Welsh Government's PPE stockpile until ....' 13 May. 2020, https://www.walesonline.co.uk/news/wales-news/gething-drakeford-coronavirus-ppe-gowns-18247239. Accessed 31 Oct. 2020.
8. 'People are still getting letters by mistake saying they're at a ....' 15 May. 2020, https://www.walesonline.co.uk/news/local-news/people-still-getting-letters-mistake-18259124. Accessed 31 Oct. 2020.

'Welcome to the Opticians, If You Would Please Start Your Engine We Can Begin'

1. 'The three signs of coronavirus UK government are urging ....' 18 May. 2020, https://www.walesonline.co.uk/news/politics/symptoms-coronavirus-smell-

fever-cough-18267971. Accessed 31 Oct. 2020.

2. 'Welsh Government cordons off area where Vaughan Gething ....' 18 May. 2020, https://www.walesonline.co.uk/news/wales-news/vaughan-gething-chips-fence-lockdown-18270812. Accessed 31 Oct. 2020.

3. 'Welsh Government cordons off area where Vaughan Gething ....' 18 May. 2020, https://www.walesonline.co.uk/news/wales-news/vaughan-gething-chips-fence-lockdown-18270812. Accessed 31 Oct. 2020.

4. 'The great mystery of Wales' missing nurses - Wales Online.' 22 Jul. 2018, https://www.walesonline.co.uk/news/wales-news/great-mystery-wales-missing-nurses-14936268. Accessed 31 Oct. 2020.

5. 'Health boards which failed to report 115 coronavirus deaths ....' 8 May. 2020, https://www.walesonline.co.uk/news/politics/coronavirus-system-hospital-betsi-dda-18219996. Accessed 31 Oct. 2020.

6. '"Loving, kind and generous" care home nurse dies after ....' https://www.walesonline.co.uk/news/health/loving-kind-generous-care-home-18207138. Accessed 31 Oct. 2020.

7. 'The man leading Wales' coronavirus lockdown strategy on ....' 19 May. 2020, https://www.walesonline.co.uk/news/politics/drakeford-wales-lockdown-rules-parks-18278418. Accessed 31 Oct. 2020.

8. 'Dominic Cummings investigated by police after breaking ....' 22 May. 2020, https://www.mirror.co.uk/news/politics/dominic-cummings-investigated-police-after-22072579. Accessed 31 Oct. 2020. See also: 'Pressure on Dominic Cummings to quit over lockdown breach ....' 22 May. 2020, https://www.theguardian.com/politics/2020/may/22/dominic-cummings-durham-trip-coronavirus-lockdown. Accessed 31 Oct. 2020.

9. 'Grant Shapps accused of editing Wikipedia pages of Tory rivals.' 21 Apr. 2015, https://www.theguardian.com/politics/2015/apr/21/grant-shapps-accused-of-editing-wikipedia-pages-of-tory-rivals. Accessed 31 Oct. 2020.

10. 'Covid-19: UK government's defence of senior aide ... - The BMJ.' https://www.bmj.com/content/bmj/369/bmj.m2109.full.pdf. Accessed 31 Oct. 2020.

A Five Mile World

1. 'Report of the Independent Review of Deaths and Serious ....' 6 Jan. 2017, https://assets.publishing.service.gov.uk/government/uploads/system/uploads/attachment_data/file/655401/Report_of_Angiolini_Review_ISBN_Accessible.pdf. Accessed 30 Jul. 2020.

2. 'UK car journeys down 80% during coronavirus lockdown - Air ....' 16 Apr. 2020, https://airqualitynews.com/2020/04/16/car-journeys-down-80-during-coronavirus-lockdown/. Accessed 30 Jul. 2020.

3. 'Analysis: UK renewables generate more electricity than fossil ....' 14 Oct. 2019, https://www.carbonbrief.org/analysis-uk-renewables-generate-more-electricity-than-fossil-fuels-for-first-time. Accessed 31 Oct. 2020.

4. 'Coronavirus: Simon Hart's exercise claims "not correct", says ....' 22 May.

2020, https://www.bbc.co.uk/news/uk-wales-politics-52778622. Accessed 31 Oct. 2020.

5. 'Delyn MP Rob Roberts investigated after being accused of ....' 21 Jul. 2020, https://www.itv.com/news/wales/2020-07-21/delyn-mp-rob-roberts-investi-gated-after-being-accused-of-asking-intern-to-fool-around. Accessed 31 Oct. 2020.

An Attack on the Fundamentals of Humanity

1. 'UK abandoned testing because system "could only cope with ....' 30 May. 2020, https://www.telegraph.co.uk/news/2020/05/30/revealed-test-trace-abandoned-system-could-cope-five-coronavirus/. Accessed 10 Aug. 2020.

2. 'Meat plants—a new front line in the covid-19 pandemic | The ....' 9 Jul. 2020, https://www.bmj.com/content/370/bmj.m2716. Accessed 10 Aug. 2020.

3. 'Staff walk out of food factory in protest over concerns about ....' 3 Apr. 2020, https://www.dailypost.co.uk/news/north-wales-news/staff-walk-out-food-factory-18038472. Accessed 10 Aug. 2020.

4. 'The full recriminations over re-opening schools in June as ....' 4 Jun. 2020, https://www.walesonline.co.uk/news/education/full-recriminations-over-re-opening-18365652. Accessed 31 Oct. 2020

5. 'Man jailed for urinating at PC Keith Palmer memorial ... - BBC.' 15 Jun. 2020, https://www.bbc.co.uk/news/uk-england-london-53051096. Accessed 10 Aug. 2020.

6. 'Channel 4 News on Twitter: "If the other three police officers ....' 14 Jun. 2020, https://twitter.com/channel4news/status/1272188213705297920. Accessed 10 Aug. 2020.

7. 'Locked down in Butetown: What isolation looks like at the ....' 13 Jun. 2020, https://www.walesonline.co.uk/news/wales-news/butetown-coronavirus-lock-down-bame-black-18391552. Accessed 11 Aug. 2020.

8. 'Johnson makes U-turn on free school meals after Rashford ....' 16 Jun. 2020, https://www.theguardian.com/politics/2020/jun/16/boris-johnson-faces-tory-rebellion-over-marcus-rashfords-school-meals-call. Accessed 11 Aug. 2020. And see "Marcus Rashford on Twitter: "I don't even know what to say ...." 16 Jun. 2020, https://twitter.com/marcusrashford/status/1272863210207694848. Accessed 11 Aug. 2020.

9. 'Persistence and clearance of viral RNA in 2019 novel coronav ....' https://journals.lww.com/cmj/fulltext/2020/05050/persistence_and_clear-ance_of_viral_rna_in_2019.6.aspx. Accessed 11 Aug. 2020.

The First Wave Ends

1. 'House of Commons - Parliament (publications).' 6 Mar. 2013, https://publi-cations.parliament.uk/pa/cm201213/cmselect/cmwelaf/95/9504.htm. Accessed 12 Aug. 2020.

2. 'Covid-19: UK Government confirms antibody tests in four ....' 21 May. 2020, https://www.conservatives.wales/news/covid-19-uk-government-confirms-

antibody-tests-four-nations-approach-pandemic. Accessed 12 Aug. 2020.

3. 'Leading Wales out of the coronavirus pandemic: a framework ....' 24 Apr. 2020, https://gov.wales/leading-wales-out-coronavirus-pandemic-html. Accessed 12 Aug. 2020.

4. 'Coronavirus: "Don't rush to beauty spots" plea after PM ... - BBC.' 11 May. 2020, https://www.bbc.co.uk/news/uk-england-52615443. Accessed 12 Aug. 2020.

5 . 'How lockdown now compares across the UK as England lifts ....' 23 Jun. 2020, https://www.walesonline.co.uk/news/wales-news/wales-england-lock-down-coronavirus-rules-18470589. Accessed 12 Aug. 2020.

6. 'People are claimed to be cancelling summer holiday bookings ....' 17 Jun. 2020, https://www.walesonline.co.uk/news/people-claimed-cancelling-summer-holiday-18437571. Accessed 12 Aug. 2020.

7. 'Anne Cori on Twitter: "I see a lot of discussions about ....' 22 Jun. 2020, https://twitter.com/dr_anne_cori/status/1275176017804525568. Accessed 13 Aug. 2020.

8. 'Chief nurse was dropped from briefings after refusing to back ....' 20 Jul. 2020, https://www.theguardian.com/politics/2020/jul/20/englands-chief-nurse-dropped-from-covid-19-briefing-after-refusing-to-back-cummings-ruth-may. Accessed 13 Aug. 2020.

9. 'Coronavirus latest: Health experts "banished" from Downing ....' 12 Jun. 2020, https://inews.co.uk/news/politics/coronavirus-latest-health-experts-ban-ished-downing-street-briefings-explained-dominic-cummings-445004. Accessed 13 Aug. 2020.

10. 'Coronavirus latest: Health experts "banished" from Downing ....' 12 Jun. 2020, https://inews.co.uk/news/politics/coronavirus-latest-health-experts-ban-ished-downing-street-briefings-explained-dominic-cummings-445004. Accessed 13 Aug. 2020.

11. 'Stanley Johnson says Greece visit is essential to "Covid-proof ....' 4 Jul. 2020, https://www.theguardian.com/politics/2020/jul/04/stanley-johnson-says-greece-visit-is-essential-to-covid-proof-villa. Accessed 13 Aug. 2020.

PPE: Left Undefended

1. 'Offline: COVID-19 and the NHS—"a national scandal" - The ....' 28 Mar. 2020, https://www.thelancet.com/journals/lancet/article/PIIS0140-6736(20)30727-3/fulltext. Accessed 28 Aug. 2020.

2. 'Unrelenting demand, no PPE and staff driven to the point of ....' 5 Jun. 2020, https://www.walesonline.co.uk/news/health/coronavirus-wales-pharmacy-ppe-prescriptions-18368189. Accessed 28 Aug. 2020.

3. 'Newport council workers ask local businesses for help in ....' 13 Apr. 2020, https://www.walesonline.co.uk/news/wales-news/newport-council-coron-avirus-ppe-covid-18083870. Accessed 28 Aug. 2020.

4. 'NHS staff "wearing goggles from DIY shops" due to scarcity of ....' 26 Mar. 2020, https://www.walesonline.co.uk/news/health/nhs-staff-wearing-goggles-

diy-17985511. Accessed 28 Aug. 2020.

5. 'Nurse who died after contracting coronavirus was treating ....' https://www.walesonline.co.uk/news/wales-news/nurse-65-who-died-after-18087828. Accessed 28 Aug. 2020.

6. 'Inquiry into the impact of the Covid-19 outbreak - Senedd ....' 1 Jul. 2020, https://senedd.wales/laid%20documents/cr-ld13304/cr-ld13304%20-e.pdf. Accessed 28 Aug. 2020.

7. 'GPs in Wales, as at 30 September 2018 - GOV.WALES.' 30 Sep. 2018, https://gov.wales/sites/default/files/statistics-and-research/2019-03/general-medical-practitioners-as-at-30-september-2018-354_0.pdf. Accessed 28 Aug. 2020.

8. 'UK missed three chances to join EU scheme to bulk-buy PPE ....' 13 Apr. 2020, https://www.theguardian.com/world/2020/apr/13/uk-missed-three-chances-to-join-eu-scheme-to-bulk-buy-ppe. Accessed 28 Aug. 2020.

9. 'Coronavirus: personal protective equipment – IN BRIEF.' 5 May. 2020, https://seneddresearch.blog/2020/05/05/coronavirus-personal-protective-equipment/. Accessed 28 Aug. 2020.

10. 'People are saying that PPE is being prioritised for care homes ....' 16 Apr. 2020, https://www.walesonline.co.uk/news/wales-news/ppe-carehomes-coronavirus-supplies-covid19-18096491. Accessed 28 Aug. 2020.

11. 'Tory backers net £180m PPE deals | News | The ... - The Times.' 9 Aug. 2020, https://www.thetimes.co.uk/article/tory-backers-net-180m-ppe-deals-xwd5kmnqr. Accessed 28 Aug. 2020.

Care Homes: Wales' Predictable Disaster

1. 'The future of care in Wales - Cardiff University.' 4 Aug. 2020, https://www.cardiff.ac.uk/__data/assets/pdf_file/0019/2427400/social_care_final2_aug20.pdf. Accessed 29 Aug. 2020.

2. 'Valuing Carers 2015 - Carers UK.' 12 Nov. 2015, https://www.carersuk.org/for-professionals/policy/policy-library/valuing-carers-2015. Accessed 29 Aug. 2020 and 'The Economic Value of the Adult Social Care sector - Wales.' 5 Jun. 2018, https://socialcare.wales/cms_assets/file-uploads/The-Economic-Value-of-the-Adult-Social-Care-Sector_Wales.pdf. Accessed 29 Aug. 2020.

3. 'Increase in NHS funding in new Welsh Government budget ....' 16 Dec. 2019, https://www.itv.com/news/wales/2019-12-16/increase-in-nhs-funding-in-new-welsh-government-budget. Accessed 29 Aug. 2020.

4. 'Care Forum Wales awards "terrible ten" local authorities ....' 3 Jul. 2020, https://careindustrynews.co.uk/2020/07/care-forum-wales-awards-terrible-ten-local-authorities-care-home-news-coronavirus-wales/. Accessed 29 Aug. 2020.

5. 'Care homes market study - GOV.UK.' https://www.gov.uk/cma-cases/care-homes-market-study. Accessed 29 Aug. 2020.

6. 'Investing 2% of GDP in care industries could create 1.5 million ....' 21 Nov. 2016, https://wbg.org.uk/analysis/investing-2-of-gdp-in-care-industries-could-

create-1-5-million-jobs/. Accessed 29 Aug. 2020.

7. 'Projections of older people living with dementia and ... - LSE.' 1 Nov. 2019, http://www.lse.ac.uk/cpec/assets/documents/Working-paper-5-Wittenberg-et-al-dementia.pdf. Accessed 29 Aug. 2020.

8. 'Why were 1,097 hospital patients discharged to care homes ....' 21 Jun. 2020, https://www.walesonline.co.uk/news/politics/care-homes-wales-coronavirus-deaths-18462208. Accessed 29 Aug. 2020.

9. 'Nosocomial Transmission of Coronavirus: Research and ....' 31 Mar. 2020, https://www.gov.uk/government/publications/nosocomial-transmission-of-coronavirus-research-and-management-31-march-2020. Accessed 29 Aug. 2020.

10. 'Why were 1,097 hospital patients discharged to care homes ....' 21 Jun. 2020, https://www.walesonline.co.uk/news/politics/care-homes-wales-coron-avirus-deaths-18462208. Accessed 29 Aug. 2020.

11. 'What was Exercise Cygnus and what did it find? | World news ....' 7 May. 2020, https://www.theguardian.com/world/2020/may/07/what-was-exercise-cygnus-and-what-did-it-find. Accessed 29 Aug. 2020.

Testing Times

1. 'South Korea pioneers coronavirus drive-through ... - CNN.com.' 3 Mar. 2020, https://www.cnn.com/2020/03/02/asia/coronavirus-drive-through-south-korea-hnk-intl/index.html. Accessed 30 Aug. 2020.

2. 'WHO Director-General's opening remarks at the media ....' 16 Mar. 2020, https://www.who.int/dg/speeches/detail/who-director-general-s-opening-remarks-at-the-media-briefing-on-covid-19---16-march-2020. Accessed 30 Aug. 2020.

3. 'Coronavirus: 'Collapsed' Roche testing deal correspondence ....' 9 Jun. 2020, https://www.bbc.co.uk/news/uk-wales-politics-52977589. Accessed 30 Aug. 2020.

4. 'Majority of Scots back Nicola Sturgeon's handling of ....' 26 May. 2020, https://www.dailyrecord.co.uk/news/politics/majority-scots-back-nicola-stur-geons-22085984. Accessed 30 Aug. 2020.

5. 'Health, Social Care and Sport Committee 07/05/2020 - Welsh ....' 7 May. 2020, https://record.assembly.wales/Committee/6198. Accessed 31 Oct. 2020.

6. 'Coronavirus home test: step-by-step guide - Gov.uk.' https://assets.publish-ing.service.gov.uk/government/uploads/system/uploads/attachment_data/file/907961/Coronavirus_home_test_step-by-step_guide.pdf. Accessed 31 Oct. 2020.

7. 'Scottish man sent Welsh woman's Covid-19 test results by ....' 16 Jun. 2020, https://www.walesonline.co.uk/news/health/scottish-man-sent-welsh-womans-18429430. Accessed 30 Aug. 2020.

'The Impact of Coronavirus on People of Colour

1. 'and the Black, Asian and Minority Ethnic (BAME) - GOV.WALES.' 22 Jun. 2020, https://gov.wales/sites/default/files/statistics-and-research/2020-

06/coronavirus-covid-19-and-the-black-asian-and-minority-ethnic-popula-tion-154.pdf. Accessed 31 Aug. 2020.

2. 'ICNARC report on COVID-19 in critical care Wales 31 July 2020.' 31 Jul. 2020, https://www.icnarc.org/DataServices/Attachments/Download/6d6ef7d8-3dd3-ea11-9128-00505601089b. Accessed 31 Aug. 2020. And see also 'Coronavirus: What do the stats tell us in Wales? - BBC News.' 28 Aug. 2020, https://www.bbc.co.uk/news/uk-wales-52380643. Accessed 31 Aug. 2020.

3. 'Disparities in the risk and outcomes of COVID-19.' 11 Aug. 2020, https://assets.publishing.service.gov.uk/government/uploads/system/uploads/at tachment_data/file/908434/Disparities_in_the_risk_and_outcomes_of_COVI D_August_2020_update.pdf. Accessed 31 Aug. 2020.

4. 'and the Black, Asian and Minority Ethnic (BAME) - GOV.WALES.' 22 Jun. 2020, https://gov.wales/sites/default/files/statistics-and-research/2020-06/coronavirus-covid-19-and-the-black-asian-and-minority-ethnic-population -154.pdf. Accessed 31 Aug. 2020.

5. 'and the Black, Asian and Minority Ethnic (BAME) - GOV.WALES.' 22 Jun. 2020, https://gov.wales/sites/default/files/statistics-and-research/2020-06/coronavirus-covid-19-and-the-black-asian-and-minority-ethnic-population -154.pdf. Accessed 31 Aug. 2020.

6. 'Overweight adults - GOV.UK Ethnicity facts and figures.' 19 May. 2020, https://www.ethnicity-facts-figures.service.gov.uk/health/diet-and-exercise/overweight-adults/latest. Accessed 31 Aug. 2020.

7. 'Written Statement: COVID-19 and BAME Communities | GOV ....' 21 Apr. 2020, https://gov.wales/written-statement-covid-19-and-bame-communi-ties. Accessed 31 Aug. 2020.

8. 'Launching risk assessment to support BAME workers | GOV ....' 26 May. 2020, https://gov.wales/launching-risk-assessment-support-bame-workers. Accessed 31 Aug. 2020.

9. 'first minister's bame covid-19 advisory group report of the ....' 2 Jun. 2020, https://gov.wales/sites/default/files/publications/2020-06/first-ministers-bame-covid-19-advisory-group-report-of-the-socioeconomic-subgroup.pdf. Accessed 31 Aug. 2020.

10. 'Wales hasn't kept a record of how many BAME people died ....' 22 Jun. 2020, https://www.walesonline.co.uk/news/wales-news/coronavirus-racial-inequalities-bame-deaths-18467037. Accessed 31 Aug. 2020.

11. 'The shockingly low amount of BAME police officers in Wales ....' 17 Aug. 2020, https://www.walesonline.co.uk/news/politics/police-black-bame-repre-sentation-race-18784578. Accessed 31 Aug. 2020.

12. 'Report of the Independent Review of Deaths and Serious ....' 6 Jan. 2017, https://assets.publishing.service.gov.uk/government/uploads/system/uploads/at tachment_data/file/655401/Report_of_Angiolini_Review_ISBN_Accessible.p df. Accessed 31 Aug. 2020.

13. 'Stop and search - GOV.UK Ethnicity facts and figures.' 19 Mar. 2020,

https://www.ethnicity-facts-figures.service.gov.uk/crime-justice-and-the-law/policing/stop-and-search/latest. Accessed 31 Aug. 2020.

Cardiff Bay and Westminster Relations - Walking in Lockstep?

1. '"We are all on the same team in the battle against coronavirus ....' 19 Apr. 2020, https://www.walesonline.co.uk/news/politics/matt-hancock-coronavirus-ppe-wales-18113343. Accessed 31 Oct. 2020.
2. 'Welsh government begins preparing for lockdown exit - New ....' 17 Apr. 2020, https://www.newstatesman.com/2020/04/welsh-government-begins-preparing-lockdown-exit. Accessed 31 Oct. 2020.
3. 'A four-nation exit strategy - The Institute for Government.' 20 Mar. 2020, https://www.instituteforgovernment.org.uk/sites/default/files/publications/four-nation-exit-strategy-coronavirus.pdf. Accessed 31 Oct. 2020. See also 'Consideration of lockdown restrictions to be "primary focus" for ....' 4 May. 2020, https://www.itv.com/news/wales/2020-05-04/coronavirus-briefing-wales-drakeford-monday-may-4th. Accessed 31 Oct. 2020.
4. 'Top Welsh Government figures take shots at England's testing ....' 3 May. 2020, https://www.walesonline.co.uk/news/politics/gething-drakeford-coronavirus-testing-england-18191492. Accessed 31 Oct. 2020.
5. 'Top Welsh Government figures take shots at England's testing ....' 3 May. 2020, https://www.walesonline.co.uk/news/politics/gething-drakeford-coronavirus-testing-england-18191492. Accessed 31 Oct. 2020.
6. 'Relationship between UK and Welsh Governments over ....' 8 May. 2020, https://www.walesonline.co.uk/news/politics/coronavirus-drakeford-westminster-covid19-virus-18221681. Accessed 31 Oct. 2020.
7. 'First Minister claims lockdown meetings with Boris Johnson's ....' 15 May. 2020, https://www.walesonline.co.uk/news/politics/coronavirus-uk-welsh-government-lockdown-18257808. Accessed 31 Oct. 2020.
8. '"For the first time, Wales has been able to flex its muscles ....' https://www.theguardian.com/uk-news/2020/jun/17/for-the-first-time-wales-has-been-able-to-flex-its-muscles-could-coronavirus-tear-england-and-wales-apart. Accessed 31 Oct. 2020.
9. 'Wales will remain largely shut to tourists this summer, warns ....' 7 Jun. 2020, https://inews.co.uk/news/uk/wales-shut-tourists-summer-first-minister-mark-drakeford-434873. Accessed 31 Oct. 2020.
10. 'Coronavirus: Welsh minister attacks UK government on ... - BBC.' 17 Jun. 2020, https://www.bbc.co.uk/news/uk-wales-politics-53077578. Accessed 31 Oct. 2020.
11. 'ITV Wales News on Twitter: "Support grows for Welsh ....' 4 Jun. 2020, https://twitter.com/itvwales/status/1268592747956535304. Accessed 31 Oct. 2020.

The State of the UK

1. 'Michael Gove to oversee UK constitutional review | Financial ....' 14 Feb.

2020, https://www.ft.com/content/6ac426a6-4f55-11ea-95a0-43d18ec715f5. Accessed 4 Nov. 2020.

2. 'Jamaica deportation: Home Office flight leaves UK ... - BBC.' 11 Feb. 2020, https://www.bbc.com/news/uk-51456387. Accessed 4 Nov. 2020.

3. 'Government launches independent panel to look at ... - Gov.uk.' 31 Jul. 2020, https://www.gov.uk/government/news/government-launches-independent-panel-to-look-at-judicial-review. Accessed 4 Nov. 2020.

4. 'Legal aid spending in England and Wales 2019 | Statista.' 5 Mar. 2020, https://www.statista.com/statistics/1098628/legal-aid-spending-in-england-and-wales/. Accessed 4 Nov. 2020.

5. 'Robert Jenrick: What did housing secretary do and ... - Sky News.' 7 Jul. 2020, https://news.sky.com/story/the-1bn-development-and-the-tory-donor-the-robert-jenrick-controversy-explained-12014447. Accessed 4 Nov. 2020.

6. 'Coronavirus: Public Health England to be scrapped - with ....' 18 Aug. 2020, https://news.sky.com/story/coronavirus-public-health-england-to-be-scrapped-health-secretary-confirms-12051592. Accessed 4 Nov. 2020.

7. 'Government creates new National Institute for Health ... - Gov.uk.' 18 Aug. 2020, https://www.gov.uk/government/news/government-creates-new-national-institute-for-health-protection. Accessed 4 Nov. 2020.

8. 'The funding from energy and property tycoons that bankrolled ....' 15 Mar. 2020, https://www.walesonline.co.uk/news/wales-news/alun-cairns-temerko-donations-tobacco-17922733. Accessed 4 Nov. 2020.

9. 'Simon Hart - TobaccoTactics.' 8 Jun. 2020, https://tobaccotactics.org/wiki/simon-hart/. Accessed 4 Nov. 2020.

10. 'The Dominic Cummings affair reveals UK government's ....' 26 May. 2020, https://www.ft.com/content/df904fd8-9f54-11ea-b65d-489c67b0d85d. Accessed 4 Nov. 2020.

11. 'The Tories' factcheckUK Twitter stunt was cleverly ... - Wired UK.' 20 Nov. 2019, https://www.wired.co.uk/article/factcheckuk-twitter-cchqpress-debate. Accessed 4 Nov. 2020.

12. 'Political journalists boycott No 10 briefing after reporter ban ....' 3 Feb. 2020, https://www.theguardian.com/politics/2020/feb/03/political-journalists-boycott-no-10-briefing-after-reporter-ban. Accessed 4 Nov. 2020.

13. 'Mirror barred from Boris Johnson campaign battle bus - Press ....' 21 Nov. 2019, https://www.pressgazette.co.uk/mirror-barred-from-boris-johnson-campaign-battle-bus/. Accessed 4 Nov. 2020.

14. 'Did "the Whole of London" Protest in Support of Far-Right ....' 12 Jun. 2018, https://www.snopes.com/fact-check/tommy-robinson-protest-photo/. Accessed 4 Nov. 2020.

15. 'Trust in politicians has fallen to an all time low in the UK.' 27 Nov. 2019, https://www.thelondoneconomic.com/news/trust-in-politicians-has-fallen-to-an-all-time-low-in-the-uk/27/11/. Accessed 4 Nov. 2020.

16. 'How much do we trust journalists? | YouGov.' 26 Mar. 2020, https://yougov.co.uk/topics/politics/articles-reports/2020/03/26/trust-news-

paper-journalists. Accessed 4 Nov. 2020.

17. 'Attitudes to Devolution and Welsh Independence - Cardiff ....' 5 Jun. 2020, http://blogs.cardiff.ac.uk/electionsinwales/2020/06/05/attitudes-to-devolution-and-welsh-independence/. Accessed 4 Nov. 2020.

Acknowledgements

First and foremost I want to pay tribute to the people who have lost their lives during the pandemic, some of whom are named within these pages. I also acknowledge everyone in Wales who has been affected by the Covid-19 crisis and thans those who did anything, however small, to make this time in our lives better.

There are so many people who helped make this book a reality.

I want to thank Mick and everyone at Seren Books for taking a chance on a new author.

I am also very grateful to all my colleagues at WalesOnline, the *Western Mail, South Wales Echo* and *Evening Post*. It is a privilege to be given the platform I have. To be part of a team of such talented people, who care about what they do is a real blessing. You do not get the credit you deserve. Particular thanks to Paul for offering me so many opportunities and to Dave for making my journalism better and saving me from myself.

Also to Mike, Cathy and Sandra at Cardiff School of Journalism for all their training and encouragement.

A big thank you to Gwyn, for keeping my head in the game.

I am immensely fortunate to have friends and family who seem to have a bottomless and unconditional well of support and love. Thank you all so very much.

There are few people in particular who deserve a shout out for getting this over the line.

To Jimmy, Laura, Bobalina and Rachel K. Your support through this was immense. I can't put into words how thankful I am to call you my friends.

To my brother Dan, for providing me with encouragement and plenty of distractions.

To my wonderful girlfriend Rachel, who has lived and breathed every page of this with me. You really believed in me and there is no way I could have done this without you.

To Dad, for being my mate, endlessly supportive and the most principled human being on earth.

And to Mum. My hero. For every brainstorming conversation and for your unwavering commitment to the thankless job as proofreader-in-chief for a dyslexic.

The Author

Will Hayward is a multi-award winning journalist and columnist based in Wales specialising in politics and investigative journalism. He is the Acting Political Editor of WalesOnline, the *Western Mail* and *South Wales Echo*. He has a passion for reporting on a huge range of issues around equality, poverty, climate change and domestic violence. For Will political reporting is not about the politicians but the people their day to day decisions affect. Will didn't realise he wanted to be a journalist until he was twenty-five. In his four year career Will has been nominated for nineteen journalism awards and was named Welsh Journalist of the year in 2019.